The Magic Years

The Magic Years

Scenes from a Rock-and-Roll Life

Jonathan Taplin

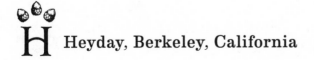 Heyday, Berkeley, California

Library of Congress Cataloging-in-Publication Data
Names: Taplin, Jonathan T., author.
Title: The magic years : scenes from a rock-and-roll life / Jonathan
    Taplin.
Description: Berkeley : Heyday, 2021.
Identifiers: LCCN 2020015947 (print) | LCCN 2020015948 (ebook) | ISBN
    9781597145251 (cloth) | ISBN 9781597145268 (ebook)
Subjects: LCSH: Taplin, Jonathan T. | Impresarios--United
    States--Biography. | Concert tours--United States--History--20th
    century. | Motion picture producers and directors--United
    States--Biography.
Classification: LCC ML429.T26 A3 2021 (print) | LCC ML429.T26 (ebook) |
    DDC 781.66092 [B]--dc23
LC record available at https://lccn.loc.gov/2020015947
LC ebook record available at https://lccn.loc.gov/2020015948

Cover Photo: Festival Express, 1970, author center right. © John Scheele. All rights reserved.
Endsheet Photo: Woodstock Festival, 1969. © Elliott Landy. All rights reserved.
Cover and Interior Design/Typesetting: Ashley Ingram

Published by Heyday
P.O. Box 9145, Berkeley, California 94709
(510) 549-3564
heydaybooks.com

Printed in East Peoria, Illinois, by Versa Press, Inc.

10 9 8 7 6 5 4 3 2 1

To Maggie

and to Daniela, Nicholas, and Blythe

Contents

In its refusal to accept as final the limitations imposed upon freedom and happiness by society, in its refusal to forget *what can be*, lies the critical function of the artist.

—Herbert Marcuse

Show a little faith, there's magic in the night.

—Bruce Springsteen

Prologue

Strapped to a Fender Stratocaster electric guitar, Bob Dylan launched into the opening chords of "Maggie's Farm" almost before the band was ready. The Newport Folk Festival of 1965 was going to close with a commotion. I had just turned eighteen, and was an apprentice road manager for Dylan's manager. This explosive moment launched me on a lifelong journey, one beyond anything I could have imagined at the time.

I was standing in the stage wing, transfixed, ten feet from the band. Mike Bloomfield, acting like bandleader, brought his Butterfield Blues Band rhythm section—drummer Sam Lay and bassist Jerome Arnold—into some approximation of sync with Dylan's rhythm. Al Kooper, in a loud polka-dot shirt, hunched over the Hammond organ and did his best to fill in the spaces, but wasn't starting well. I ran out toward the mixing booth in front of the stage, where Peter Yarrow had commandeered the board. It was worse out front. In his nervousness, Bloomfield kept raising his guitar volume and was now drowning out everything else. The first tune ended on a sour note and there was only light applause from the audience. I gazed behind me and a look of shock seemed to be the dominant emotion in the sea of blue work shirts and peasant blouses. The man in the tight pants, orange shirt, and dark glasses was not their Bob Dylan. What was going on?

A chorus of boos filled the air before Bob started his radio hit "Like a Rolling Stone," but by the end the fans were still booing. Voices from the crowd called for their favorite tunes from the folk era. The band looked nervous, but without a word to the audience Bob plunged into "It Takes a Lot to Laugh, It Takes a Train to Cry." The band found their groove, but when the tune ended, the booing got worse. Dylan turned to Bloomfield and said, "Let's split." To the surprise of the other musicians and the road crew, he unplugged his Fender and walked off the stage.

Instantly the crowd went silent. People started yelling at each other in the aisles. "Look what you did!" "He's gone, asshole." Peter Yarrow bolted from the mixing console and I followed him backstage. Dylan was sitting on the bottom steps of the stairway leading up to the stage. He was clearly shaken, rubbing his eyes. Peter ran up onto the stage and seized the microphone. "Hey, show Bobby that you love him. Let's get him back." The audience roared approval. Dylan sat still on the steps. The audience began to clap in rhythm. Dylan refused to budge. Peter appeared at the top of the stairs, pleading with him to return.

Johnny Cash wandered out of the artists' tent holding an acoustic guitar. For a minute he watched the triangular drama of Peter, Bob, and the crowd. He moved over to Bob and handed him the guitar. "Play them a song, son." Bob took the guitar and slowly walked up the thirty steps to the stage. When he appeared in a lone spotlight holding the acoustic guitar, the cheers from the audience were deafening. He leaned toward the microphone, raising his harmonica holder. "Does anyone have a D harmonica?" Out of the crowd, three of Hohner's finest sailed through the air onto the stage. Dylan danced out of the way and, grinning, picked up one and placed it in the holder. He started to strum the guitar.

> *You must leave now, take what you need,*
>
> > *you think will last.*
>
> *But whatever you wish to keep, you better grab it fast.*
>
> *Yonder stands your orphan with his gun,*
>
> *Crying like a fire in the sun.*
>
> *Look out, the saints are comin' through*
>
> *And it's all over now, Baby Blue.*

When he finished the song, he rushed through "Mr. Tambourine Man," then turned and, without a word, walked quickly off the stage. He had said his piece. They did not own him and, like a lover leaving a bad relationship breakup, he would not turn back.

Great cultural movements are not developed in clarity and order. I could feel that I had just witnessed something profoundly important, but I had no idea what its long-term effects would be. And as I chased the intensity and freedom that Dylan's Newport set had allowed me to taste, my life also unfolded in a series of random acts of good fortune—being in the right place at the right time. I experienced some of the great rock-and-roll moments of the sixties from one of the closest vantage points possible, I found myself in the middle of a new movement in film during the seventies, and I stopped in several more unexpected places on the way to the present. I could never have foreseen where I am now. My current business card carries the title Director Emeritus, Annenberg Innovation Lab, University of Southern California, and I dedicate most of my time to writing and speaking about Big Tech monopolies and examining the great contradictions of the tech revolution. Maybe it seems strange to connect our current culture all the way back to a divisive show Bob Dylan played in 1965. But they're part of a common story about our culture, and in these pages I tell my version of it.

In 2015 and 2016 I wrote a book called *Move Fast and Break Things*, which considers the monopolization of the Internet and its destructive effects on society, and especially on artists. That story has become more common in the years since, and here I intentionally do not tell it again. In many ways, this book is the complete opposite.

Move Fast and Break Things is about technology, oligarchy, determinism, and our ruthless present. The story I tell here is about art, democracy, serendipity, and history. It's about the messiness and chance that are essential to the development of culture, even when aspects of that process age better than others. But the daring messiness of the period from the early sixties to the fall of the Berlin Wall in 1989 contrasts strongly from the nihilistic cultural and political stagnation of the current moment. The great cultural historian Jacques Barzun wrote a book titled *From Dawn to Decadence*. In it he described a moment that feels very true right now: "The forms of art as of life seem exhausted, the stages of development have been run through. Institutions function painfully. Repetition and frustration are the intolerable result."

At this very moment, as I am finishing this book, those painfully functioning institutions are putting our society—savaged by a pandemic, a financial depression, and a racial justice crisis—into danger. How we emerge from the crisis, and the role an optimistic culture could play in that renaissance, will be a lesson hopefully learned from the thirty years of upheaval depicted in this story. The business analyst Peter Drucker famously said, "Culture eats strategy for breakfast." This book is about the sense of possibility that allows culture to be its most vital and powerful, even in difficult times. It's about culture eating politics for breakfast.

The history of America is filled with periods of upheaval like the one we are experiencing now. They tend to show up every fifty years. From 1850 to 1865 we fought over slavery. From 1902 to 1915 we fought over the power of corporate monopoly and women's right to vote. From 1962 to 1970 we fought over the civil rights of our Black citizens. And today we are fighting for those same civil rights and battling new corporate monopolies that threaten our democracy. And though the battles seem never to end in permanent victory for the forces of freedom and equality, in each generation progress is made. In each of these earlier battles American artists were at the barricades, refusing, as Marcuse said, "to forget what can be." But right now the voice of the progressive artist is kept at the periphery, as the critic A. O. Scott makes clear, noting that much of our popular culture—especially our movies and TV—"has been authoritarian, anti-democratic, cynical, and pseudo-populist. That much of the politics of the past decade can be described with the same words is hardly an accident."

Rather than lamenting *what is*, this book explores *what was*, so that we might understand *what can be*. For as Thomas Paine reminded us at the beginning of this long American experiment in freedom and equality, "We have it in our power to begin the world over again."

1. Lord of the Flies

1962

Sometimes I wonder how different my life would have been if my brother Randy had not brought home from college Bob Dylan's first album. I certainly would never have encountered it listening to the radio in Cleveland. When I went to the local record store to buy my own copy, they had never even heard of Bob Dylan. So I went home and played Randy's copy like it was on a loop. It drove my mother crazy. She couldn't stand Bob's voice.

Running our family was a balancing act for my mother. My sister, Susan, and my brother Randy had both been born before World War II, and then my father departed for the navy in 1942 and my mother, Constance Huntington Taplin, lived the gypsy life of an officer-in-training's wife. My dad, Charles Farrand Taplin, Jr., lieutenant on a destroyer escort that would be deployed to hunt Japanese submarines, trained in Florida, with my mom and two young kids stuck in one tiny motel room in a complex the navy had requisitioned. I was one of the early postwar babies, born in July of 1947, and my younger brother, Bob, arrived in 1950. We grew up in a big clapboard house in Shaker Heights, outside of Cleveland. My mother described my father returning from the war and ordering the family about as if they were subordinates on his navy crew.

My father's side of the family, the Taplins, had French Huguenot roots and had fled to Ireland from France during the purge of the Protestants only to have to flee to America in the 1840s under conditions of oppression and famine. They arrived as immigrants with no real savings. My grandfather Charles Taplin and his brother Frank both were lower-middle-class strivers, trying to get into the inner circle of John D. Rockefeller's Cleveland enterprises. Frank eventually became Rockefeller's private secretary in 1912, before going off on his own to start a company with his brother. All of my life growing up in Cleveland, I heard rumors of a blood feud between Charles and his brother Frank. Although it was never discussed in our family, I did know that Frank's side of the family was tremendously wealthy and ours was not and that somehow my grandfather had gotten screwed out of his fortune.

One day in 1990, while researching a documentary in a Santa Monica library, I was flipping through the *New York Times Index*, the massive bound volumes cataloging every article ever published by the *Times*. I opened up the volume for the 1920s and on a lark looked up the name Taplin. I was shocked to find thirty-five articles listed under that name. When I went to the microfilm, I found article after article detailing the rise of the Taplin Brothers in the railroad and coal businesses in the twenties. They controlled the Wheeling and Lake Erie Railroad, which appeared to be an important route for shipping coal to the steel mills of Cleveland and Pittsburgh. At the same time, the New York Central and the Pennsylvania were locked in an epic battle to control the freight traffic east of the Mississippi. At a critical point in the late summer of 1929, the Taplin Brothers sold a major portion of their stock in the Wheeling line to a group called Pennco for $45 per share. The sale, however, was not revealed until October 10, a week after the great stock market crash, when shares of the Wheeling had fallen to $19 per share. The deal was immediately attacked on two fronts: by the minority shareholders who hadn't gotten the good price and by the Interstate Commerce Commission, which said that Pennco was simply a front for the Pennsylvania Railroad and therefore the Pennsylvania Railroad would have a monopoly on the transport of coal in the eastern United States.

Whereas in the early articles my grandfather Charles was always quoted as the public spokesman, after the deal was announced his older brother Frank began speaking for the company. He maintained that he was still running the Wheeling and West Virginia and had merely sold some stock. It wasn't until three years later during the Pecora hearings in the Senate that the real story emerged. Evidently my grandfather and the head of Pennco had drawn up a document that ceded operating control of the Wheeling to Pennco on the sale. After the crash, when the ICC began looking into the deal, the Pennco attorneys had torn up their copy of the document. When Frank asked his brother to tear up their copy, he refused. Frank had loaned Charles the money to buy into the Wheeling trust and he demanded repayment while withholding the proceeds from the Pennco sale, claiming that it might have to be undone given the lawsuits. Charles couldn't come up with the money, so Frank took all of Charles's shares in the North American Coal Company (their other holding) as repayment, locked his brother out of his office (where the Pennco contract was in a safe), and never spoke to him again.

Twenty-five years after my father's death I realized that this whole tragedy had taken place during his junior and senior years at Princeton. His family had been ripped from total security and forced to start all over again, just at the very point when his life could have been carefree. When my father graduated from Harvard Law School in 1933, he went to work with his father in a two-man law firm. My sense is that my father felt that his dad was weak and that he should have stood up to his brother. But that was not to be. The brothers never spoke for the rest of their lives. This sense that his father was weak was a constant source of pain for my father.

After the war, my father and my grandfather slowly rebuilt their law practice and then merged into a larger firm. My father's specialty, antitrust law, was of particular importance in the wake of Cleveland's connection to the Standard Oil monopoly. He was ambitious and worked very hard to become a pillar of the community, determined both to undo the hurt that had been caused his father and to never himself be seen as weak.

What I remember most was his sense of style. His closet was like Gatsby's: rows of shirts in white, blue, and (for weekends) pink. He must have had fifty striped repp ties and ten bow ties, twenty pairs of shoes, polished perfectly, and ten different hats, including straw boaters for summer. The only time he would not wear one of his twenty suits was on weekends, when he dressed in flannels and blazers or, if he was really casual, a pair of perfectly creased khakis. I once took one of his thirty white handkerchiefs to wear in my pocket to a dance. He noticed it was missing.

I don't think living with my father was ever easy for my mother. He was obsessed with regaining his family's position in Cleveland society and therefore felt it crucial to be in the company of the men that ran the big businesses in town. What money my parents had—a good portion of which was my mother's inheritance from her father—was spent on memberships at the Kirtland Country Club, the Tavern Club, the Union Club and, most gallingly, a bird-shooting club called Winous Point. My mother once acidly remarked that the fee for the last of these came to about $2,000 per duck my father would bring home for Sunday dinner.

When he was home, my father was a real disciplinarian. I hold an image of my seven-year-old rebellious self, having been sent to my room, listening as my father ascended the stairs and knowing I was in for a spanking with his belt. In his defense, this was common practice in the 1950s, and when it was over my mother would enter the room to comfort me.

When I was nine years old, my mother was finally overcome with the tension of holding the family together with no help from her spouse. I was in the supermarket with her when she fainted, collapsing into my arms. The fear of not knowing what to do only grew as I rode by her side in the ambulance to the hospital. With my brother and sister away at boarding school and college, and my father out of town, I felt even more deeply scared of losing my mother. It was not until a few years later that I realized how important her daily counsel was to my life.

In the fall 1961, at the age of fourteen, I was sent away by my father to Brooks, a boarding school for boys in Massachusetts. The headmaster, in the tradition of English "public schools" like Eton, believed every young man needed grounding in the Classics, and so not only did we study Latin and Greek as languages, we also became versed in the Classical philosophers and playwrights. Thus it was that, at the age of fourteen, I came upon the philosophy of Epicurus. As a young man far away from my home in Cleveland, friendless and adrift, I took readily to Epicurus's view of what made a good life, which he broke into three elements:

- The company of good friends.
- The freedom and autonomy to enjoy meaningful work.
- An "examined life," built around a core faith or philosophy.

At the moment I came upon Epicurus, I had none of the three elements, and no idea how to obtain them. I would spend my life trying to achieve all three (with varying levels of success), and over time I came to understand that enjoying autonomy and an examined life in particular are more elusive than they appear, especially to a fourteen-year-old.

I had been sent off to boarding school because my father had my whole life planned out for me. I would go from boarding school into Princeton and then to Harvard Law School, following the track he had taken. I would then come home to Cleveland and join his law firm. For my father, boarding school was a prerequisite, and although I think my mother had second thoughts, I was not opposed to the idea, as I had no great attachment to Cleveland and no real friends—both conditions serving as evidence that I had always lived more in my imagination and books than in the real world of the city. I had been a loner since the fall of 1953, when I was misdiagnosed with polio and quarantined in a hospital ward for three months. From then on, I found it preferable to make my own way. Headed off to boarding school, I knew I would miss my mother's advice about how to navigate life, but I was anxious to get away from the constant arguments with my father. Although I was "sent away" to Brooks School, I went willingly.

The Reverend Endicott Peabody, headmaster of the Groton School for Boys (one of the most elite boarding schools in the nation), had founded Brooks as a sort of "junior varsity Groton" at the height of the Roaring Twenties. The first headmaster of Brooks was a twenty-five-year-old Groton and Yale graduate named Frank Ashburn, and he was still headmaster when I arrived in the fall of 1961. We named him Prune, and his wife Phyllis we called Fille. They were both tightly wound and spoke with the Boston version of a British upper-class accent. Ashburn had the kind of slicked-back hairstyle you might see in a silent movie from the 1920s, and he wore small wire-frame glasses. His pinched-in mouth lent itself to the nickname Prune. He had the appearance of a stodgy old man, but, as I eventually found out, he was, unlike many of his station, open to new information.

I showed up at Brooks for third form, the equivalent of ninth grade. Most of my schoolmates had been there since second form, so I was the odd man out from the start, not a great position to be in considering that the British traditions of boarding school that Groton and Brooks followed brought out the innate cruelty in young men of fourteen. To begin with, the prefect system assigned older students to monitor and discipline the dormitories filled with younger boys. One freezing January night, for the sin of talking after lights-out, two of us were taken to the second-floor fire escape in our underwear and forced by a prefect to kneel back and forth on the metal grate, our hands clasped behind our heads, until our knees bled into the snow below. There was no appealing to a higher authority; the prefect was judge and jury. When I went back into the dorm, the chief bully in my class saw my bleeding legs and named me Night Crawler.

For the first year and a half, I found myself a complete outsider, with no one to turn to. Certainly Frank Ashburn was not interested in my sadness and alienation. "Buck up, boy" was his favorite riposte at dinner to a long-faced kid. It was a real *Lord of the Flies* situation. Having come from the Midwest, I was unused to the sarcasm that the other boys had grown up with in their East Coast hometowns. It was a foreign concept to me that a person would say something and mean just the opposite, and it took me quite a while to adapt to the utter cynicism that was the code at Brooks. What was so strange to me was that, on the surface, and especially in front of "the masters," everyone at Brooks was terribly polite. They all knew how to play the game of upper-class gentility. Among my classmates were the great-grandsons of J. P. Morgan and Henry Clay Frick; Jamie Auchincloss, Jackie Kennedy's half-brother, lived in my dorm. The word "manners" was used several times a day, but the cultivated displays of civilized behavior only masked a deep streak of cruelty. I began to live in a state of continual anticipation, wondering where the next round of abuse would come from. No event had any meaning except as a way station to the future—college, a job—anything that would be an escape from my present reality.

My isolation was so profound that I, a generally unreligious person, took to prayer. Brooks had a chapel service every evening, and although attendance wasn't mandatory, the chapel became a place of quiet sanctuary for me. I would get down on my knees and pray to God for some guidance out of the hell I found myself in. I don't know if God heard me, but the very hope that someone might listen to my plight was perhaps all I was looking for. Perhaps I was even then in search of Epicurus's "examined life," but I didn't yet appreciate that, in order to realize the goals of his philosophy, I would have to break away from the place I had first encountered them as an ideal worth striving for.

Despite what the Episcopal values of Brooks would have me believe, prayers were not always answered and the meek did not inherit the Earth. I was trying so hard to fit in at Brooks, but nothing was working. I had the Brooks Brothers tweed jackets and gray flannels, the Bass Weejuns, the blue button-down shirts, and the striped repp ties. Why was I such an outsider? When I got older and read Hemingway and Fitzgerald, I realized that fighting might have been a way to make my mark, but I was a small kid, so even that would have been a longshot. The only sport I excelled at was swimming, and Brooks had no swimming team. Instead, I became a coxswain on the crew team, and for a couple hours every day in the spring, I found a small measure of camaraderie with four upperclassmen oarsmen.

In my dormitory, the variety of the nastiness I saw, especially as dealt out by a ringleader named John Leake, would constantly catch me by surprise. I remember him picking on the fact that I had long eyelashes, which he took as evidence that I was secretly gay. There was no rational response to bullying like that, so I just suffered in silence.

My only respite from the unkindness of prep school was a little coffeehouse in Harvard Square called Club 47 (now Club Passim). This was the center of the folk music revival in the Northeast. I had been introduced to the genre by my older brother, Randy, who was a sophomore at the University of Virginia. Randy had been introduced to the scene by Paul Clayton, who was a UVA ethnomusicologist ranked up there with Alan Lomax as one of the great collectors of songs from the field. Clayton's methodology was to hike through the Shenandoah Valley and the Blue Ridge Mountains with a backpack, a wooden banjo made by the old-time Appalachian banjoist Frank Proffitt, and an Uher portable tape recorder. When he came to a mountain cabin he would ask for a drink of water and try to see if any musical instruments were hung on the wall. If he spied the odd guitar, mandolin, or banjo, he would work his way around to getting the occupants to play a song with him. Eventually they would come to a tune he'd never heard, and at that point Paul would ask if he might turn on the tape recorder. Between 1961 and 1965, he'd put out fourteen records on the Folkways label, and his great joy was in making sure the mountain players got their surprise royalty checks by postal money order.

Randy had met Paul at a civil rights sit-in at a lunch counter near the UVA campus, and although taking part in this and similar actions did not endear my brother to his fellow university students, it did win him an invitation to Paul's weekend retreat in the mountains above Charlottesville. There he met Bob Dylan, Odetta, Richard Fariña, and Carolyn Hester, the young folk singer who brought Dylan to the attention of John Hammond at Columbia Records. The singers would come to Clayton's to listen to his latest finds, looking for material. (The tune for Dylan's song "Don't Think Twice, It's All Right" came from one of Clayton's tapes.) In June of 1962 my brother brought home Dylan's first record.

By February of 1963, I was allowed (because my grades were good) to take the train to Boston twice a month, ostensibly to visit a mythical great aunt but in actuality to spend evenings at Club 47. The only way to describe Club 47 faithfully is to ask you to imagine the Paris of Hemingway's *Moveable Feast*. If you combined the Café de Flore with Sylvia Beach's bookstore Shakespeare and Company, you might approximate the importance of Club 47 to folk music culture of the early 1960s. It was there I found myself listening to Joan Baez, Lightnin' Hopkins, the Jim Kweskin Jug Band, the Charles River Valley Boys, Tom Rush, Eric Andersen, Flatt and Scruggs—the whole panoply of American folk music that was coming out of the woodwork in 1963. You could nurse a cappuccino for hours and be in the company of friends who understood the richness of this music, and its sadness too. I would go back to school on a Sunday night, high from my forty-eight hours of expatriate life in Cambridge, knowing there was a world of wondrous art and friendship and courage that I could live in once I fulfilled my educational duty to my family. It was the first of the "scenes" I was introduced to as a kid.

I think of a scene as a magical gathering of artists that pushes everybody's work to a higher level, and Club 47 was a perfect example. One evening after a show, I was invited back to the Cambridge apartment of John Cooke, who played and sang in the neo-bluegrass group the Charles River Valley Boys. (John was the son of Alastair Cooke, the BBC commentator on all things America.) John had a huge iron lung parked in the hallway, and in the small hours you might spy couples making out inside. But what I remember from that night is a singer named Eric Von Schmidt teaching John Cooke and Geoff Muldaur the fingerpicking chords to a song called "Baby, Let Me Follow You Down." Earlier that year, he had taught the song to Bob Dylan, who'd used it on his first album. This was the folk tradition: four or five players with acoustic instruments at two in the morning teaching each other songs they had found. This one is from the blind gospel and blues singer Reverend Gary Davis, and you have to wonder how he got the moniker "reverend" with lyrics like these:

> *Baby, let me follow you down,*
> *Baby, let me follow you down,*
> *Well, I'll do anything in this God-almighty world*
> *If you just let me follow you down.*

The time I spent in Cambridge also introduced me to a new politics, not just because of who I was hanging out with but because Boston was a center for the civil rights movement in the north. It's hard to explain what happened that spring, but for many of us, May 2, 1963, was a turning point. That was the day Sheriff Bull Connor of Birmingham, Alabama, unleashed the dogs and firehoses on the Children's Crusade. For months Martin Luther King's Southern Christian Leadership Conference had been teaching high school kids the principles of nonviolence. Local school principals had tried to lock their young Black students in school so they couldn't get into downtown

Birmingham for sit-ins protesting segregation, but as the kids jumped school walls, they faced police dogs and powerful streams of water, and hundreds were arrested, all of it happening on national TV. A correspondent for the *Huntley–Brinkley Report* news program said that the events in Birmingham disturbed him more than any military action he had seen.

The abuse I suffered in boarding school aside, I had led a pretty sheltered life, and the violence of the pictures created a visceral anger inside of me that I had never experienced. I joined the civil rights movement soon after the successful Birmingham Children's Crusade. As a prep school kid, deeply lonely and alienated from my peers, there was no one in my school who was interested in civil rights causes, but down in Cambridge the movement and the music were one. There was no split between culture and politics, and whenever there was a civil rights march in the summer and fall of 1963, Dylan's songs were sung. I was drawn to the charisma of John Lewis and Bob Moses, who seemed to be the public face of the Student Nonviolent Coordinating Committee (SNCC), and I would use the word "magical" to describe the sense of inclusion even white students felt in the movement. By the time of the March on Washington in August of 1963, there was a sense that a new world was at hand.

The importance of music to the movement cannot be overstated. When, in the early years, many civil rights actions in the South took the form of sit-ins—some with as few as twenty brave young people, Black and white together—good songs like "Blowin' in the Wind," "The Times They Are a-Changin'," and "We Shall Overcome" did much to help keep courage up in a generally hostile environment.

There is a moment in Martin Scorsese's 2005 Dylan documentary, *No Direction Home*, where Bob is singing to a voting rights rally in Greenwood, Mississippi, in the summer of 1963. What you see is a group of young Black kids listening intently to Dylan's song, but what might not be apparent is that the people listening to Dylan at that rally were literally risking their lives to be there. A year later and not far away, the local sheriff and the KKK would kill three young civil rights workers, and violence against protesters and supporters was not uncommon.

This was all part of a profound political and cultural shift that seemed to strike like lightning in my consciousness. Out of my sight, folks like Martin Luther King and Rosa Parks had been struggling against segregation since the early 1950s. But for me, the summer of 1963 was a point of political and cultural cleavage. Bobby Rydell's saccharine "Forget Him" was number one on the Cleveland Hit Parade, and yet I was trying to get my friends to listen to Bob Dylan's protest anthem "Blowin' in the Wind." Elizabeth Taylor's *Cleopatra* movie was being advertised ubiquitously, and yet in a small art theater the burgeoning counterculture was being entranced by another take on Roman life: Fellini's *8½*. Everywhere there was a disconnect between mass culture and the underground. As an outsider in my own life, I felt a natural affinity to the latter. The political culture of the civil rights movement and the musical culture of folk music—much of it based on the country blues genre of the American South—merged perfectly, and both spoke to me on a personal level. The movement gave me a place to stand, a place where I felt that others shared both my alienation and my idealism.

In July of 1963, my father planned a special journey as a way to make peace within our family, and perhaps also to make peace with a God he didn't believe in. In that summer of political chaos and personal repose he chartered a yacht in the Greek port of Piraeus, and for the next two weeks he, with my mother, myself, and my two older siblings, sailed around the Aegean. The trip is forever burned into my consciousness not just because it was my first time abroad but because it allowed me to regain a friendship with my dad.

Under the spell of Epicurus's quest for freedom and Martin Luther King's quest for justice, I had spent the previous five months arguing vehemently with my father about politics and culture over the phone and in passionate letters. The anger that had sparked in me the moment I saw Bull Connor on TV unleashing his dogs and water cannons on the kids had since grown into a bonfire. I believed in the grassroots force of the civil rights movement, but my father believed you changed the world through changing the laws. The idea of changing laws by defying law enforcement infuriated him to his core, and he did not approve of my joining SNCC or my older brother participating in sit-ins in Charlottesville, Virginia. We wanted to know which side he was truly on, and he booked that sailing trip in part as a way to turn down the heat between the three of us.

I think my father wanted to make peace because he genuinely saw me as the prodigal son. My older brother, Randy, had no interest in the law; my sister, Sue, had shown she wanted to be a writer and teacher (she wrote us incredibly beautiful letters describing her life as a teacher in Bangkok in the early sixties); and perhaps even then my dad and mom knew that my younger brother, Bob, was probably going to be an artist of some kind. So my dad's vision of having a son join his law firm turned on me like a laser. It meant going to prep school and then Princeton and then Harvard Law—the exact route he had taken—and I could see stretching before me almost a decade more of measuring up, and then probably a whole lifetime of the same after that. There was always the temptation to say the hell with it, but I knew such a decision would be costly. As much as my dad and I had fought over politics, long hair, and manners, I still felt bound to him by a sense of duty and a desire to live up to his expectations.

One early example of this sense of obligation happened when I was thirteen and on a train with him from Cleveland to Washington, D.C., to watch him plead an antitrust case in front of the Federal Trade Commission. My father's client was an oil service company called Dresser Industries. Long before Halliburton (which eventually acquired Dresser), the company dominated the Texas market for valves, pumps, drill bits, and, most importantly for my father's case, "drilling mud," the special lubricant critical to oil exploration. Dresser had a 90 percent share in the Texas market and had proposed to acquire a Pennsylvania company that had a similar share in its market. The trick for my father was to convince the FTC that nothing would change in each market if the two firms merged. I read his brief on the way down, and it caught my father off guard when I pointed out one missing piece of information in the brief. He and his colleagues were surprised by my question and did some research on it, and it later turned out to be the first question the commission asked my father after his opening presentation. Thanks to me, he had the answer prepared, and when we arrived home in Cleveland he couldn't stop boasting to my mother about my contribution. She remarked that since I sure liked to argue a lot, I might be a very good lawyer. My father thought my long hair and protest music was just a phase I would grow out of and set his sights on having me join his firm one day.

My mother, on the other hand, was curiously tolerant of my musical ambitions, and I can trace that to her long family history of art and commerce living together harmoniously. Her father, Robert Huntington, had a conservative job as an insurance executive, but a spirit of liberalism infused Hartford in the thirties, and he mixed with all types of people. The family's next-door neighbors in Hartford were Dr. Thomas Hepburn and his wife, Kit, a leading suffragist and promoter of birth control and, with Margaret Sanger, cofounder of the organization that became Planned Parenthood. (One of the couple's six children, Katharine, named after her mother, became the most successful actress of her generation.) During his summer vacations in Camden, Maine, my grandfather would paint watercolor landscapes, and this helped him forge a friendship with realist painter Edward Hopper (not to mention that he was able to buy eight of Hopper's early watercolors for $500 a piece). My mother once told me about the time she saw the poet Wallace Stevens (whose day job was working as an insurance executive) walk by their house in the morning on the way to the office, sometimes pausing, taking a step back, and then beginning again; she imagined he was figuring out the rhythm of a poem in his head. Perhaps these experiences account for the tolerance my mother had for her sons' political activities and cultural tastes.

Politics wasn't really discussed much in my house in the 1950s. I think my dad and most of his friends were Eisenhower Republicans. They had fought in World War II, and Ike was a hero to them. Like Ike, they were suspicious of big business "war profiteering," but they all believed in American Exceptionalism— the idea that the United States has the right to impose its will on other countries because it knows more and lives on a higher moral plane than other nations. That idea would be put to the test in the next decade.

As for me, I have always been a curious mix of liberal and conservative. I was brought up by my mother to be liberal minded—open to new ideas and embracing a deep belief in equality of opportunity—but since the age of thirteen I have also been religious, a fairly consistent keeper of the Episcopalian faith, much to the puzzlement of many of my friends and academic colleagues. As to conservatism, much of my life has been dedicated to conserving what might be called "folk traditions"—I love the music of Louis Armstrong, Duke Ellington, the Stanley Brothers, and Muddy Waters—but is that instinct conservative or something else? Can open-mindedness and reverence for the past dwell in one consciousness without repercussions?

My own political awareness was first raised during the presidential campaign of John F. Kennedy in 1960. I will never forget when, during a cocktail party my parents were hosting, they and their friends invaded the kids' playroom, where the only TV was located, and changed the channel to the first Nixon-Kennedy debate. When it was over, the men left the room, fully confident that Nixon had won, but my mother stayed with me to watch some brief commentary. I told her I thought Kennedy was much better than Nixon. I think she agreed, but she said nothing.

Even though politics was not a major force in my household growing up, it was causing tension during my teen years, and the trip to the Aegean was to be a respite from current events and the constant arguing with my father. It was my first trip abroad, and new horizons arrived on a daily basis. As a fierce mistral blew over the Aegean Sea on my sixteenth birthday, we went to port on the island of Mykonos, and our skipper, Sam Barclay, a former British naval officer who had fallen in love with the Greek islands when he was stationed there during World War II, took me out for a beer at a bar that was filled with college kids from all over Europe. It was loud, and a record called "If You Wanna Be Happy," by Jimmy Soul, was playing over and over in the background. The boys and girls were tanned and good-looking, with a kind of looseness that was so foreign compared to the boarding school dances I had attended. The joyful music, combined with the beer and the beautiful bodies, induced a strange ecstasy in my head. Somehow I ended up dancing with a girl named Kari, who said she was nineteen and from Norway. She had a fairly decent grasp of English and was dressed in a tight blue-and-white-striped T-shirt and cutoff jeans. She moved like a cool breeze. I was entranced, and when I finally looked away from her after two or three songs, I noticed that Sam Barclay had disappeared. I turned back to Kari and saw her nipples were showing through her sweaty T-shirt.

Fifty-five years later, the rest of the night feels caught between recalled desire and faded memory. I remember my first French kiss, the shock of Kari's tongue on mine, and I remember leaving the bar and following her down to the beach and off to some deserted corner where the lights of the town could hardly be seen. Then more kissing and her peeling her T-shirt off and my lips on her beautiful small breasts and her pulling my shorts off, pushing me down on my back and lowering herself onto me. She took my virginity with the greatest gentleness. I remember waking up in her arms at the crack of dawn and panicking, knowing we were leaving for Spetses that morning. Had my father sent out a search party?

I got dressed. Kari wrote down her address in Oslo and I ran back to the boat. No one was stirring, and I snuck on board and crashed on the long bench on the afterdeck. When Theodore the cook came up from below at seven, he handed me a cup of coffee. I felt like I had just been initiated into a secret society. Not a word about the evening was ever uttered to my family, but when I got home to Cleveland I wrote to Kari in Norway. I learned "Jeg elsker deg"—"I love you" in Norwegian—but in my heart I knew it had been a one-night stand and I would never see her again.

When I returned to prep school in the fall, I saw everything in a different light. The beginning of my understanding of Epicurus's freedom from fear had begun. Was it the sexual confidence or was it the rebellious stance I had begun to adopt? Over the summer, I had had a remarkable growth spurt and literally had to buy new shirts every four months. Maybe that was part of it—I wasn't so easy to pick on anymore.

On the afternoon of November 22, 1963, I was leaving class, headed toward my dorm, when I saw the Volkswagen van from which a local man used to sell candy and magazines. As I picked up a Mounds bar I heard through his transistor radio the words "The president has been shot." The outside world came crashing in. A secret service agent arrived to pick up Jamie Auchincloss not more than two hours after President John F. Kennedy, his brother-in-law, was killed. The initial feeling was a sort of numbness—the aftermath of shock.

This was followed by what seemed like a week of watching the television as the bizarre events unfolded: Lee Harvey Oswald captured and then paraded through the Dallas police headquarters by beefy men in cowboy hats; Oswald shot by Jack Ruby on live TV, with the same cops looking aghast; then the funeral procession, with my schoolmate Jamie walking right behind Bobby Kennedy. It all seemed unreal, and none of it made sense. I had been studying Lincoln's assassination in history class, and the words of Walt Whitman's elegy "O Captain! My Captain!" haunted me.

> Here Captain! dear father!
>
> This arm beneath your head!
>
> It is some dream that on the deck,
>
> You've fallen cold and dead.

The JFK assassination separates my generation from those that came after. At the very beginning of my generation's engagement with the larger world (I was sixteen), it was deeply troubling to have a paranoid sense that your government is hiding the truth about the murder of your political hero. That lack of trust has remained with us our whole lives, and to this day many of us do not believe the Warren Commission findings that a pathetic, attention-seeking loser named Lee Harvey Oswald was the sole gunman. In the summer of 1965, when I was visiting Jamie Auchincloss in Newport, Rhode Island, he noted that even Bobby Kennedy did not believe that Oswald had planned and executed the killing on his own. Bobby knew more than most the incredible ties between the mafia, the Cuban exile community, and the CIA—all of whom viewed the Kennedys as existential threats. To the end of his life Bobby wondered if his zealous prosecution of mafia leaders had led to his brother's death, and his close aide Robert Morgenthau said he wrestled with questions such as "Was there something I could have done to prevent it? Was there something I did to encourage it? Was I to blame?"

Don DeLillo, who has written more eloquently than anyone on the effect of the JFK assassination on the American psyche, had a character in his novel *Underworld* contrast the broadcasting of the 1951 Giants/Dodgers "shot heard round the world" baseball game to the news of the JFK assassination. When the former happened, DeLillo claimed, everyone in New York ran into the streets, becoming a united crowd. When the latter happened, everyone went inside to commune with their radios and TVs, isolating themselves in response to the news. That contrast evokes something powerful about the psychic effect of the assassination: the forces organizing the world had become unreliable in a new way, and a more mysterious strain of mistrust entered American life.

Because Jamie Auchincloss was a student at Brooks, the mourning at the school felt more personal, and it lasted through the beginning of 1964, when something quite magical happened that shook us all out of our stupor. The headmaster gave the whole school permission to watch *The Ed Sullivan Show* on that Sunday night in early February when the Beatles first appeared. I kept a journal during that period and here is what I wrote:

> As cloistered as we are, we still know that the arrival of The Beatles is a pretty big thing. I guess it's the first happy news since the President was killed. Even though I'm a folk music fan, I really like their songs and their look. Its funny watching a bunch of stuck up preppie's trying to look cool when such craziness was going on in the audience of the Sullivan show.

It was such a different spirit on the stage of the *Sullivan Show* from what was happening on the American Top 40. Our spirits were lifted by the band's humor, and all of a sudden London seemed like the coolest place in the world. This was reinforced when, a few weeks later, our history professor Richard Holmes chose the new John Schlesinger film *Billy Liar* as the Saturday night movie at the school. I loved the British New Wave sensibility and left the theater with such a crush on Julie Christie, whose attitude defined the hip girl for the next ten years of my life.

A different kind of passion was stirred up in me a few months later when our school was visited by Yale University's chaplain, the Reverend William Sloane Coffin, who gave a guest lecture to the whole school. Brooks headmaster Frank Ashburn was a Yale bulldog through and through and also an Episcopalian lay minister, so the idea of inviting the Yale chaplain to deliver a bit of moral uplift to his students in the spring of 1964 must have been a no-brainer. My guess is that the traditionalist headmaster had not really done his homework, however, because Coffin was a world-class disrupter. In 1961 he had been the first prominent white clergyman to get involved with the Freedom Rides conducted to integrate the interstate bus services in the South.

Coffin did not sugarcoat his message, reproduced below thanks to Warren Goldstein's biography *William Sloane Coffin, Jr.: A Holy Impatience.* Five months after John F. Kennedy's assassination, and with the dead president's brother-in-law in the audience, Coffin said, "At his best, John Kennedy exemplified freedom both at home and abroad. If we would be true to the best memory of this man, we might now on his behalf . . . take up the unfinished business of freedom. America is not free, not in terms of the 14th or even the 1st Amendment; our press is not free, it's private and far from free; many of our citizens are free only to sleep in the cold water tenement of their choice; and none of us are free of the greed, trivia and superficiality that mark so much of our national life." I looked around me and saw the Morgans and Fricks staring at their shoes. Coffin finished his talk with a prayer: "Grant us grace not to find reasons to support what we already hold, but to seek a truth greater than anything we have as yet conceived. . . . Remind us that our neighbors suffer from injustices we too were born to correct, for the world is now too dangerous for anything but truth, too small for anything but love."

I staggered out of the hall. I felt he had been talking directly to me, handing me a philosophy to live by. I had to meet him. I waited outside until the slightly shaken headmaster had said his goodbyes and Coffin started to walk to his car. I came up beside him and introduced myself. I told him I had joined SNCC and was trying to figure out how to make a difference in a school that was totally oblivious to the civil rights movement. Coffin was clear: "I didn't see any negro students in the audience tonight. Are there any in the school?" He knew the answer, but I also realized he was handing me a mission. This was the beginning of my examined life, and I set out to convince the headmaster to integrate the school.

People show up in your life just when you are open to change. If you have the ears and heart to hear what they are trying to tell you, your life will be rich. If you ignore them or shut them out, you will get stuck.

I wrote my mom and dad a letter filled with the fervent intensity Coffin had unleashed. My father called me and we had a passionate argument over the tactics of nonviolence. He still believed laws should be changed through legislation and not civil disobedience. To him, Coffin was leading me down the path to chaos. I hung up, furious, figuring that at Easter vacation I would straighten him out in person.

Three weeks later, everything changed. I was summoned to the headmaster's office, where he told me that my father was sick and that I should call my mother right away. I called her. She was trying to be brave but I could hear her crying, and she said that Dad had cancer and it was pretty bad. I should come home.

When I got to Cleveland my father was acting like everything was going to be fine. He would get radiation treatment for the cancer in his pancreas and his stomach. He looked okay, but my mother was really worried. I think the doctors were more pessimistic than my dad. He did not know that he was marked for death, but he did know that although he was only fifty-two, he had lived hard—a pack of cigarettes a day and a pitcher of strong martinis before dinner—and had also worked hard, sometimes going to his law office on Saturdays. He had left the raising of his children to his wife and he sought now to make amends. Dad asked me up to his study and he said that we needed to turn over a new leaf. He promised he wouldn't criticize me for my hair or my politics. He said, "We just have to be friends and care for each other." I felt like I had been storing up months worth of gripes, planning to have it out with him at Easter, and now I would just have to stuff them all back down. He was right about taking care of each other.

When I got back to school, I set out on the mission Bill Coffin had given me, by using my position as managing editor of the school paper to suggest that Brooks should integrate by the fall of 1966. I wrote an editorial and showed it to the faculty advisor to the paper, Mike King. King knew my editorial was going to be explosive and so he had decided to give the headmaster a heads-up before the paper went to press. Ashburn was furious and ordered King and me to a meeting in his study. He began by outlining how much backlash this was going to cause. I know he had listened to Bill Coffin and he knew that the Christian thing to do was to let me publish, but he also wanted me to know just how dependent the school was on alumni donations from people who would disagree with my message. From his office he called my house in Cleveland. Fortunately for me, it was midday and my father had already left for work. Ashburn explained to my mother his "pickle," but she was amazing in her response to this formidable man. She totally took my side and told Ashburn he had a moral duty to let me publish the editorial. I think the history of troublemakers in her family had given her the courage to back me.

The next morning, I was called to Ashburn's office again. He said this was going to hurt his fundraising drive, but he wasn't going to stop me. The paper came out and the bombshell reverberated throughout the Brooks community. The mere suggestion that Black students should be admitted inside the WASP citadel provoked outrage among parents, some of the faculty, and many of my fellow students. "Nigger Lover" was scrawled on my dorm room door. In the next issue of the paper, a history teacher named Keany wrote an outraged letter to the editor about my column, which we published side by side with my reply. For me, everything changed that day. When you express yourself forcefully, you'll usually find your enemies, but hopefully you'll also uncover allies you didn't know were there.

As alone as I felt, a handful of allies did show up in early April, when Martin Luther King announced he was going to march in Boston to protest segregation in schools and public housing. School busing to achieve desegregation was a hot-button issue for many working-class whites in that city, and so we knew there could be violence. I was given permission to take a small group of students to join in the march, and Bob Dean, Jamie Auchincloss, and Grey Ferris, a classmate from Georgia, joined me. When we arrived at the staging ground, we were given written instructions:

THIS IS A NONVIOLENT DEMONSTRATION, therefore,

1. You are expected to refrain from any hostile act or word, even when provoked.

2. The march will be quiet, orderly and serious.

3. You are expected to follow the instructions of the trained marshals, who are easily identified and stationed at regular intervals in the march. Marshals will remove any inappropriate signs.

The march went through several sections of Boston where the crowd reaction was hostile, but no violence broke out. We would march mostly in silence but then once in a while a song like "This Little Light of Mine" would break out and spread through our ranks. At one point during the march I got separated from my classmates and was walking next to three young Catholic priests and four nuns. Five young men who seemed to know one of the priests poured out of a nearby bar and started to aggressively confront him, calling him "nigger lover" and "fag." He calmly said, "Boys, Jesus would be marching with us today," and the bullies shut up. In the rain at Boston Common, Dr. King gave a great speech, making it clear that "this is not a battle of white people against Black people. It is a struggle between the forces of justice and injustice." And as he had before, he ended the speech with the cadences of a church sermon, saying, "Now is the time to make real the promise of democracy. Now is the time to make brotherhood a reality. Now is the time."

At my school, it was a moment of change. When I reported back to Frank Ashburn, I sensed that even if Bill Coffin had upset him a year earlier, the tide of history had changed and he knew it. Within two weeks he told the assembled school at Sunday Chapel he agreed with me, and the school set out to recruit some qualified Black students. By the time I graduated, the school had begun to transform itself into the wonderfully diverse institution it is today. In a final acknowledgment of my part in that transformation, he awarded me the Allen Ashburn Prize, with a dedication that read in part, "He has become the articulate voice of conscience for the school. Many have disagreed with him, but I know of no one who does not respect him." When Ashburn died in 1997, at age ninety-four, the *New York Times* published a long obituary, the last paragraph of which seemed aimed at me.

> As he explained shortly before his death, he loved the bad boys as much as the good boys, maybe more. After all, he said, the bad boys needed more guidance, and from Mr. Ashburn at Brooks they got it.

What I learned from him is that sometimes the people you worry might hold you back can turn out to be your greatest allies. And if they want to believe it was *they* guided *you*? Cool.

But was it guidance and respect that I wanted or just comradeship? I was in a hurry to abandon adolescence and innocence. I hated the loneliness of my youth. I was looking for my own band of brothers, a group of likeminded people who believed in justice and loved folk music. I found them at Princeton after a long, hot summer.

2. Dylan Goes Electric

1965

I graduated from Brooks in June of 1965 and would go to Princeton in the fall. After a strange and violent spring, from Selma to Washington, the summer of 1965 had turned hot and sultry. A new form of rock and roll was being manifested, and I wasn't quite sure how I had ended up in the eye of the storm, but on Sunday night, July 25, 1965, I was at the Newport Folk Festival when Bob Dylan decided for the first time to play rock and roll in the hallowed acoustic cathedral of folk music.

The folkies were very serious that music played on acoustic instruments—"old-timey music"—was a counter force to mainstream rock and roll. Much of the early raw energy of rock—Elvis, Chuck Berry, Little Richard—had been replaced by a kind of saccharine pop—Fabian, Frankie Avalon, Bobby Darin. "Authenticity" was a word often heard at Newport. But for me, Dylan's break with the folkies formed a crack in my known universe, even though I did not understand at the time that I was both at a cultural beginning and a political ending. That would only become clear much later. When you are eighteen, the line "I was so much older then, I'm younger than that now" doesn't really make sense. Dylan, who was twenty-four that summer, seemed to have concluded that the life of a folk music polemicist was not for him. He wanted the youthful fun of rock and roll.

I was standing just off the main Newport stage, behind the Leslie speaker cabinet of Al Kooper's Hammond B-3 organ, when the explosion hit. I watched as Jerome Arnold, the bass player, checked the back of his bass one more time for the chord changes for "Maggie's Farm." Bob Dylan trotted up the steps to the waiting area. He had on tight black pants over high-heeled English boots. A bright orange shirt buttoned to the collar glowed under a black leather jacket. He took off his dark glasses to slip his harmonica holder over his head. Both he and Mike Bloomfield, the guitar player, exuded nervous amphetamine energy. Bob gave a nod to Chip Monck, the lighting director, and the lights went up as he, followed by his pickup band, walked quickly onto the stage of the Newport Folk Festival. The crowd came to its feet, the prodigal son returning to where it had all started for him in 1963, when he had sung "A Hard Rain's a-Gonna Fall" to universal acclaim. Coming just six months after the Cuban Missile Crisis, Dylan's poetic antiwar anthem set him apart from all the other topical singers. The show that night in 1963 culminated with Dylan, Joan Baez, Pete Seeger, the Freedom Singers, and Theodore Bikel linking arms and singing "We Shall Overcome."

I had arrived at this position in the wings of the Newport stage by a somewhat circuitous route. Paul Clayton, the friend of my brother Randy, had promised to get me a backstage pass. My private life was in semi-chaos—I had graduated from Brooks and my father was dying—and just how I could make a living in this world was still a mystery. I hadn't known it at the time, but meeting Paul Clayton was the first step to freedom.

Clayton introduced me to Jim Kweskin and Maria and Geoff Muldaur of the Kweskin Jug Band. They needed to hire someone to help them with equipment for the festival, and I gladly signed on. Two days before Dylan's electric debut, Geoff had taken me over to meet the band's manager, Albert Grossman, and to listen to a couple of workshops that were being conducted in the open space behind the main stage. The festival was held in a huge field, with a main stage arena holding about twelve thousand seats. Arrayed around the outside of the main stage were several small "workshop" stages, where the audience would sit on the ground and enjoy the wide variety of subgenres that made up what we called folk music. One was a country blues workshop with Son House, Mississippi John Hurt, and Skip James. These three gentlemen, then in their sixties and seventies, had been "rediscovered" by Dick Waterman and John Fahey, who acted like forensic detectives of the blues revival. The Festival Foundation had financed many of these rediscovery missions. Son, who had recorded a couple of 78s in the 1930s, had been found in Rochester, New York, on the same day in 1964 that Skip was located in Mississippi. Both he and Skip, who sang in a high, beautiful tenor, could not believe their good fortune when they suddenly found themselves with new recording contracts and gigs at festivals and blues clubs around the country that paid $500 a night.

But on this afternoon, the mentor of the blues revival, Alan Lomax, was in a foul mood. Not three hundred yards from the stage where Son was fingerpicking his old Martin guitar, the Paul Butterfield Blues Band was tuning up for a workshop on the urban blues. The amplified wail of Butterfield's harmonica could be heard under Son's plaintive song "Make Me a Pallet on Your Floor."

Geoff and I looked toward the far-off stage and decided to check it out. But for Lomax, Butterfield was nothing but a rude intrusion. He had been recording blues for the Library of Congress since the mid-thirties and had adamantly opposed inviting the Butterfield Band to Newport, on the grounds that this was not a place for electric music. He marched over to the stage where Butterfield was just beginning "Shake Your Moneymaker" and insisted that they turn off the power. Albert Grossman, the most important manager in the folk world, who had just signed the Butterfield Band, confronted Alan. Both men weighed in above 230 pounds, so it was at least a fair fight. As Mike Bloomfield's guitar solo wailed across the field, these two titans wrestled in the dust over an electric cable. Geoff Muldaur, whose group was also managed by Grossman, egged his man on, but eventually the fight kind of petered out. Lomax slinked back to his roots stage, and Grossman brushed himself off. Geoff then made an introduction, and I took the measure of a man who was to be an important part of my life for the next ten years.

Albert was stocky and had very long hair that was going prematurely gray. His small wire-rimmed glasses made him look like a hip Ben Franklin. The three of us walked back to the main artists' tent, and Muldaur immediately began to regale the Grossman artists with the tale of the wrestling match. Off in the corner, Bob Dylan was tuning up his acoustic guitar, getting ready for the singer-songwriter workshop with Phil Ochs, Donovan, and Eric Andersen. I saw him smile listening to Muldaur's story and a few minutes later whisper something to Grossman, who was his manager too. There was a glint of mischief in Bob's eyes that I was to observe many more times over the next seven years. Even today I wonder if this was the moment that he decided to play rock and roll at the summit meeting of folk music and change the music business forever. The poet-philosopher of sixties rock, Pete Townshend of the Who, once told the *New York Times*, "We don't have the brains to answer the question of what it was that rock 'n' roll tried to start and has failed to finish." I could dispute that, but the true part is that the larger project of rock may have started in this moment at Newport—this effort to blend the kinetic energy of rhythm and blues to the political poetry of folk music. Bob had already recorded "Like a Rolling Stone" with a backing band, so it was only a matter of time before he introduced similar music onstage. But to choose the Newport Folk Festival to debut his new sound was a fairly aggressive move.

Whatever the impetus, it became clear to Grossman's circle by Saturday morning that Dylan was going to "go electric" on the main stage on Sunday night. Albert arranged for Al Kooper to be flown up to Newport by private plane (despite Al's abject fear of small aircraft). I heard a rumor there was going to be a rehearsal Saturday night at a house in the country, but no one seemed to know if it ever got serious. All I know is that on Sunday afternoon as the ushers worked to clear the arena for a sound check, it was obvious that the band Dylan had chosen to back him was *not* rehearsed in the traditional sense. Jerome Arnold and Sam Lay were blues musicians through and through—they both had played with Muddy Waters, and the twelve-bar progression was their stock in trade—but to understand how far this was from "Maggie's Farm," you could look at the back of Arnold's bass, where he had taped a kind of odd notation showing that the song proceeded for almost the entire first verse with only two chord changes before an abrupt change to a third chord. To Jerome, the timing of these changes seemed random, and so during the sound check he focused on Bloomfield's chording hand to the exclusion of everything else. I worried that if Mike ever turned his back to Jerome, the whole thing would collapse.

To make matters more chaotic, Dylan seemed restless. Bob Neuwirth, Dylan's road manager, was the master at keeping Bob calm, but even he and Peter Yarrow (of Peter, Paul and Mary, Grossman's biggest act), who took charge of the sound mix, could not seem to get Bob to play more than a couple of verses of each tune. Some years in the future, I would be in Neuwirth's shoes, trying to get Bob to do a proper sound check, but in this moment, I was an eighteen-year-old kid in a near dream state. I hovered behind the big Hammond Leslie speaker watching Dylan's every move. I felt that rush of excitement that comes from being in the right place at the right time.

Nine months earlier, in the fall of 1964, I had been this close to Bob by total chance, but I had been on the outside looking in. Dylan was playing a sold-out gig at Boston's Symphony Hall. At the last minute they put up for sale two hundred seats on the stage, and I was lucky enough to get one. By the first chorus of the first tune, "The Times They Are a-Changin'," I was as spellbound as one could possibly be with an artist. I was in the presence of genius.

> *Come mothers and fathers throughout the land*
>
> *And don't criticize what you can't understand*
>
> *Your sons and your daughters are beyond your command*

Your old road is rapidly agin'.

Please get out of the new one if you can't lend your hand

For the times they are a-changin'.

I had written my senior paper at boarding school on T. S. Eliot, and I considered Dylan to be rightly held as one of our great poets. Songs like "Masters of War" and "The Death of Emmett Till" spoke deeply to my political concerns. New songs seemed to pour out of him on a daily basis. His need to compose was as compulsive as lust. In later years, Bob would deride the importance of what he brought to that year of cultural and political transformation. He told critic Nat Hentoff in a 1965 interview for *Playboy* magazine, "If you want to send a message, go to Western Union." But regardless of his intentions, the deed had been done.

Of course, the artistic and political eruption of the 1960s wasn't simply delivered from the heavens by gods or aliens—it was the work of men and women, many of whom understood that they were part of an American tradition of "counterculture." Bob Dylan was no more a rebel than Henry David Thoreau, Mark Twain, Louis Armstrong, Billie Holiday, or Orson Welles. But as the political establishment of America became more conservative in the 1980s, it has served the culture warrior's purpose to paint the artists of the sixties—the people who made American music and film the envy of the world—as dangerous desperadoes. And in a sense they were. The spiritual godfather of the movement, Henry David Thoreau, wrote, "It is not desirable to cultivate a respect for the law, so much as for the right"—to which Bob Dylan replied, "To live outside the law, you must be honest."

The most important concept to grasp here is that culture leads politics. It is not that the art *causes* the political reform but rather that it opens the collective mind to the idea that rebellion is healthy. And it also sketches out the forms that rebellion might take, as in the lyrics of Pete Seeger's union hymn "Which Side Are You On?"

> *Oh workers can you stand it?*
>
> *Oh tell me how you can?*
>
> *Will you be a lousy scab*
>
> *Or will you be a man?*
>
> *Which side are you on?*

Four months before Dylan's appearance at Newport he had toured England for three weeks. Every night he and Neuwirth would return to their hotel suite at the Savoy in London, overlooking the River Thames. Most every night John Lennon would show up to trade stories and songs, smoke some hash, and sit at the feet of the man he considered the real artist. And out of those weeks Lennon wrote most of his songs for *Rubber Soul*. The time gap between "I Want to Hold Your Hand" (released three weeks after JFK's assassination) to "Nowhere Man" was less than eighteen months, but the emotional distance was a lifetime. And John Lennon would have been the first to credit Bob Dylan for helping him grow up.

After the chaos of the Dylan concert at Newport, there was a party at one of the mansions that lined the shore. In a salon with high ceilings, groups of musicians gathered on couches and on the floor, smoking cigarettes and drinking red wine. I moved around the room as if swimming in a cool lake, plunged into the world I had before then only dreamed about. I listened but didn't talk much, afraid I would be jettisoned for my youth, my lack of understanding of the code words being passed. Somehow, I had made it inside the walls of the castle, and I wanted to remain in the warm comfort of the musical fraternity. Dylan was off in a corner, hiding behind dark glasses at midnight, laughing with a small group of friends. It was as if the craziness of the night's concert had never occurred.

Around 2 a.m., slightly inebriated from the wine, I drove myself to Hammersmith Farm, the palatial home of my prep school classmate Jamie Auchincloss. As I slinked back through the grand foyer in my dusty cowboy boots and jeans, the spirit of the American establishment was in the air. In prep school I had read a novella by Thomas Mann called *Tonio Kröger*, in which Mann depicts the anguish of the young Tonio, caught between a passionate mother who encourages his artistic ambitions and a cold, businesslike father who has planned Tonio's whole career and future for him. Mann calls Tonio a "bourgeois manqué"—a future pillar of middle-class life who got on the wrong track. The duality of my life and ambitions felt so close to Tonio's in that moment at Hammersmith Farms. I knew something important had taken place that night, but I wasn't sure exactly what, or what I was supposed to do with it. It took a few months for the full gravity of the night to reveal itself.

3. The Summer of Love
1967

Epicurus taught that the root of all human neuroses was death denial, and watching my father, with stage IV cancer, try to achieve *ataraxia*—the Ancient Greeks' word for peace and freedom from fear—brought me closer to him. Up until the last two months of his life, my father refused to admit he might die; he was very brave, but he never escaped the fear. In the end, all the complications of chemo and radiation made existence unbearable, and after two years of struggle he surrendered to death. In the spring of 1967, I came home from my sophomore year at Princeton and found myself standing in front of an oxygen tent as his life slowly slipped away. He was fifty-six. I was nineteen. You don't expect to be confronted with the death of a parent so soon.

I reached under the tent and grasped his hand. He gave me a weak squeeze, acknowledging my presence but without words. His breath was labored, his skin almost translucent. I looked around at my brothers and sister and there was nothing to say. My mother sat at the end of the bed, trying to control her sense of my dad's fade-out. We maintained the vigil until 11 p.m., and then we kids went home while my mother stayed at the hospital, in the other bed in his room. By the morning, he had died and my mother, at the age of fifty-three, was alone.

The following days were filled with preparations for the funeral at St. Paul's Church. My dad was not a religious man, but his funeral filled the building. When I think of the shaky foundation on which his early career in Cleveland had started, it was clear by the turnout at his funeral that he had made a real name for himself. I was proud and also sad, and yet something was keeping me from the deep grief my mother was showing.

Perhaps it was my knowledge that my father went to his grave holding on to an illusion; he believed that just as I had followed him to Princeton, I would follow him to Harvard Law and then come home and join his firm. Maybe even I had believed that back when I got accepted to Princeton in the spring of 1965, but after Newport I knew I was never going to be a lawyer. But as he was so sick, I never saw the point in telling him the truth. Now, in the wake of his death, I had a strange sense of anticipation, as if I had just crossed some shadowy line dividing past and future, obligation and freedom. I didn't fully understand how his death would give me the autonomy to find my own meaningful work, but the day after his funeral, as I headed back to Princeton, I told my mother I had taken a summer job offered by Albert Grossman to road manage the Kweskin Jug Band. I don't think she had a clue of what I was talking about. She had other things on her mind. The feelings of liberation and guilt stuck with me for a couple of months, but the world was beginning to move a lot faster and I was soon racing toward my future.

I arrived in San Francisco on June 15, 1967, with the Jug Band. We had been booked to open for a new act called the Doors at the Fillmore Auditorium. There was a feeling of innocence and innovation in California then, and the very fact that promoter Bill Graham had paired the Kweskin Band with the Doors gives a good sense of the eclectic spirit in the air. The sidewalks of the Haight-Ashbury District near the Fillmore were jammed with hippies of all colors and sexes. You could stroll down the street and smell the pot in the air mixed with a hit of patchouli oil. There was a great coffee place near the Fillmore called Patisserie Delanghe where the croissants were flaky and you could get a real cappuccino. That was rare in those days. Mostly it was Maxwell House, with or without milk. You could sit there for an hour and read a book while nursing your coffee.

One of Muldaur's friends that we met there, a guy named Bruce Conner, was a great conceptual painter but also a real send-up artist. He had published a five-page spread in a major art magazine with fifteen pictures depicting the steps to make a peanut butter, banana, bacon, lettuce, and Swiss cheese sandwich. He was also doing some of the early light shows at the Avalon Ballroom, a rival to the Fillmore. In those days we would have breakfast with Bruce around 1:30 in the afternoon, since musicians went to sleep at 3 a.m. after long nights of drinking and playing.

We reached San Francisco to find that the Doors' song "Light My Fire" was being played about every fifteen minutes on every radio station. You couldn't escape it. It drove Muldaur crazy. It's not that he didn't love pop music, he just had very specific taste. Did he think that Jim Morrison was a pretentious songwriter? Did "Our love become a funeral pyre" just send him over the edge? My guess is that, in Geoff's reverence for the great

American songwriters from Irving Berlin to Carole King, he could never see Jim Morrison joining that club.

The night before our first show we got a copy of *Sgt. Pepper's Lonely Hearts Club Band* and spent the evening smoking some good sensimilla and marveling at the Beatles' luminosity. It is a miraculous record, full of wit and invention, and everybody was amazed by it. Jim Kweskin, being a scholar of jazz, likened it to some of Duke Ellington's innovations, and at least at that time all things seemed possible.

I think I learned more about the history of American music that summer than in the twenty years preceding it. Both Muldaur and Kweskin had mined the American songbook from Stephen Foster to Chuck Berry, and they had immersed themselves in the history of New Orleans jazz and held Louis Armstrong as the giant of our history. This was new for me, because Armstrong was associated in my mind with the song "Hello, Dolly!," a pop ditty of little consequence. But Muldaur and Kweskin played me Armstrong's "West End Blues" from 1928, and Kweskin once said it was the most perfect three minutes in American music. It starts with Louis's solo horn, improvising in a way that was new, and eventually moves to the style of singing that made Armstrong famous—"scat," in which the voice is used as a musical and rhythmic instrument.

Muldaur had gone to school on the country blues singers of the 1930s and '40s—Sleepy John Estes, Blind Lemon Jefferson, Charley Patton, Son House, and Robert Johnson. Geoff told me the story of the famous Johnson recordings like "Crossroads Blues." Some of Johnson's songs had been recorded in 1937 in a hotel room with a single mike and a crude wax disk recorder. The sound is almost as raw as the early Edison wax cylinder recordings. Eric Clapton recalled (for an English music magazine) the first time he heard the record, at the age of sixteen: "It was a real shock that there was something that powerful . . . . It led me to believe that here was a guy who really didn't want to play for people at all, that his thing was so unbearable for him to live with that he was almost ashamed of it. This was an image that I was very, very keen to hang on to." I think that's how Geoff Muldaur felt as well. He was able to channel these old guys in a remarkable way, using his own tenor with amazing range. But he also could take a song like Chuck Berry's "Memphis" and totally transform it. Geoff's wife, Maria, was also an amazing blues singer, steeped in Billie Holiday, Bessie Smith, and Ma Rainey. They were both competitive and harmonic; sometimes moody, sometimes sarcastically funny.

But it was the introduction to Louis Armstrong that really changed my whole view of American music that summer, and a big part of that was learning about his history. Armstrong had come up to Chicago from New Orleans in the summer of 1922 to rejoin with his musical mentor, King Oliver, and for a long moment in the steaming heat of a Southside evening in August, gazing at the huge marquee of Lincoln Gardens Café advertising "King Oliver & the Creole Jazz Band," the twenty-year-old Armstrong was paralyzed with self-doubt. "I could hear the King's band playing some kind of real jump number," he wrote later in his autobiography, "and believe me, they were really jumpin' in some fine fashion . . . . I said to myself, 'My Gawd, I wonder if I'm good enough to play in that band' . . . and hesitated about going inside right away." In the next six years, the nervous New Orleans cornet player would transform American music in ways he could hardly understand on his first night in Chicago. As the jazz critic Gary Giddins noted to director Ken Burns, for the 2001 documentary series *Jazz*, the highbrow critics had, since the 1920s, been "looking for an American Bach," but they didn't realize he had arrived because "he doesn't fit their description. He's black. He is by their standards musically illiterate."

Fortunately for the future of music, Joe "King" Oliver knew Louis Armstrong was special and, as Louis said in his 1954 autobiography *Satchmo*, "Papa Joe came outside and when he saw me, the first words he said were 'Come on in heah you little dumb sumbitch. We been waitin' for your black ass all night.'" Armstrong had arrived in Chicago following two years on his own after King Oliver had left New Orleans. He had plied the riverboat trade, playing for Black and white audiences off the pleasure boats as far north as Davenport, Iowa, where a young white cornet player named Bix Beiderbecke heard Louis and decided to abandon everything to pursue a life of music. In time, Armstrong had become such a big deal in New Orleans that the New York bandleader Fletcher Henderson had tried to lure him to New York to join his big band. Louis declined the offer, but when Joe Oliver asked him to come up to Chicago, Louis told his friends, "The King sent for me and it didn't matter to me what he was doing, I'm going to him just the same." Louis may have felt like an uneasy country boy in Chicago, but he had seen enough in New Orleans to avoid some of the bad drinking habits that had brought down players like Buddy Bolden, and since his mother was a sometime hooker, he had also been around the gangsters in Storyville enough to know he should always watch his back.

But he was arriving in Chicago in the second year of Prohibition, and to be in the entertainment business at that time was to be in a business pretty much controlled by racketeers.

For the new popular form of music called jazz, Prohibition was a godsend. Overnight "speakeasies" that sold smuggled booze sprang up in every city and town, and along with drinking went music and dancing. And once Louis Armstrong got up on the bandstand at the Lincoln Gardens, things really began to jump. In the two years that he had been away from King Oliver, he had made quantum leaps in his technique. But more importantly, he began to extend the notion of the solo to several choruses long, a style unheard of at that time; the stability of the blues twelve-bar form, which Armstrong codified as the basis of his music, allowed him to extend his solos without confusing the rest of the band. The second thing he brought to the music was a new sense of time. He would begin a solo "just a fraction behind the melody" and then sometimes surge ahead of the 4/4 beat. As Giddins told Ken Burns, "Armstrong invented what for lack of a more specific phrase we call swing. He created modern time. The approach to time that was completely divorced from marching band time."

If you listen to the Kweskin Jug Band records from the late 1960s you can hear that same idea of time—of swing—and touring with them that summer allowed me access to the canon of popular music from 1920 through 1955. This sense of carrying on a tradition was everywhere that summer. If you sat with Jerry Garcia, he could play country licks from Bob Wills in the forties and blues solos from Lightnin' Hopkins in the fifties. The musicians of San Francisco also carried on other parts of music history, including Louis Armstrong's love affair with marijuana. "I was actually in Chicago when I picked up my first stick of gage," Louis wrote, "and I'm telling you I had myself a ball." It became Armstrong's recreation of choice. He had shunned the rotgut booze the gangsters would serve musicians in the clubs, and for him a couple of tokes before playing was part of the ritual of "jazz musicians [who] are so glad to see one another they'll call one another almost any kind of name (but affectionately) just to get that good handshake. After all this knowing each other, why, out of a clear sky a stick of gage would touch the palm of my hand or the tip of my finger." Louis smoked pot pretty much every day for the rest of his life, even when it was dangerous for him to do so.

A story told to me by Miles Davis in a dressing room at the Hollywood Bowl in 1970, as he was waiting to go on as the opening act for the Band, may be apocryphal, but it gives a good sense of Louis. According to Miles, in the summer of 1959 Armstrong was asked to play in Moscow at the opening of the American National Exhibition, in the hope of relieving some of the incessant bad news about the United States' race relations, which had become a daily feature of *Pravda* headlines. Armstrong had previously refused a request by the State Department to tour the Soviet Union in 1957, saying, "The way they're treating my people in the South, the [U.S.] government can go to hell." Louis had also been one of the earliest financial supporters of Martin Luther King, which had led FBI director J. Edgar Hoover to start a file on him.

According to Davis, as Louis and the band were waiting for their flight in the VIP lounge at Paris's Orly Airport, in walked Vice President Richard Nixon and a small group of staffers who were also going to Moscow. (This is the trip that resulted in Nixon's famous Kitchen Debate with Khrushchev.) Nixon was a huge jazz fan and an amateur pianist, and he immediately approached Louis and starting fawning over him—"Satchmo, you are a national treasure. If there is anything I can do for you while we're in Moscow, you let me know?"

Armstrong thanked the vice president and then they were all escorted on board, taking up the whole first-class section of the Pan Am Clipper. When they finally arrived in Moscow, Nixon once again asked Louis if there was anything he could do for him. Louis looked down at the two cases at his feet, one for his trumpet and the other a valise with some sheet music and his stash. He turned to Nixon and said, "Why, sure, Mr. Vice President, you could carry my valise." Nixon was thrilled, and when they met on the other side of the Russian customs check, Louis retook possession of his valise (and his stash), and Nixon shook his hand firmly, telling him what a pleasure their meeting had been. "The pleasure is all mine," said Satchmo.

To walk into the Fillmore Auditorium on a Friday night in the summer of 1967, with the pot smoke drifting through the air, was to enter a world of what the English would have called "dandies." We had grown up with women dressing extravagantly, but now the men were competing like young peacocks. Long velvet morning coats, striped pants, and paisley shirts seemed to be the favorites. The smell of sex and pot and incense coursed through the slightly smoky light, filtering from the high ceilings with red and blue washes, covering young bodies dancing wildly. How much of the wildness was LSD was hard to tell. It was my first real view of the Other America—San Francisco, so different from the political atmosphere of a college campus. The world of anger and impotence about the war in Vietnam seemed distant—it was as if I had moved to another country. Novelist Ken Kesey, who ran the communal LSD festivals he called the Acid Tests—got it right when he made the metaphor in *One Flew Over the Cuckoo's Nest*: It was getting harder to tell who was sane and who was not.

I took two days off from the Jug Band tour to go to the Monterey Pop Festival with Albert Grossman. The brainchild of Lou Adler and John Phillips (of the Mamas and the Papas), the festival was set up as a nonprofit foundation. For one weekend, most of the great bands in the world were assembled in one place, working for minimal pay. For me there were three great moments: hearing Otis Redding, Jimi Hendrix, and Janis Joplin—Otis because he brought the unfettered Stax/Volt sound into the center of the hipster culture and won every heart with his epic version of "Try a Little Tenderness"; Jimi because, faced with playing after the Who on a night when he knew his career in America would either soar or crash, rose to the occasion with a truly scary performance of "Are You Experienced?" that ended with the operatic fury of setting his guitar on fire; and finally Janis, who, despite a mediocre backup band in Big Brother and the Holding Company, brought the spirit of Etta James, Billie Holiday, and Big Mama Thornton into a weekend dominated by men.

Albert Grossman fell in love with Janis's music that weekend, and I had never seen him work harder to sign an artist. Janis teasingly told him the final assessment of whether she would sign with him was if he was good in the sack. Albert was happily married to Sally Grossman, but I had the feeling he would have taken Janis's test if she had pushed the matter. He came home with her signature on a contract and a major personality that would take much of his focus over the next few years. He was having trouble communicating with Dylan, so maybe he needed a new star. Bob had an accountant named Naomi Saltzman who was constantly reminding him how much he was paying Albert Grossman, and she'd gotten him so worked up about money that Bob proposed they renegotiate their music publishing deal. Albert, who was never afraid to renegotiate an artist's contract with a record company, was uninterested in the same tactic being applied to *his* share of Bob's music publishing. Over the next year, this rift would get worse.

I want to take a break from my own story and go a little deeper on these three artists. Hendrix was a virtuoso. More than any other guitarist, he brought a range of sound from the guitar that was totally original. He was a rock-and-roll star—deeply sexual and a true dandy—but also deeply immersed in the traditions of Black music—from Louis Armstrong and Charley Patton to Howlin' Wolf. I think he must have studied John Coltrane, and certainly the jazz musicians I met, like Miles Davis, had a deep respect for Hendrix. In fact, I believe Miles would have never made *Bitches Brew* if it hadn't been for Hendrix. The guitarist John McLaughlin described taking Miles Davis in 1968 to see the film *Monterey Pop*, in which Jimi Hendrix lights his guitar on fire in an orgy of chaotic destruction. Miles turned to John with a glint in his eye and said, "We need to go there." And go there he did over the next three years. It was not that Miles was unfamiliar with the god of intoxication—after all, he had a serious heroin habit in the early 1950s—but his music had nevertheless always had a particular clarity to it. The ordered arrangements of Gil Evans, the meticulous timbre of Miles's muted horn in *Sketches of Spain* . . . these approaches were all abandoned post-Hendrix, starting with the wildness of *Bitches Brew* and continuing with everything beyond.

Jimi was like Miles Davis in the sense that his music was so astonishingly original that it seemed to come from some internal place. It was not like the folk tradition, where you could trace the roots of a song back to an earlier tune. Unfortunately, also like Miles, Jimi Hendrix battled the demon of heroin, and in the end it got him.

Just like it got Janis.

I always thought that Janis was a wounded child. One time at the Newport Folk Festival we shared stories of being bullied as kids, and although we had some things in common (both of us were called "nigger lover"), her stories were worse than mine. Janis grew up in Port Arthur, Texas, an ugly oil port on the gulf, just east of Houston. She went to a high school filled with crackers and was bullied relentlessly. Somehow she met a girl who had some Bessie Smith recordings, and it changed her life. She was a pimply, overweight teenager, but she learned how to sing the blues, and this made her want to see real blues singers, a challenge, since this was not the sort of act likely to visit Port Arthur. She eventually got to see Mance Lipscomb in Austin, where she briefly attended UT.

Almost from the start of her adult life, she had an affection for shooting speed or heroin. At one point, her speed habit was so bad that her fellow musicians in San Francisco took up a collection to send her to her parents in Port Arthur. She always made it back to the Bay Area, though, and Monterey was the moment that moved her into stardom. Alas, fame doesn't cure bad habits.

I remember being on an epic trans-Canada train journey with her in the summer of 1970, when I was tour managing the Band. A Canadian promoter had booked the Band, Janis, the Grateful Dead, Buddy Guy, and Delaney and Bonnie for what he called the Transcontinental Pop Festival. The original plan was to play Montreal, Toronto, Winnipeg, Calgary, and Vancouver, riding between shows on the Festival Express, a private train chartered from the Canadian National Railway that consisted of fourteen cars: two engines, one diner, five sleepers, two lounge cars, two flat cars, one baggage car, and one staff car. What was most memorable for those of us on the tour was not the concerts but the endless hours of jam sessions in the lounge cars, fueled by pot and Janis's favorite drink, Southern Comfort—a rather vile sweet whiskey liqueur flavored with fruit and spice.

Janis and the Band's Rick Danko led many of the jam sessions, favoring country tunes from the Hank Williams era. At some point we ran out of pot and even Jerry Garcia and Bob Weir (confirmed potheads) began consuming whiskey. In the late afternoon, halfway between Toronto and Winnipeg, we ran out of booze. Janis was outraged and insisted that we stop at the next viable burg to replenish the bar. It happened to be a township of about a thousand residents called Chapleau—just big enough to have a decent liquor store. We convinced the conductor that this was a genuine emergency, and he stopped the train in a tiny station. Janis's road manager John Cooke and I took up a collection and brought $500 into the local liquor store, put it on the counter, and told the proprietor to let us know when we had spent the whole wad. Miraculously, the locals who frequented the store seemed to have a taste for Southern Comfort, as well as tequila and Johnnie Walker. We returned triumphant to the train and partied on into the night.

The thing about Janis was that she wanted to prove she could drink any of the boys under the table. Jerry Garcia and Rick Danko passed out long before Janis retired to her sleeping quarters. She had a tough exterior, but I kept thinking: How fragile is her lived presence? Like her hero, Billie Holiday, Janis had a romantic notion about heroin, believing it would lead her deeper into the true blues. But it was a lie, and as Miles Davis, who fought his own battles to quit smack, wrote in his autobiography, "When somebody gets backed up with that dope— using, stopping, using, stopping—and then when it gets into your system you die. It just kills you and that's what happened to Billie and Bird [Charlie Parker]; they just gave in to all the shit they was doing. Got tired of everything and just checked out." Janis fought to get clean, but in moments of loneliness she would score again. That's what had happened when she died— she was alone in a sad hotel in Hollywood between recording sessions.

Of the three musicians that blew me away at Monterey, however the loss of Otis Redding was the most tragic for me personally. Otis was only twenty-six when, six months after his Monterey triumph, the private plane carrying him and his band stalled on its approach to the airport in Madison, Wisconsin. The plane plunged into Lake Monona, killing all but one of the eight people on board. Redding had been performing for five years and was just beginning to write and arrange his own material. On stage he was the most powerful and charismatic soul singer of his generation. Bob Weir of the Dead had said after the Monterey performance, "I was pretty sure I'd seen God onstage." When Otis's "(Sittin' on) The Dock of the Bay" was released after his death, it was clear that here was an artist whose best work was yet to come. He had such a combination of strength and sensitivity that you can feel, especially in songs like "Respect" and "Try a Little Tenderness," how beautiful an example he provided for other performers and his young fans to emulate.

It was at Monterey that I really got to see Albert Grossman in action. He was the opposite of the classic show-business bonhomme. No hugs or slaps on the back, just a very contained and often wry set of comments on a musician's work. Sometimes when he wanted a new client, he would ask them about their current record contract or publishing arrangement, all with the ultimate aim of showing them how much better they could do under his management. Albert had been born and raised in Chicago, the son of Russian Jewish immigrants who both worked as tailors. He managed to graduate in 1948 from Roosevelt University in Chicago and get a job working for the city housing authority. He went to see the early folk performer Bob Gibson at the Off-Beat Room in early 1956 and immediately sensed that folk music could move beyond the confines of the few college "folk societies" that provided the meager living for singers like Pete Seeger and Jean Ritchie.

When I first began listening to folk music, the most important record label was Vanguard, owned and run by a socialist academic named Maynard Solomon. Defying the anticommunist
blacklist, Solomon signed the Weavers and Paul Robeson. As
folk music began to get popular, he signed Joan Baez in 1960 and
the Kweskin Jug Band in 1962. In a way, Vanguard was as much
a political project as a commercial venture. When folk music
started to really sell, Vanguard had Baez, the Jug Band, Ian &
Sylvia, and Baez's sister Mimi, who sang with Richard Fariña, a
close friend of Dylan's. But Albert Grossman had a more commercial vision of what folk music could be.

He opened a club in Chicago called the Gate of Horn in
1956 and helped performers like Odetta and Dave Van Ronk
find a wider audience. I think Albert felt that fifties culture was
lacking a certain authenticity that was inherent in folk music.
Although today we associate Elvis with fifties music, his reign
at the top of the charts was only from 1956 to 1958, when he
was drafted into the army and went to Germany. And Elvis was
anything but "authentic," as you can see in his early television
appearances, especially the one when he jokes with Milton Berle
about his hip-shaking shtick, revealing it to be an affectation put
on for audiences. Neither Van Ronk nor Odetta was slick like
that. Their voices were rough, and Van Ronk looked like a home-
less painter. Grossman knew that this kind of authenticity was
important to the genre, but he also knew that if folk music was
really to become mainstream, it would need better messengers.

He produced (with George Wein) the first Newport Folk Festival in 1959, giving Joan Baez her first national exposure. He
tried to sign Baez, but she stayed with her original manager. In

1961 he formed the group Peter, Paul and Mary in an attempt to get folk to cross over into pop music. He had Peter and Paul wear suits and ties, and Mary looked like she just stepped off the Vassar campus. They were well-dressed, marketable beatniks, and with that the folk boom took off. By 1963 Albert was the most important manager in the folk music business, but his next client wasn't about to just fall in line with his new manager's vision.

Bob Dylan had no interest in a stage costume. Blue work shirts, Levi's, and cowboy boots were what he wore onstage and off. Albert learned then that notions of authenticity were mutable; he never again made any wardrobe suggestions to his clients. By then the role of the songwriter was ascendant, having moved beyond merely serving as an interpreter of traditional music, and audiences were invested not in the look of the performers but in folk's genuine message, especially when the lyrics deviated from what they were used to hearing in pop music.

In 1963 Albert had enough money to buy a weekend house in a town called Bearsville, right outside of Woodstock, New York. Pretty soon both Peter Yarrow (of Peter, Paul and Mary) and Bob Dylan followed him to Woodstock and bought houses. It was a modern version of the old artists' retreat in the Catskill Mountains that had spawned the Hudson River School of landscape painting in the mid-nineteenth century. The artists came to the mountains around Woodstock to celebrate (in the words of the most famous artist of the school, Thomas Cole) "a natural world defined as a resource for spiritual renewal and as an expression of cultural and natural identity." For myself, having been raised in Cleveland, where the Cuyahoga River caught on fire and the steel and iron ore mills poured a thick smoke into the air, the transition to the green mountains of Woodstock was a blessing. When I moved to Bearsville in 1969 after graduation to manage the Band full-time, I came to value the view that looked remarkably similar to Thomas Cole's *Sunrise in the Catskills* painting of 1826. America was already turning into the commercialized McWorld we know today, but mall culture had not come to Woodstock. The very weather of the town seemed to have a quality of the past, faded climate of Cole's paintings from a century before. In the course of a summer afternoon, the color of light on the mountain across from my house might change three times.

Albert Grossman intimidated a lot of my friends who would visit me in Woodstock. He was stout, with long gray hair sometimes pulled back in a ponytail. He wasn't outgoing, but once he took to you, he could be warm and funny. He smoked weed by placing the joint between his third and fourth finger and then cupping both hands around it. It took me a while to get his confidence, but when I came to know him better, we would sit on the stools in his Woodstock kitchen while he prepared toast and espresso. The bread was a special recipe he got the local Bearsville Bakery to make for him. He was a proponent of local self-sufficiency and had a large vegetable garden that was tended for him by a young couple that had fled the city. He took real pride and joy in the taste of samples from his new tomato crop.

Over the years, Albert slowly began to build the amenities that would keep us closer to our mountain colony. The property had a world-class French restaurant and a theater, as well as a wonderful recording studio. Slowly the community of artists, both competing with and encouraging each other, began to build. Paul Butterfield, Geoff and Maria Muldaur, Jimi Hendrix, and Leslie West moved in, and Janis Joplin came to record. On any given evening there were informal music parties at which artists traded songs and honed their craft. In that sense, it was just as Albert had imagined it.

4. Dylan and the Hawks

1967

I first came up to Woodstock in the fall of 1967 to visit with Albert. I had ulterior motives in that I had heard that Bob Dylan and his band, the Hawks, were beginning to make music again as Bob slowly recovered from the horrible motorcycle accident that had almost cost him his life.

As Bob described the accident to the *New York Times*'s Richard Shelton, "It happened one morning after I had been up for three days." Amphetamine and grass were the musician's drugs of choice in the mid-1960s: speed to give you an energy boost to write new songs or perform the same material onstage night after night, and pot to chill you out after the concert, when the only question was if you were going to be alone or have company in your bed. A friend told about one memorable night in 1966 in the back room of Max's Kansas City, the all-night New York hangout. It was 2 a.m., and there in a booth under a red neon light were Dylan, artist Andy Warhol, Brian Jones of the Rolling Stones, Robbie Robertson of the Band, actress Edie Sedgwick, and a couple others. The banter was going fast and furious, driven by Dylan. At one point my friend looked over at Edie and saw she had bitten off the edge of a wine glass and was grinding the shard between her speed-powered teeth. A small trickle of blood slipped toward her chin.

But Edie was just one player in an endless real-life movie Andy Warhol was making that would transform New York culture. Warhol's influence on late-sixties New York cannot be overstated, and in fact much of what characterizes that time and place started with him. "As Warhol was fond of telling us," the art critic Dave Hickey wrote in *Air Guitar*, "the strange thing about the sixties was not that Western art [music, film, painting, photography] was becoming commercialized but that Western commerce was becoming so much more artistic." And of course Dylan played an equally important role in this transition.

In 1965 and 1966, Bob Dylan was living as close to the edge as artists ever do. I admired Dylan for his courage, and he was as near to my Greek ideal of autonomy as anyone I had ever observed. In the face of the hostile reaction from his fans after Newport in 1965, he pressed forward and found himself a band. John Hammond, Jr. (son of the Columbia Records A&R man who discovered Dylan, Billie Holiday, Aretha Franklin, and Bruce Springsteen) had told Dylan about a group called Levon and the Hawks that had backed him on a record of R&B classics. John gave Dylan a number for Robbie Robertson in Toronto, and eventually the Grossman office tracked the group down playing in a bar on the New Jersey shore called Tony Mart's.

The Hawks were essentially low-rent journeymen when Dylan called. For them, Tony Mart's was just one more stop on an endless cycle of bars and clubs from Toronto to New Orleans that had been their meager sustenance for five years since

Ronnie Hawkins, Canada's answer to Jerry Lee Lewis, had lured them into leaving their families and joining his rock-and-roll circus. Robbie later told me that Hawkins's pitch was, "You won't make much money, son, but you'll get more pussy than Frank Sinatra." He had been right on both counts. From Jack Ruby's Dallas dive featuring the one-armed go-go dancer to the honky-tonks of New Orleans, they had seen the underbelly of America, and her innocence too. As time went on, the girls seemed to get prettier and the band could afford better matching suits, but they never saved any money or got a record deal. Eventually Ronnie Hawkins's act got old so Levon and the boys decided to tour on their own.

When Albert Grossman asked the Hawks to do two concerts with Dylan in August of 1965, they were so skeptical that they kept their roadhouse gig going while sending Robbie and Levon to the Forest Hills Stadium to check out the venue. The two of them went up to New York, rehearsed for a day with Dylan, Al Kooper, and Harvey Brooks on bass, and then played in front of seventy-five hundred fans at Forest Hills. Dylan played the first half of the show by himself on acoustic guitar and then brought the band on for the second half. There was still some resistance from the folkies to the rock-and-roll set, but the preparation was much better than at Newport, so it sounded good. Robbie and Levon convinced the rest of the Hawks that Dylan was the real deal, and they quit Tony Mart's the next day and came up to Woodstock to rehearse for a big Hollywood Bowl concert on September 3 in Los Angeles. The city's rock and movie royalty showed up, and there was even less resistance to the rock half of the concert.

L.A. was just recovering from the physical and psychic damage of the Watts riots three weeks earlier. Not just in California but all across the country there was a profound shift in the movement toward racial justice, but I didn't really understand what that meant until I showed up for my first year at Princeton, in September of 1965. The third week of classes I went to an informal meeting of SNCC on campus. Things had definitely changed since the Boston march I had participated in six months earlier. The foundations of nonviolence were being contested from within the civil rights movement. Perhaps it was the Watts riots, or maybe the aftermath of Bloody Sunday in Selma, Alabama, when armed policeman beat hundreds of civil rights marchers, but the nonviolence vision of leader John Lewis was clearly being tested at SNCC. At the meeting at Princeton, some Black students were talking about another SNCC leader named Stokely Carmichael, who had managed over the summer to register twenty-six hundred Black residents of Lowndes County, Alabama, three hundred more than the registered white population of that county. He had started a party called the Lowndes County Freedom Organization, which used a black panther as its mascot. But what had really struck these students was that Stokely and his organizers openly carried guns, because they didn't trust the federal marshals to protect them from the KKK.

By May of 1966, Stokely Carmichael, with his vision of Black Power, would be chairman of SNCC, and by December of 1966, white members were asked to leave the organization. The implication was that we should join Students for a Democratic Society (SDS) and continue to fight the power structure from that base. Carmichael openly embraced working with SDS, but for many of us, something important had changed. My connection with the civil rights movement was so deeply framed by the religious gospel of love that the Reverends Martin Luther King and William Coffin had been preaching that I felt alienated by the cold political-secular calculations of Stokely Carmichael, with a gun on his hip. In retrospect, I think Carmichael's decision was a mistake that the leaders of our contemporary Black Lives Matter movement need to study. Martin Luther King had written in his "Letter from a Birmingham Jail," "White moderates have marched with us down nameless streets of the South. They have languished in filthy, roach-infested jails, suffering the abuse and brutality of policemen who view them as dirty nigger lovers." What has thrilled me since the spring of 2020 is the inclusion of all races and genders in the BLM movement. That must be maintained. But back then, Dr. King's efforts had relied on SNCC to organize the students, so there was nowhere for white kids to go if they were not interested in joining SDS.

Where we went was into music. This raises an interesting question: Had I been drawn to the civil rights movement partly because Bob Dylan's songs had inspired me, or had I been drawn to Dylan because he embraced the justice movement I felt the country needed? For this, I don't have an answer. I do know that by 1966 it felt like many of the great civil rights battles had already been won. Hundreds of thousands of Black voters were registering in the South, and schools were being integrated across the land. At the time I'm writing this, when Republican legislatures are erecting new barriers to voting rights, I can see I was naive then to have thought we were so close to achieving racial justice and equality. But at the time, our successes felt huge, and even

Dr. King was turning his attention away from civil rights and toward fighting against the Vietnam War.

As for the great singer-songwriters I was drawn to, their focus turned inward. Some cultural historians have suggested that radical politics became irreconcilable with the increasingly profitable business of rock, but I don't think that's true. One only has to look at John Lennon's career trajectory during this period to know that a rock star with controversial opinions could not be silenced. Even if J. Edgar Hoover wanted it. Lennon had made it clear that he wanted nothing to do with the more violent factions of the left, like the Weathermen, singing in the Beatles' "Revolution": "But when you talk about destruction / Don't you know that you can count me out." Instead, he kept up his chant of "Give peace a chance," and by 1971, when Lennon was living in New York, his political opinions had inspired Hoover to have U.S. immigration officials try to deport him.

I had great dreams of organizing folk concerts at Princeton, and so I found my band of brothers: Lindsay Holland, Cam Ferenbach, and Nick Hoff. All of them could play guitar better than me, and all of them loved folk music. Lindsay was from Fort Worth, Texas, and Cam from Nashville, Tennessee. Lindsay's dad ran a small oil services company and Cam's dad ran a carpet company. Nick grew up on Long Island and his dad worked on Wall Street. They were upper-middle-class prep school kids, able to get a Princeton education through family money or scholarships.

One of my other new friends at Princeton, Peter Kaminsky, loved music as well but was spending more time getting involved in the antiwar movement that was just starting up at Princeton. Peter was a high school kid from New Jersey and would later be both our class president and the president of the Princeton chapter of SDS. (His grandfather was from Russia and had been a good socialist in the 1930s, but Peter's father had foresworn politics and ended up writing for *The Jackie Gleason Show* in Miami. That's the American dream.) Peter managed to get along well with both the prep school kids and the smart high school kids, and my class was divided evenly between the two types.

In May of 1966, an advanced copy Dylan's new album, *Blonde on Blonde*, had just arrived for me from the Grossman office. It was a double album, and we played it from one end to the other. I thought it was the best thing he had ever done. The song "Sad Eyed Lady of the Lowlands" was more than ten minutes long, and every verse was better than the last. When it was all over we all voted to play it again. It was at this point I revealed I had a surprise for my new friends. I put a towel under my door, pulled out a joint, and lit it up. Cam hadn't ever smoked pot before, but he liked it a lot. He was almost crying the second time we heard "Sad Eyed Lady of the Lowlands." I was studying Wallace Stevens, T. S. Eliot, and W. H. Auden in my classes, but when I listened to Dylan gently spin out this tale of broken love, it was as if the poet was right there in the room with me.

> *Now you stand with your thief, you're on his parole*
>
> *With your holy medallion which your fingertips fold,*
>
> *And your saintlike face and your ghostlike soul,*
>
> *Oh, who among them do you think could destroy you?*

The song ends in a very long harmonica solo with which Bob achingly brings the denouement to a close. He has offered his gifts to his love, but the question is never answered: "Should I leave them by your gate, / Or, sad-eyed lady, should I wait?"

As much as I still loved folk music, I was caught up in Dylan's new direction. Because I had worked for Albert Grossman over the summer, I was able to get great seats to Dylan's Carnegie Hall concert in October of 1965, and I went with Paul Clayton, who had moved to New York. Paul was spending time with Tim Leary and a light show designer named Rudi Stern, and together they were creating a sort of experimental multimedia experience in the East Village on Tuesday nights at one of the last of the Yiddish theaters, called the Village East Theater. As Stern described it to a *Village Voice* reporter, "We put up *Psychedelic Celebration Number One with Timothy Leary, Light Projections by Jackie Cassen and Rudi Stern.* The crowds on Tuesday night stopped traffic on Second Avenue. The police came because there were more people than the place would hold. And there was a line around the block." Paul explained to me what Leary was trying to accomplish by combining drugs and art in a new way. Clayton was filled with the ardor of a new convert to the church of LSD.

Bob played the opening half of the show with just an acoustic guitar and a harmonica. After the intermission, the Hawks, dressed in black suits and thin ties, walked on the stage and plugged in their instruments. Their hair was short, and had it not been for the instruments, they could have been mistaken for a group of accountants. Rick Danko, the bass player, had grown up in Simcoe, Ontario. His father chopped firewood for a living, and Rick was headed for a similar fate until he found music.

Levon Helm, the drummer, was a native of Springdale, Arkansas, and had watched Sonny Boy Williamson play every afternoon on a small stage for the *King Biscuit Flour Hour*, a local radio show. Though born two thousand miles apart, Rick and Levon were as "country" as if they had been neighbors, and they not only knew all the same songs but their harmony singing blended perfectly, and it paid as much homage to Hank Williams and the Stanley Brothers as to any of the rockabilly singers that Ronnie Hawkins liked. Those harmonies could be traced to the influence of WSM radio in Nashville, a 50,000-watt behemoth that beamed the Grand Old Opry as clearly to Ontario and Arkansas as to the room next door.

Richard Manuel was the Hawks' piano player. Smart, handsome, and with a beautiful tenor voice, he was the trickster of the group. His specialty onstage had been Bobby "Blue" Bland covers like "Stormy Monday" and melting the hearts of the girls in the audience. Garth Hudson was a good five years older than the rest of the band, and Robbie had had to plead with Hawkins to hire him originally. Garth could play almost any instrument well, and when he left home he told his parents that he had been hired to be a touring music teacher. Somehow this was seen as more acceptable to his father than saying he was joining a rock-and-roll band. Garth played organ primarily, and he also got each of the other band members to pay him $10 per week for music lessons on their own instruments.

The last person to plug in before Dylan was Robbie Robertson. His mother, Rosemarie Chrysler, was from the Cayuga and Mohawk tribes, and she raised her son on the Six Nations reservation east of Toronto. She was married to Jim Robertson, who worked plating jewelry, and it wasn't until the couple separated that Robbie's mother revealed that Robbie's biological father was Alexander Klegerman, a Jewish gambler who had been killed in a car accident right before Robbie's birth. These slightly strange beginnings informed his worldview—skeptical, but believing in Lady Luck. Robbie had developed a guitar style that was almost completely original. Most of his contemporaries played the Fender Stratocaster, which had a mechanical tremolo arm that gave the effect of minor pitch variation, a kind of musical wavering. Robbie, however, used the much simpler Fender Telecaster, which had no vibrato arm, and so to create a similar effect, Robbie would bend the strings on the neck, providing a much rougher version of the tremolo sound. He had grown up listening to Muddy Waters and Bo Diddley and he had participated in "cutting contests" (dueling guitar solos) with Toronto's legendary Roy Buchanan, but his style was so different that Dylan once called him a "mathematical guitar genius."

When Bob walked onstage at Carnegie Hall that night, he was yet another bastion of originality, now from a sartorial standpoint. Perhaps influenced by the Hawks' notion that a professional musician should wear a suit, Dylan was wearing a green-and-brown suit with an outsize houndstooth pattern. Still shrouded in dark glasses, and skinny as a rail, he looked like an extra from the Mad Hatter's tea party. But as soon as they started to play, we were blown back in our seats. The music was scary and tight and LOUD. Carnegie Hall is not big, but the Hawks had the volume turned up as if they wanted to fill the Hollywood Bowl. Robbie would do solos that soared, and Bob would face him, six inches from his guitar, egging him on. Sometimes Dylan would dance around on his high-heeled boots, his long curly "Jewish afro" glinting in the backlight.

The whole experience was extraordinary, and over the next eighteen months Bob and the Hawks would tour the world, evoking both anger from the folk purists and admiration from the rockers who understood that some sort of new music was being birthed. In a sense, this was one of those breaking points where technology actually changes the nature of the art form, just as, for instance, the invention of photography changed the portrait. Take a song like "One Too Many Mornings," which Bob had recorded for *The Times They Are a-Changin'* with just a guitar and harmonica. Where it was once a plaintive lament, now, with electric guitars and drums, it became a harsh accusation: "You're right from your side / I'm right from mine." The technology of the music fit the psychological state of the song, and in a way that mirrored how Dylan's mood changed from 1963 to 1965.

As time went on, the Hawks personal style got wilder. Their hair got longer and their suits got cooler. To make touring easier, Dylan had borrowed Peter, Paul and Mary's airplane, a Lockheed Lodestar, which Danko called "the Volkswagen Bus of the sky." Although it was slow (135 knots, or 155 m.p.h., at top speed), the plane could carry the drums, amps, and guitars in its rather large cargo section, as well as all the band members. Up front there was a couch, six regular seats, and a small restroom. Garth Hudson regularly grabbed the couch to sleep on. Levon and Danko later told me this story of how Levon had taught Garth not to hog the couch.

The most recent issue of *Life* magazine had featured an article describing how astronauts trained for weightlessness, which involved sending a conventional airplane into a parabola. With Garth snoring loudly on the couch, 15,000 feet in the sky, Levon took the *Life* graphic of the plane's flight path up to the pilots and asked if they could approximate the experience. They were game to try, and when everyone but the sleeping organist was well strapped in, they made the arc. Sure enough, as they reached the apex of the parabola, Garth began to float up off of the couch. This is the point at which Levon shouted for Garth to wake up, and for the next thirty seconds, Garth found himself floating a foot in midair before he fell back down as the wings strained to pull out of the dive.

Traveling on the road in 1966 with Bob Dylan was a desperado experience. Walking into the best hotel in the town backed by an entire crew felt vaguely like a scene from a Western movie, where a group of outlaws comes into a saloon and the whole rowdy room goes silent. Dylan himself had the attitude to match. He was talking in a language within a language—the way he spoke defined by the audacity of his metaphors, the breadth of his scorn. You either got it or you didn't. His song "Ballad of a Thin Man" summed up the perspective:

> *You've been with the professors*
> *And they've all liked your looks*
> *With great lawyers you have*
> *Discussed lepers and crooks*
> *You've been through all of*

F. Scott Fitzgerald's books

You're very well read

It's well known

But something is happening here

And you don't know what it is

Do you, Mr. Jones?

What's so astonishing about the music Dylan and the Hawks made in the eighteen months they were on tour is that it prefigured punk rock. Every night was a battle. Bob would tell his band as they went onstage, "Don't stop playing, no matter what." Occasionally, angry fans would try to storm the stage, and Robbie Robertson said he sometimes felt he might need to use his Telecaster as a weapon to fight his way off. Between tunes the mood of the audience seemed always up for grabs, but it was usually a din of rhythmic clapping and stomping from the rock fans who were trying to drown out the cries of "Play the good stuff!" from the folkies. When Bob introduced an older acoustic tune of his, "I Don't Believe You," he told the crowd, "It used to be like that, and now it goes like this," and then treated them to a version he had translated into a hearty, hard-hitting accusation of a song, now filled with screeching solos from Robbie. When the tune ended to boos and cries for "Blowin' in the Wind," Dylan's refusal to sing the protest anthem was cold: "There's a fellow up there looking for the savior, huh? The savior's backstage; we have a picture of him."

Chekhov once wrote to a friend, "I would like to be a free artist and nothing else, and I regret God has not given me the strength to be one." On their tour around the world in 1965 and 1966, however, Dylan and the Hawks found the strength and courage to get there. (It's also worth noting that it was Albert Grossman and the team of tour managers he had hired that in large part made it possible for such a venture to not implode.) What they did was nothing short of transformative. Cultural historians have noted times when works of art became seminal moments, as when the debut of Stravinsky's *Rite of Spring* in Paris in 1913 caused a riot at the theater, but that was a one-off. Imagine taking a show of that power on the road and spreading the effect in sixty cities around the world. That's what the Dylan and Hawks tour was like.

I remember being at a party one night at Albert Grossman's townhouse on Gramercy Park, and Allen Ginsberg was holding forth about how Bob Dylan was just carrying on from Jack Kerouac. In retrospect, Allen was right—without the beats, there might not have been Bob Dylan—and so perhaps a short digression on the role of the beat movement in 1960s culture is in order.

Paul Clayton once told me about the time he, Dylan, and Dylan's road manager, Victor Maymudes, took an "homage to Kerouac" trip in the spring of 1964. They had set out from Woodstock in Bob's new Ford station wagon, and they were just going to travel around America, play a few concerts, and see what trouble they could get into. They went to visit Carl Sandburg, but he didn't know who they were and sent them away. They went to New Orleans for Mardi Gras and couldn't get a room. All the time, Bob was writing songs like "Mr. Tambourine

Man" in the back seat on a little portable Olivetti typewriter. They had a pound of pot with them and stayed stoned for three weeks, almost missing Bob's concert in Denver. They finally wound up in San Francisco at the City Lights bookstore with Lawrence Ferlinghetti.

At the party, Ginsberg told us the story of the Kerouac road trip that eventually became the root of Dylan's road trip. In January of 1949, twenty-seven-year-old Jack Kerouac and his friend Neal Cassady set out from New York City to visit their friend William Burroughs in a town called Algiers, across the river from New Orleans. For Kerouac, understanding the heart and soul of America was key to both his work as a writer and his journey as a person, and so the road beckoned. His approach contrasted with that of some of the other fathers of the beat movement, including Burroughs and, to a lesser extent, Ginsberg, who considered themselves citizens of the world in the vein of Hemingway and Fitzgerald, rather than chroniclers of the American experience.

In Neal Cassady, Jack Kerouac had found a soul with a similar vision of the open road as the pathway to knowledge and salvation. While they sat on the hood of Neal's Hudson as the ferry crept toward Algiers in the evening fog of a January night, they were forging a bond as blood brothers of the beat world. Neal had been brought into the circle by Hal Chase in 1946, when Neal and his wife, LuAnne, were on their honeymoon in New York. Chase was a Columbia student and part of the group that had formed around classmates Ginsberg, Ferlinghetti, Kerouac, and their friends. Neal had been in and out of reform school, and although he had no college education he was almost as passionate about literature as he was his other two preoccupations:

cars and sex (or, as he called it, "Adventures in Auto-Eroticism"). After Cassady's first trip to New York, Ginsberg and Kerouac both picked up on the kind of stream-of-consciousness style of both his writing and his talking, a style that's on full display in *On the Road*, the book that made Kerouac famous.

By the time they got the Hudson off the ferry and crawled through the dirt alleys to Bill Burroughs's house, it was pretty late. Kerouac offered to make Crêpes Suzette for everyone while Cassidy rolled a joint and Burroughs put away the pistol he had been using for target practice on his wife's emptied Benzedrine inhalers. (She would break the inhalers open and chew the Benzedrine capsule inside.) In the morning, Burroughs confessed to Jack that he was skeptical of their whole adventure and especially suspicious of Cassady, whom he regarded as a con man. As for Cassady, once he was certain that no serious infusion of cash would be forthcoming from the "adding machine heir," he was anxious to quit Louisiana and get back to San Francisco.

The next day, Burroughs wrote to Ginsberg, confessing his doubts about the voyage, "which for sheer compulsive pointlessness compares favorably with the mass migrations of the Mayans." He also warned Ginsberg that one Herbert Huncke, another Columbia friend, was about to be sprung from the Rikers Island prison and would inevitably show up at Ginsberg's door looking for Burroughs. Burroughs asked Ginsberg to turn Huncke away because "the more obligations Huncke is under to anyone, the more certain he is to steal from or otherwise take advantage of his benefactor." Ginsberg did not heed the warning, and within a month Huncke was running a moderate-size fencing operation out of Ginsberg's apartment, and within two months they were all busted for going the wrong way on a one-way street in a stolen car.

Kerouac shared some of his writing with Burroughs, especially parts of *The Town and the City*, a sprawling historical novel that was deeply influenced by his fascination with Thomas Wolfe. Although Burroughs admired the work, he urged Jack to try to write in the more modern vernacular that was so much a part of his conversational style. Already the basis for *On the Road* was filling Kerouac's journals, and Burroughs felt it was just a matter of getting it all organized into a novel. With that charge in mind, Jack relented to Neal's desperate need to move on, and with $25 wired from his mother, they left for San Francisco. The rest is history: the trip and the journals would end up changing American literature and creating a beat culture that artists like Bob Dylan were anxious to follow. The beats showed what it was to challenge the mainstream and forge a new path, especially in the context of the conservative 1950s. While Kerouac was writing *On the Road* in a mad three-week, amphetamine-fueled fury in late 1951, the House Un-American Activities Committee was in its second round of Hollywood hearings to ferret out suspected communists, asking people from the movie industry to name names. Already ten prominent writers had been sentenced to prison for contempt of Congress after refusing to turn others in to the committee. In the context of that paranoia (which only increased with the rise of Republican senator Joe McCarthy), the beat's rejection of standard narrative values in favor of "radical" philosophies—which included the embrace of Eastern spirituality, the promotion of antimaterialism, the support of open experimentation with psychedelic drugs, and the welcome of both gay and straight sexual liberation—was an affront to American middle-class values. Their courage prepared the way for the counterculture that would arise in the early 1960s.

Being "on the road" was liberating, yes, but for Dylan in 1966, touring for months at a time and facing hostile crowds proved it could wear down even the most courageous musician, and perhaps his motorcycle accident on July 29 of that year was the universe's way of calling a halt to the madness. By the time I went up to Woodstock in the fall off 1967, Dylan was still recovering under the loving care of his wife, Sara. Sara was pregnant with their second child, and Bob was doing a lot of painting and listening to the quiet music of an earlier era. I would go up to Woodstock from Princeton to visit Robbie Robertson in a little cabin on Albert's estate, and the pace of life was so antithetical to the insanity of the tour of 1966 that I could hardly sense that both Bob and Robbie were in one of the most creative times of their lives.

In the town of Saugerties, right outside of Woodstock, the Hawks had rented a house that they named Big Pink. Garth had set up a crude two-track recording machine, and every day around 10:30 in the morning, Dylan and the Hawks gathered, drinking coffee and slowly getting around to working on some new songs. Robbie had played me two songs: "I Shall Be Released" and "Mighty Quinn." It was very clear that Bob was back in rare form, and his lyrics were more touching than ever. But also, in a deep way, Dylan was really schooling his band on the roots of American folk music, a powerful tradition that moved them from their rockabilly training into a much deeper well of feeling and folklore. As Robbie noted to Greil Marcus, "Bob was educating us a little. The whole folkie thing was still very questionable to us . . . but he remembered too much, remembered too many songs too well. He'd come over to Big Pink . . . and pull out some old song—he'd prepped for this." Eventually Dylan would give both Rick Danko and Richard Manuel new lyrics he had written, and they created two wonderful songs, "This Wheel's on Fire" from Rick, and "Tears of Rage" from Richard. And Robbie picked up on the lessons as well. He wrote a song called "The Weight" that delighted me. He wrote it in one afternoon and they recorded it the next day.

Those Big Pink sessions were fruitful, but when the group moved from the intimacy of the house to a real recording studio in New York City to make their first album (as the Band), they found they had to fight the conventions of the recording industry to record "The Weight" as they wanted it. Modern recording depended on isolating each of the instruments and thus each of the players, but that setup wasn't crucial in this case because the Band didn't rely on overdubbing. Nevertheless, Levon was walled off behind high baffles, and Robbie and his guitar amp were put in a corner, again behind sound baffles. The intricate timing of the choral harmonies on "The Weight," however, required that everyone be able to see each other, so they rebelled and gathered in a circle in the middle of the studio and created the sound they wanted—a different sound than what was being produced at the time. When Robbie played it for me in Woodstock, it didn't sound like any record I had heard since the 1950s.

My early visits to Woodstock also proved that young men up in the country can get wild. Certainly Rick, Levon, and Richard tended toward drink and drugs as soon as the sun sank behind the mountains. I remember thinking as I drove back to Princeton through the red splendor of the Catskills fall that the philosophy course I was taking on Nietzsche was not as irrelevant as my roommates had suggested. We were all battling the dialectic of the Apollonian and Dionysian forces within us. The ecstatic moments of smoking a joint, drinking a good Beaujolais, and listening to some new music kept pulling us back toward intoxication. Nietzsche was right that music was the essence of everything. When you are young, sex and music lead you around like a pony.

For me, Princeton was my Apollonian attempt to make order of an increasingly chaotic world. My good friend Lindsay Holland, who was also an English major, used to joke about how little time I put into my college work, and he was right. In many ways my heart was already up in Woodstock, and at Princeton the seriousness of the academy was compounded by my daily awareness of the riots in the streets of many cities, the fact that the Vietnam War was closing in on my generation, and the sometimes harsh reality of my personal life. My father was dead and life was complicated by the intricacies of friendship and "success," and yet the phrase "Which side are you on?" kept echoing in my head. The Beatles hit "All You Need Is Love" had become the anthem of the summer and fall, and yet my poetry professor, Walton Litz, had moved me to tears when he read these lines from W. H. Auden:

> Waves of anger and fear
>
> Circulate over the bright
>
> And darkened lands of the earth,

Obsessing our private lives;

The unmentionable odor of death

Offends the September night.

The year ahead would shatter the Beatles prophecy, and by the spring of 1968 the odor of death would be a stink we could not escape. But the Apollonians had been routed. Allen Ginsberg and Abbie Hoffman performed an exorcism (metaphorically) on the Pentagon. Stokely Carmichael threw the white kids out of SNCC. The velocity of the shift was startling. I couldn't have anticipated how the Vietnam War would loom over our heads for the next two years and change the whole nature of the non-violence protest movement I had been a part of.

The sad personal coda to this time was the suicide of Paul Clayton. Clayton had been living in a small flat near the Village East Theater. He got in the bathtub and pulled the electric heater in after himself. LSD or depression? I will never know. Paul was the third member of Dylan's circle to die within a few months. Richard Fariña went off a motorcycle in California, and then Geno Foreman, who had hung out with Bob and Victor Maymudes in Woodstock, died of an overdose. I owed Clayton my gratitude for the introduction to Dylan and the Hawks. I was so sorry I didn't get to say thank you.

5. Princeton in Rebellion

1967

Grossman told me that Dylan and the Hawks were not going to tour, so I began working for Judy Collins as a road manager in the fall of 1967. She was tremendously popular on the college circuit, and we toured with two backup musicians, Paul Harris on piano and Bill Lee on bass. I would leave Princeton on Thursday night, get on a plane Friday morning, and do one college concert Friday night and another one on Saturday night. I'd be home in Princeton by Sunday evening. It was better than spending weekends swilling beer on Prospect Street, Princeton's version of fraternity row.

Bill Lee (filmmaker Spike Lee's father) and Paul Harris regaled me with wonderfully funny stories of the life of the journeyman musician. They were also personally protective of me, worrying about the looming draft after I graduated. Paul gave me the name of a shrink in New York who had written a long letter to his draft board explaining Paul's inability to sleep in a barracks with a lot of other soldiers.

Bill made a very good living as a session musician, and he always had the best pot. One night we were on a double bill with the Modern Jazz Quartet, and Bill took Paul, myself, and Percy Heath of the MJQ out for a little pre-concert "meeting." After about fifteen minutes of talking, laughing, and smoking, Percy complimented Bill on the weed: "This tastes just like the 'long green' that blew through Harlem in '48." I thought to myself, "There's a man with a sense of history."

Judy Collins's manager was a wonderful old leftie named Harold Leventhal. Harold had been the manager of the Weavers, the original folk group that flourished in the fifties under the guidance of Pete Seeger. Seeger's father was a distinguished composer and folk music scholar, and Pete had gone to boarding school and then Harvard. But in his sophomore year, he left. "I wasn't sorry to leave Harvard," he told the *New Yorker*'s Alec Wilkinson in 2006, "I was disgusted by what I considered the cynicism displayed by one of my professors. He would say, 'Every society has a spring, a winter, a summer, and a fall,' and scoff at us trying to stop Hitler. He said, 'All you can do is accommodate.' I was young and idealistic."

In 1940, Seeger met Woody Guthrie at a "Grapes of Wrath" benefit for farmworkers. Guthrie and Seeger hit it off immediately, and Seeger invited Woody to join a communal singing group he had organized called the Almanac Singers. The group was a loose cooperative of people all living in what they named the Almanac House in Greenwich Village. All meals, chores, and rent were shared, and once a month the group would host a rent party they called a "hootenanny." Along with Woody, the other regular members of the Almanacs were Millard Lampell and Lee Hays, and in classic socialist style they all agreed to share the song copyrights equally. But Woody wrote one song on his own during this period that would be his most lasting contribution to the American music canon: "This Land Is Your Land." As war fever built during 1940, Guthrie told Seeger that he was tired of hearing Kate Smith's version of Irving Berlin's "God Bless America" being played over and over on the radio. The Berlin song did not represent the America he had seen traveling on railroad boxcars during the depression, so he wrote his own. The depth of his feelings for his country are apparent in this verse that's hardly ever sung:

> *In the squares of the city,*
>
> *In the shadow of a steeple,*
>
> *By the relief office*
>
> *I'd seen my people.*
>
> *As they stood there hungry,*
>
> *I stood there asking,*
>
> *Is this land made for you and me?*

Seeger had joined the Communist Party in 1936, and he often appeared with the Almanacs under an assumed name so as not to cause trouble for his father, Charles, who was employed by the Library of Congress as an ethnomusicologist. By 1942 Pete had joined the army and Guthrie had gone off to the Merchant Marine with his friend Cisco Houston. The Almanac Singers dissolved, although Seeger and Hays would reconstitute it after the war, but without Guthrie and under the name the Weavers. By the spring of 1950, the Weavers had a hit single with Lead Belly's

"Goodnight, Irene," and by the end of the year they had sold four million copies of their first album.

But Seeger knew it was too good to last. In September of 1947 the House Un-American Activities Committee had subpoenaed forty-three Hollywood writers, directors, and actors to appear in early October to answer questions about the influence of communism in the movie business. The blacklisting campaign was aided by the June 1950 publication of the pamphlet *Red Channels* by an organization calling itself American Business Consultants Inc. (ABC), which claimed to be staffed by former FBI agents. For a hefty fee ABC would scrutinize the payrolls of the studios and TV networks to purge them of communists. *Red Channels* was their opening salvo, and in it they named 151 entertainers ABC claimed were "Reds." The Weavers had just concluded a very successful engagement at the nightclub Ciro's in Hollywood and were preparing their first network television show when their manager called to say that Seeger had been cited in *Red Channels*. "*Red Channels* came out," Seeger told Wilkinson, "and the contract was torn up. I expected it, so I didn't really feel resentful. We assumed that sooner or later they'd get us."

For Seeger, the trouble with HUAC was just beginning. The Weavers disbanded, and essentially the commercial potential of folk music was put on hold for ten years. As much as I believe culture paves the way for political change, this period reminds me that a certain kind of authoritarian politics can block culture completely. If one imagines an alternative history in which Bob Dylan started his career in 1950 instead of 1960, would the Red Scare have buried Dylan's genius? And if so, would the whole course of music have changed dramatically?

The man who might have been able to answer that question was Harold Leventhal, who had managed both Seeger and Guthrie in the time of the blacklist. Neither singer was able to get a recording contract because of their alleged communist pasts. And then in 1956, Guthrie developed Huntington's chorea and went into permanent hospitalization. Two months after Woody died, in October of 1967, Harold asked me if I would help him in the staging of a Guthrie Memorial Concert. The concert, held in January of 1968 at Carnegie Hall, would benefit the Huntington's Chorea Foundation. Harold was excited because Bob Dylan had agreed to come out of his two-year self-imposed exile and appear with the Hawks. Despite his break with the larger folk music community, Bob's commitment to the legacy and work of Woody Guthrie never waned. The concert came off without a hitch. Bob Dylan and the Hawks, Judy Collins, Pete Seeger, Odetta, Woody's twenty-one-year-old son Arlo, Joan Baez, Ramblin' Jack Elliot, and Tom Paxton all played Guthrie tunes.

Albert Grossman, who was a bit pissed that his rival Leventhal had managed to get Bob out of retirement, decreed that there would be no photographs of Dylan allowed and that every single bag of every single audience member had to be searched for cameras. Bob and his band had all grown beards, and they definitely looked like the mysterious mountain men that was becoming their legend. They played three Guthrie songs, including a brilliant version of "Ain't Got No Home" that brought down the house. The feeling of being present at the creation of this new music coming out of Big Pink was almost overwhelming for me. I was just offstage calling the light cues that night, and the sense of joy that Bob and the Hawks were exuding kept bringing a smile to my face. The next morning the front cover of the *Daily News* featured a full-page grainy picture of Bob, obviously taken from the balcony with a tiny Minox camera. The headline read "Dylan Emerges."

At the end of the concert, Robbie Robertson took me aside and said the Hawks had been recording an album on their own for Capitol Records and might want to tour in the summer. He asked me if I would be interested in managing their tour, and I told him I would. I asked what they were going to call themselves, and he smiled. "Levon wants to call us the Crackers, but I'm not sure everyone would get the joke. Bob just calls us the Band. Do you think we could get away with that?"

I went back to Princeton, excited that a new horizon awaited. I had no way of knowing then how consequential the Band's first record, *Music from Big Pink*, would be. Musicians like George Harrison and Eric Clapton regularly cited *Music from Big Pink* as the seminal influence in developing their new direction, and it didn't escape me that they both grew beards like Levon and Robbie. It was as if the psychedelic sound that had dominated since the Summer of Love was running out of steam and a fresh take was just around the corner. Even Clapton was tired of the ten-minute solos he was doing at the Cream live shows. And the Beatles, post *Sgt. Pepper*, began to pare down their music to the point that the style of *Let It Be* is remarkably close to the Band's sound. The San Francisco bands like Jefferson Airplane and the Grateful Dead continued on their own path, but it was clear that even Jerry Garcia was inspired by the Band's first album.

Big Pink created its own genre, which we now identify as Americana, but in 1968 that genre didn't exist. *The Basement*

Tapes and *Music from Big Pink* were sui generis. Dylan had taught the Band that there was so much to learn from the history of American music. For many rock musicians, that history started in the early 1950s, but Bob had learned from Woody Guthrie and others that it really stretches back into the nineteenth century. Listen to Mavis Staples singing Stephen Foster's "Hard Times Come Again No More," published in 1854. That a Black woman could interpret a song from the king of minstrel music says a lot about the porous boundaries of class and race that make Americana such a rich tapestry. Dylan, giving his acceptance speech for the 2015 MusiCares Person of the Year Award, said, "If you'd listened to Robert Johnson singing 'Better come in my kitchen, 'cause it's gonna be raining out doors' as many times as I listened to it, sometime later you just might write 'A Hard Rain's a-Gonna Fall.'"

When I returned to Princeton, the gentle pace of Woodstock was obliterated. The Tet Offensive in Vietnam had shocked everyone. All the lies about "the light at the end of the tunnel" were being revealed as just wishful thinking on the part of Westmoreland and Johnson. In my American history course, I had read a famous John Quincy Adams speech from 1821 in which he said, "[America] goes not abroad, in search of monsters to destroy" and then concluded by saying that if America undertook foreign wars, "the fundamental maxims of her policy would insensibly change from *liberty* to *force*." The wisdom of the Founders is lost on the living; in 1967, the possibility of having to fight this foreign war seemed inevitable.

As part of its antiwar effort, SDS attempted to close the Institute for Defense Analysis (IDA), a Defense Department–funded think tank that had a presence at Princeton and on other university campuses. IDA was working on new forms of warfare, and there is a fair amount of evidence that napalm was conceived there. The photograph coming out of Vietnam of a local girl running naked along a road with her skin badly burned by napalm was enough to turn many students to the task of staging a sit-in at the IDA offices, making it very hard for them to get any work done. A *New York Times* report said that IDA was also developing crowd-control technologies, such as a super water pistol that could squirt pepper spray long distances.

In October, Peter Kaminsky led a group of thirty Princeton students to block the entrance of IDA. The president of the university arrived and asked them to disband, but they refused. None of the IDA employees tried to go into the building, and so the president said it would be a matter between IDA and the local police. Thirty minutes later the police arrived and told the students they had five minutes to leave, at which point Kaminsky asked, "Does anyone have a five-minute cigarette?" Using billy clubs, the cops carted them all off to jail.

Peter was the first friend to try to teach me about what Eisenhower had called the military–industrial complex. Peter had been schooled by a great political scientist at Princeton named Michael Walzer (still the editor of the quarterly magazine *Dissent*), and they felt that IDA was the nexus of the military–industrial cabal. Corporations like Dow Chemical needed university research scientists to invent vicious weapons like napalm, and then each university would subsequently lean on its local congressperson to secure grant funding from the Pentagon. The defense companies would in turn make sure to spread their production plants all over the country so there would be many congressional districts needing defense funds to keep local employment going. At the height of the war, the unions were co-opted as well, so we were in fact building the modern corporate state with the help of big business, big government, *and* big labor. What a con.

When Peter got out of jail, SDS turned its focus to getting the ROTC ejected from our campus. Here I found myself caught between two friendships. On one side, my roommate Cam Ferenbach went into NROTC so that the navy would pay for his very expensive Princeton education. As the war intensified and the campus got more militant, Cam became more and more ambivalent about his service, but he was going through with it despite his desire to hang out with the rest of us who were smoking pot and dreaming of the freedom that was waiting at the end of college. Peter Kaminsky was another story. He was able to confront the president of Princeton with humor, good manners, and passion and somehow move his agenda without causing a backlash, but he *did* want to throw ROTC off campus, so there was tension whenever we hung out with both him and Cam. It helped that Cam wasn't dedicated to the ideals of the ROTC but was just using it as a way to pay for college, and eventually Peter and Cam figured that friendship trumps politics and the pair are still friends to this day.

Peter held SDS together despite the presence of some Progressive Labor types who were puritanical and without an ounce of humor. They all had short hair, thought that rock and roll and drugs were bourgeois, and were committed to a more violent vision of revolution than Peter was ever going to lead. Late one night at the farm that Peter and many of his communards lived at outside of Princeton, I told one of the PL guys, "If there ever is a revolution, it's guys like Bob Dylan who you will throw in jail for causing trouble." He didn't crack a smile or dispute the assertion.

SDS was a curious case study in the failure of the left. Like many of my classmates who toyed with joining SDS, I read the Port Huron Statement, a 25,000-word manifesto of the movement written by SDS member Tom Hayden and some colleagues. They addressed "the felt powerlessness of ordinary people [and] the resignation before the enormity of events," and wrote that "the decline of utopia and hope is in fact one of the defining features of social life today." Looking back, it's obvious that these feelings still plague our democracy, and yet in the fall of 1967 we still had reason to believe that some sort of utopian future might await our generation. We didn't realize the power fear had to freeze politics in place. This sentence early in the Port Huron Statement gives the drift of our resignation to the apocalypse: "Our work is guided by the sense that we may be the last generation in the experiment with living." Faced with the threat of nuclear war, this "New Left" had an almost bipolar approach to politics: On the one hand there was a desire to achieve an authentic self—to break through the apathy and conformity—and then we also wanted to build a communal life dedicated to social justice at home and a foreign policy in which the military–industrial complex no longer called the tune.

Though some of the Port Huron Statement can seem dated, its emphasis on "participatory democracy" was extraordinarily prescient. As Tom Hayden later wrote, "There should be experiments in decentralization . . . devolving the power of 'monster cities' to local communities seeded with more developmental incentives." If only the Democratic Party had been able to reconnect with its Jeffersonian roots, with its emphasis on the innovative power to be discovered and developed at the state and local level, as opposed to believing that all wisdom flowed from a gigantic (and distant) federal government. Those of us who study innovation realize that true breakthroughs come from organizations that have pushed power out to the edges. As one of my mentors, John Seely Brown, former director of Xerox PARC, wrote, "We can now build these small, lightweight, fast-moving businesses from the edge. What that does, for those enlightened large-scale firms, is to convert the excitement on the edge into a dynamic attractor for the folks in the core." At some point in the near future, progressives will understand this dynamic and embrace a kind of New Federalism that would allow our country to thrive again.

By the spring of 1968 the Princeton campus was host to daily scenes of confrontation. There was a real awareness that we had become agents of history—that the weekly demonstrations against the war were making a difference. But then, in the beginning of April, Martin Luther King was murdered by an assassin's bullet and you could literally feel the idealism leaking out of the campus. Dr. King was the one who seemed able to bring together the civil rights movement and the antiwar movement. Without him, we were lost.

A year earlier I had seen Dr. King preach at Riverside Church in Manhattan. The sermon was about how President Johnson's "War on Poverty" was killed by the Vietnam War. I remembered one line in particular: "I was compelled to see the war as an enemy of the poor and to attack it as such." This was such a radical stance that many of King's liberal white backers moved away from him. And yet the connection he drew was obvious: the hundreds of millions of dollars we were pouring into the Vietnam War was directly related to the lack of funds we needed to improve living conditions and eliminate poverty at home. If Dr. King were alive today, he would be fighting this same battle still; only the location of the war has changed.

Some of my professors dismissed the "great man" theory of history and said that world events move forward irrespective of the major personalities of an era. But for me, Martin Luther King was a unique voice of change, and his way of thinking about equal rights—based in the religious tradition of nonviolence—was doing nothing short of changing the course of history. I honestly didn't think that the amount of progress we had made since 1963 could have happened without him. In my deep depression over his death, I could only hope someone would step forward to continue the work of combining the strands of the civil rights movement and the antiwar movement, and to do it with the vision and effectiveness King had.

I remember watching *CBS News* playing King's speech from the night before he was murdered. He had said, "I have seen the promised land. I may not get there with you, but my eyes have seen the glory of the coming of the Lord." Did he know he was going to die the next day? Had he lived with the threat of assassination for so long that he just assumed he would be killed? In the end, I concluded that King understood John's gospel better than most of us: "Greater love has no one than this: to lay down one's life for one's friends."

In my grief, I turned my energy into supporting Bobby Kennedy's presidential campaign, which seemed a way to carry on King's work both in civil rights and in opposition to the war. Kennedy had given a speech in March of 1968 at the University of Kansas that went to the heart of a dilemma we are still facing: Is the only way to measure our prosperity by Gross National Product?

> Our Gross National Product, now, is over $800 billion a year, but that Gross National Product—if we judge the United States of America by that—that Gross National Product counts air pollution and cigarette advertising, and ambulances to clear our highways of carnage. It counts special locks for our doors and the jails for the people who break them. It counts the destruction of the redwood and the loss of our natural wonder in chaotic sprawl. It counts napalm and counts nuclear warheads and armored cars for the police to fight the riots in our cities. . . . It measures neither our wit nor our courage, neither our wisdom nor our learning, neither our compassion nor our devotion to our country[;] it measures everything[,] in short, except that which makes life worthwhile. And it can tell us everything about America except why we are proud that we are Americans.

It seemed to me that Bobby was asking the existential question we are still facing: Are we defined only by what we consume? But these were questions that were not to be answered. One night in June, I was plunged again into sadness and anger when I heard Bobby Kennedy had been killed in Los Angeles.

I wrote to my mother, "What is going on in this sick country? Every time someone steps forward trying to heal the wounds of segregation or the war, they get killed." I was in Los Angeles at the time of Bobby's death, working with Judy Collins on her new record. We were in the studio when we heard. We had to stop and cry and send the musicians home. I felt sadder about Bobby's death than that of my own father. Was that right? All I know is that I had invested a lot of hope in the possibility of liberal reforms that might set our country on a different path—specifically one that didn't involve our being the world's policeman. My emotions devolved from sadness into an attitude of "fuck politics"; experience had told me caring too much will only lead to heartbreak and sometimes even death.

The cultural-political battle was brought into even greater focus for me in the beginning of September, when Judy Collins and her new band played the Big Sur Folk Festival. Big Sur was special because Joan Baez was the host, and she had invited some of her big-name friends like Joni Mitchell, David Crosby and Stephen Stills, and of course Judy Collins. The concerts took place at Esalen, the center of the "alternative consciousness movement," with the performance area situated on a cliff overlooking the Pacific.

After the concert we all gathered in the big hall for a dinner— musicians, crew, and everyone else who was part of the show. Baez was there with her new husband, the draft-resistance leader David Harris. They had married in the spring of 1968, three months after they had met in Santa Rita Jail, both having been arrested in a large action to shut down the Oakland Armed Forces Induction Center. In June, Harris had refused induction into the army and was indicted.

It was in this context that Harris spoke to us about the struggle against the war. He was in the Dr. King tradition of nonviolent resistance and had made it clear he would not flee to Canada. There was a clear split in the room between those who were willing to put their lives on the line and those who felt that what was needed was a change of consciousness. David Harris was saying we needed to sacrifice our personal futures to stop the war, and Tim Leary was saying we needed to "turn on, tune in, and drop out." I thought I was capable of honor and sacrifice, but the idea of going to jail or to war filled me with dread.

Here we were at Esalen, the heart of the "awareness movement," discussing the important matters of the day and yet . . . the hot tubs beckoned. Here was the split: Take drugs and jump in the water with lovely naked California girls or contemplate going to jail. I made my choice to move toward Dionysus—proof that you could lose an examined life much easier than you could gain one. That said, it can be hard to tell when you are at a crossroads—when going in one direction instead of the other will change everything that comes after. When you decide to take the path that seems more scenic and beautiful in the moment, you don't always know you're also choosing to leave your old life of political commitment behind. I certainly didn't.

(Years later, my good friend the musician Van Dyke Parks wrote me his recollections of the evening: "I was happy I held forth on the keyboard in that field of forfeit. I knew a processional or two. David approved of them. My wife and I enjoyed that weekend, amused by the odors. It's entirely possible we participated in a dream escape with psilocybin, which was rife as the crowd's choice confection. The hallmark of that indelible weekend[:] she lost three precious Parks heirloom rings, set among her effects near a hot tub, about the same time the flying saucers started to dart about the crepuscular coast line.")

David Harris was arrested nine months later and spent eighteen months in prison. When he got out he said, "In prison, I lost my ideals, but not my principles." In 1968, I lost my ideals, too, but (hopefully) not my principles—and I did it without going to prison. Most of the great musicians sitting in that beautiful room at Esalen and listening to David believed then that they were going to have a greater effect on changing America through their art than through the kinds of personal sacrifices David was making. As much as I appreciated David's sacrifice, that turned out to be true. Having seen the trajectory of their careers and the impact they've made, I know that the culture led the politics.

6. The Band in Los Angeles

1969

In Woodstock, in a bleak and ashen January of 1969, the cold wind blowing down Ohayo Mountain Road, I made my commitment to rock and roll. I was six months from graduating, but I knew I was leaving behind any life my father could have imagined for me. I was riding shotgun in Rick Danko's Lincoln "Confidential" as he slammed over the snow-covered bridge with inches to spare and then, with one hand on the wheel, cut a hard left into the driveway of the clubhouse. He still wore the neck brace from his last car accident but seemed oblivious to the danger of the icy driveway.

"You know, sometimes I almost think it's lucky I broke my neck."

"How do you mean?" I said.

"Well, the Band recorded *Music from Big Pink*, and after it came out we had some offers to do some small college concerts and then I had my accident and we couldn't tour and so people began to think there was some mystery about us. The more we stayed out of sight, the more famous we got."

He sucked on his Marlboro and grinned. Then he gunned

the Lincoln up the hill and parked next to a long, low clapboard house of weathered gray.

In January, I was given the opportunity to work with the Band, the essence of American music, and the offer was too great to let pass. In Robbie Robertson's memoir he notes of me, "There was nothing he wanted more than to be affiliated with the Band." That was true. The dreams of my dead father—that I would follow his path from Princeton to Harvard Law—were now exhausted. I would not have to face him. My mother could deal with the change of plans, and she already had seen glimpses into my future when she served as a generous host to the Kweskin Jug Band in her Shaker Heights home, ignoring the roaches in the library ashtray. She had been my great defender from an early age, shielding me from my father's anger, and she was still stepping up for me. I called her to promise I would get my degree in May but, for the time being, I was headed to California.

The plan was to move the Band out to Los Angeles to record their second album. Everyone wanted to be away from the Woodstock winter, and so my first job was to organize the equipment transfer to California with the help of my roommate Lindsay Holland. Inside the clubhouse, the rest of the Band was packing their gear. When you are young and in love with music and you can't get enough of rock and roll, the time spent with masters like the Band was treasured, and I soaked up every moment of it, even when doing mundane things like boxing up household items.

In the Band's music there were songs so true that they changed you as you listened to them. They were carrying on Dylan's craft of songwriting, and Robbie Robertson was finding his own voice, which had touches of Flannery O'Connor and Levon's

Arkansas dirt farm and maybe a bit of the traveling music shows that would move up the Mississippi from New Orleans to the rough neighborhoods of West Memphis, where the old Hawks had run across Sonny Boy Williamson on his last legs, spitting blood into a can while playing some hooch joint.

I was an English major and had written my junior paper on T. S. Eliot and W. H. Auden, but the poetry of Dylan and Robertson felt like it had some dirt under the fingernails. It certainly was well removed from the seminar rooms of Princeton, and my professors would object to even comparing the songwriters with the poets, but I didn't care. The music that was coming out of Woodstock also made me feel as if the songs of San Francisco bands such as Jefferson Airplane and the Grateful Dead were no more than the artificial imaginings of some spoiled children compared to the good and simple language of a Dylan song like "I Shall Be Released."

When we got to L.A. we set up in a house on Sunset Plaza that we were renting from Sammy Davis, Jr. It had a pool house that we converted into a recording studio with the application of insulation and moving blankets on the walls. All the light switches and fixtures had been installed for someone who was five feet tall, so a six-footer like me felt like a giant in a cartoon movie.

John Simon, another Princeton grad, worked as a combination producer and recording engineer. The routine was similar to what we had done in the basement of Big Pink: sit around and drink coffee and smoke cigarettes every morning until the spirit moved us to begin recording. Robbie had written six new songs, Richard Manuel had written two, and Rick Danko had one.

The only other person in the studio was a photographer

named Elliott Landy. Once in a while a photographer gains the trust of an artist or a band and his work fuses with them in such a way that they become married in the public consciousness. One might think of David Duncan's pictures of Picasso at work, or Alfred Wertheimer's pictures of Elvis backstage in 1956. Elliott Landy's chronicle of the Band from this period was of similar importance. One of my jobs as manager was helping Robbie and various art directors like Bob Cato make the album covers (and I was happy to, since I'd always been interested in photography), and thus for me especially, Elliott's pictures are so much a part of the early Band image that I almost can't think of those days without envisioning a photograph Elliott created.

For the second record, Robbie and John Simon had an idea for a much more homemade sound than what was being produced at the time. So much music was being compressed so it would feel loud on a cheap radio—it was all midrange and high frequencies and very little real bass. Levon had bought an antique drum set with a really big bass drum that made a kind of thud. The piano was a crappy upright, and over the course of the week, they added mandolins, fiddles, accordions, and tubas to the mix. In his 2018 memoir, *Testimony*, Robbie wrote of our improvised studio, "Nobody was thinking along these lines back then, and Capitol Records thought we were crazy. But my theory was that the Band could do something truly original if we had our own atmosphere, a music machine that ran on our course of time and creativity." The notion that you could use modern tools to recreate a more ragged sound is one of the great contradictions of this critical period of rock. We had not entered the digital age, so "fixing" something on the recording often involved physically cutting a piece of tape. With that in mind, the idea was to get what you wanted live so you didn't have to change it later. Needless to say, as the years went on and the digital tools got better, the possibility of correcting one flat vocal note in a song was easy.

But that is not what the Band was after. Four years before, when they had first met Bob Dylan, they were almost completely unaware that the "old-timey music" their parents had played was still viable. Now they were joyously reviving it, and capturing it the way they wanted, for an album Capitol Records hoped would be in the top ten. It was liberating.

But the sessions were not without conflict. Richard Manuel had picked up the habit of starting to drink beer in the late morning. The evening I left to return to Princeton to finish college (I got my degree but never went to graduation), Robbie was all over him about his inability to get the lyrics and harmony right to accompany Levon on "Up on Cripple Creek." It foreshadowed troubles to come.

By the time I returned to California in early April, Albert Grossman had booked the Band into a series of "debut concerts" with Bill Graham. We would open at Winterland in San Francisco and then play the Fillmore East in New York. The first night back in L.A., Robbie brought me down to the pool house, where they had set up a playback room in Sammy Davis, Jr.'s playroom—an elaborate bedroom straight out of a Hugh Hefner fantasy, with mirrors on the ceiling and TVs rising out of the floor. Robbie put on "The Night They Drove Old Dixie Down," loud and clear coming out of the big speakers, and by the song's end, tears were welling up in my eyes. It's strange how music can produce empathy in a way that no other art form quite can.

I had pored over James Agee and Walker Evans's book collaboration *Let Us Now Praise Famous Men* and it had opened up a window onto the life of the sharecropper, but it did not put me in the soul of loss that Levon's three-minute plaintive ballad did. As a Northern liberal who had marched with Martin Luther King, to me all crackers were like Bull Connor, the sheriff who had billy-clubbed the Black civil rights workers in Birmingham. Those scenes on TV in 1963 had seared into my forming political consciousness, but what it took me some years to realize was that in making this distinction I had left out the poor white folks who were also exploited by the politics of Southern racism. Robbie's song gave me an understanding of Levon's world that would last me the rest of my life.

Within a week we were on a plane to San Francisco to unveil the mystery that had become the Band. Everyone seemed ready for the concert debut, but by the time we checked in to the Seal Rock Inn, overlooking the Pacific, Robbie was running a 102 temperature. A year later he would write a song about the next three days called "Stage Fright," but on that Wednesday afternoon, I just put it off to bad timing and too many weeks in the studio. The rest of the Band and our crew went over to the cavernous Winterland Ballroom to do a sound check, with full confidence that Robbie would be ready for the Thursday night opening.

Bill Graham was the only serious promoter in San Francisco at the time, and he was wound tight like a German clock spring. Orphaned at the age of four, he'd fled Berlin for Paris in 1938 with his sister and stayed one step ahead of the Nazis, from Marseille across the Pyrenees to Lisbon and on to Casablanca, Dakar, and Bermuda, before finally ending up in New York City. His sister had died on the trek, and he never let you forget that he'd gone through more hell in his childhood than you would in a lifetime. We assured him that Robbie would be okay, but by Thursday at 2 p.m., the fever was worse and he had been unable to keep any food down for twenty-four hours.

Albert Grossman arrived from New York and spent a few minutes with the doctor. By 8:30, Bill Graham was pacing the halls of the hotel asking if we were going to cancel. The Ace of Cups, an all-girl band, had already played, and now the Sons of Champlin, a local favorite, had gone onstage. When Albert said he didn't want to cancel, Bill put forth the notion that maybe Robbie was just scared. If so, he had a hypnotist who had worked on a few performers. Albert suggested he call him, and within thirty minutes a small man with gray hair in a black suit with a white carnation on his lapel showed up at the hotel. We ushered him into Robbie's room, and in the presence of Bill, Albert, myself, and the rest of the Band, he proceeded to put Robbie, sitting in bed in his pajamas, under hypnosis. Once he had done that, he began his incantations, in the quietest voice imaginable.

"Your head will feel like a cool artic breeze is blowing."

"Your stomach will feel as calm as a quiet mountain lake."

"Whenever you hear the word 'grow,' these sensations will feel stronger."

"Now I'm going to bring you out of the trance."

And so he did. Robbie looked around at the assembled crowd in his hotel room. His wife, Dominique, and some of the band members' wives looked on skeptically. He said he felt better. He swung his legs out of the bed, went to stand up, and immediately collapsed on the floor. Our collective hearts sank. I had actually begun to believe in this magic show. But the hypnotist was not discouraged.

"I forgot you've been sitting in bed for three days. I have to put you back in a trance and work on your legs."

After he had repeated the process and spoken to Robbie of "legs that feel like taut springs," he brought him out of the trance again. Robbie got up and walked around the room. For the first time in three days there was a smile on his face. Levon asked him if he was ready to play, and he said, "I guess so." With that, Bill Graham was out of his seat calling the hall. The Sons were just leaving the stage. We had to get to Winterland immediately.

In ten minutes we had a police escort to the auditorium. I sat in the back of one of the limos with Robbie and the hypnotist. All the way to the hall, the little man kept up a very quiet chatter in Robbie's ear. When we got out of the car, he told me it was important for him to be positioned in Robbie's sight line. I put him backstage behind one of the massive speakers, right behind Richard Manuel's piano bench. The Band went on and played an eight-song set. It wasn't inspired, but it was damn good given the circumstances. Robbie played all of his solos as if on autopilot. The crowd was a bit disappointed that there were no encores.

As we settled into the cars to go back to the hotel, I saw Robbie look curiously at Richard Manuel.

"Richard, wasn't that weird how the hypnotist kept yelling 'grow, grow, grow' between every song?"

"What do you mean? I never heard a thing."

"That can't be. You were much closer to him than me."

"I promise you. I never heard him say a word."

The morning after, I knocked on Robbie's door. He was miraculously cured, as if the past three days had been just a nightmare. He was anxious to get out of the hotel room, which had nothing but memories of fever and claustrophobia, so we ventured out to Haight-Ashbury to see our friend Emmett Grogan, the leader of a group of anarchists called the Diggers. They had a store over on Frederick Street called Trip Without a Ticket, and near that was their free clinic and a park where they gave out food every afternoon.

Together with Peter Coyote, Emmett had taken the name Diggers from the English radicals of the 1640s who had used the chaos of the Interregnum to put forth an alternative vision to feudalism that would be free from private property and exist as a barter economy. Emmett had a clean-shaven, chiseled face and a haircut that made him look more like a biker than a hippie. He and Peter, both movie-star handsome, wore black Levi's and motorcycle boots, with tight black T-shirts under leather jackets. We left the store and went next door for coffee, and as we walked, it was obvious from the deference offered by one and all that they were local stars of the Haight. They had managed to court all the local bands into putting on free concerts, and both the Grateful Dead and Janis Joplin had given them money for the free clinic. Peter, Emmett, and Bill Graham knew each other from their work with the San Francisco Mime Troupe— Bill as an organizer—but they had gone in opposite directions when Bill went completely over to the commercial side and Peter and Emmett split off to form the Diggers, whose philosophy supported the barter economy of their namesake. Emmett had little regard for Graham anymore and asked the Band, "Why don't you guys do a free concert for us?"

"We're playing two more nights at Winterland and then we

have to go to New York to play the Fillmore," Robbie replied.

"Well, play tomorrow afternoon in Golden Gate Park for the kids," Peter countered.

I jumped in. "We are exclusive to Bill Graham in San Francisco for the next month."

"Fuck the contracts," said Emmett.

I could see this was going nowhere, so I suggested that we could give a donation to the free clinic instead. Peter and Emmett quickly accepted and then began to tell us about all of the activities they were sponsoring. They had started three years ago with the Artists Liberation Front, but the arguments about tactics had been too constraining, and so Emmett and Peter, with their cursory reading of radical history, had started the Diggers. They were essentially anarchists; they didn't want to deal with committees and the associated politics. In the wake of Richard Nixon's first great "law and order" campaign, their first manifesto portrays the jokey anarchy of their movement:

> Money Is an Unnecessary Evil
> It is addicting.
> It is a temptation to the weak (most of the violent
>   crimes of our city in some way involve money).
> It can be hoarded, blocking the free flow of energy[,]
>   and the giant energy-hoards of Montgomery Street
>   will soon give rise to a sudden and thus explosive
>   release of this trapped energy, causing much pain
>   and chaos.
> As part of the city's campaign to stem the causes of
>   violence the San Francisco Diggers announce a 30
>   day period beginning now during which all

> responsible citizens are asked to turn in their
> money. No questions will be asked.
>
> Bring money to your local Digger for free distribu-
> tion to all. The Diggers will then liberate its energy
> according to the style of whoever receives it.

Earlier in the summer they had staged a parade through San Francisco's Financial District bearing a huge coffin with a banner reading "Hippie—Son of Media" on the side. Local TV stations had carried the parade and accomplished the Digger goal of "creating the condition you describe." To my mind the Diggers represented the continuation of a long tradition of freethinking. The notion of anarchism had gotten a bad name in the United States, but the Diggers brought it back to its original meaning: "a society based on voluntary cooperation and the free association of individuals and groups." Many of the Diggers kept up the tradition over the years, and a group of them moved to the country around Bolinas and continued their barter lifestyle. Emmett showed up in Woodstock a couple of years after we'd hung out with him in San Francisco, and although he wrote a memoir about his adventures, he never really could get off the street or his smack habit, and he died too young. Meanwhile, Peter's love of street theater stayed with him, and he eventually became a well-known actor and one of the best paid voice-over artists in the West.

I remember one late night in 1967, after playing the Fillmore with the Jug Band, we went to a party at the Grateful Dead house and listened to Jerry Garcia spin tales of how they were going to establish their own record company and not sell out to "the man." Of course, that story ended with the Dead becoming a conglomerate, their records being distributed by Reprise, the old Sinatra record company, and when Jerry died in 1995, the carrying out of his will ended up proceeding with all the drama of a soap opera worthy of daytime TV.

Using our "alternative history" frame, I imagine that if the Diggers had come along today, creating their vision of a barter economy would not be hard using Internet tools. And the music industry has already been transformed by modern technology—just ask my son, Nicholas, the Alan Lomax of the DIY music scene in Oakland, California, who believes it is possible for artists to thrive without the formal structures of record companies. In defense of the Dead, in their time, there did not seem to be a good alternative to the established music business owned by the conglomerates. I saw Jerry many times over the years, and whenever I watched him pull up in his new top-of-the-line BMW, I was sure that the cultural contradictions of capitalism were always part of what he was trying to escape but ultimately couldn't.

Similarly, Bill Graham's start with the nonprofit Mime Troupe had morphed into something more mercenary. In 1974, Robbie Robertson and I happened to run into a chagrined Graham changing planes in a Paris airport, headed for Zurich. He was carrying two large briefcases, and we didn't need to ask what a man with an all-cash business was doing headed for the land of the numbered account.

The morning after the debut concert, we parted ways with the Diggers and I left them ten tickets to that evening's show at

Winterland. Robbie was anxious to make up for the shortfall of the first night's performance, and by the time we went onstage he had something to prove. As a guitarist, Robertson's style was less flashy than some of his peers; the flow of the melodic line is somewhat spare at times, and his sense of leaving holes in a solo is unique. He never put out the speed playing of Clapton or Jeff Beck, but when Robbie performed with Bob Dylan his special solo style would shine, as it does in recordings of "Just Like Tom Thumb's Blues" and "Highway 61 Revisited," where Dylan's three-chord structure gave Robbie the room to build a solo, from big chords to the continuous plucking of a high note that cut through like a knife. The Band compositions, in contrast, were built with a different kind of craftsmanship—a conscious move away from the long solos of the English bands like Cream—and so the opportunities for Robbie to show off were more limited. The irony was that it was Clapton who, in an interview with a Toronto music critic, said of the album *Music from Big Pink*, "It stimulated me, it moved me, and it upset me and made me very discontent all at the same time."

On the second night at Winterland I realized that the Band was going to be successful on the road. They were trained as a bar band, but my only live experience with them had been the Dylan tour of 1965–66, which was Bob's music, not theirs. Early on at Winterland they played "King Harvest," a song that starts off quietly with a guitar and organ vamp under Levon and Richard singing a chorus of "King Harvest has surely come," which then leads into a powerful Richard Manuel lament about a farmer facing a drought. That night the song ended with a three-chorus solo from Robbie that brought the San Francisco crowd to its feet.

A little while later they played "Chest Fever," which starts with a long, unstructured organ improvisation by Garth Hudson and then grows into the most outright rocker in the Band's repertory. Garth really was feeling loose that night, and the crowd was howling approvingly by the time Levon's big snare drum kicked in with Rick's bass run. Robbie got off a wonderful solo that wound back into a solo from Garth, and then the rhythm section took it home to huge cheers. At one point I looked up from the corner of the stage into the vastness of the ballroom— seven thousand folks on their feet, cheering and stomping. I knew I had made the right move committing to the Band.

By the time the night was over, the Band had done two encores, and any doubts about their ability to bring their recorded magic to the stage were gone. We spent some time backstage with the Diggers and then went off to a party with Jack Casady, the bassist from Jefferson Airplane, who had for all three nights taken up a seat right behind the biggest stage speakers. The party felt like a scene from Antonioni's film *Blow-Up*—a curious mix of fashionable San Francisco couples and hipsters like Lawrence Ferlinghetti and Michael McClure. The poets seemed at home in the beautiful mansion in Pacific Heights, honored, patronized, and pursued by wonderful tall girls in flowing skirts of Indian cotton over boots of Spanish leather. I wondered why any artist would want to join a liberation front. This life seemed perfect.

7. Bearsville

1969

Before I saw the dark side of rock, I saw the ecstasy of it, and I found it welcoming. In June of 1969, having graduated from Princeton, I took possession of the clubhouse out on Bearsville Road, as all of the Band's members were suddenly flush with money (and had wives with children on the way) and there was no longer any need for group living. My girlfriend Wanda Mahaffey moved up from Princeton, and sometimes her girlfriend Britt MacNamee would come stay with us. Having spent the last eight years in all-male educational institutions, developing real friendships with girls was wonderful.

My house was still treated like the clubhouse by the band members, a place to get away from family obligations and smoke the good weed they brought in from California by the suitcase load. It wasn't strong like pot is today, and it came in bricks full of seeds and stems, but it did the trick and a musician could still keep good time after the first joint of the morning.

Woodstock was not famous then. The festival bearing its name had not yet occurred, and except for the small group of artists and musicians surrounding Dylan, it was pretty much off the radar. There was a café run by a French émigré we knew only as Bernard where you could nurse an espresso and play chess all afternoon without anyone bothering you. All summer, musicians and filmmakers would come up to visit. Miloš Forman, Dennis Hopper, and Jerry Garcia were just three visitors in the month of July 1969. Robbie Robertson had bought a house on a beautiful piece of land with a great studio building that we used to rehearse in.

For a man who had left school at sixteen to play rock and roll, he had an incredible desire to educate himself. He read voraciously about America, his adopted land. William Faulkner and Flannery O'Connor deepened his understanding of the mystical South and the weird sense of being a permanent outsider to the American mainstream that the Pentecostal Christians carried with them. The paradox that a kid from Toronto like Robbie was somehow able to have a different view of America's strengths and her foibles was fascinating to me. He was like a sponge, and the fact that I had been a lit major at Princeton was part of our relationship. He was never afraid to admit he didn't know the work of a poet like Auden or William Carlos Williams. I was glad I had transported much of my poetry library from Princeton to Woodstock.

We also took to getting the local Woodstock movie theater to book films we wanted to see. One of Robbie's favorite films was Marcel Carné's *Children of Paradise*, and on one weekend we watched it twice. Set in 1828 Paris, its demimonde of actors, swindlers, pickpockets, and impresarios was one that Robbie would return to many times in his own songs, including "Life Is a Carnival" and "The W. S. Walcott Medicine Show." But maybe more importantly, we were fascinated by the story behind the movie. The film was shot in France during the Nazi occupation, and several of the key creative talents were Jewish. By making a period film about defiance, and by moving the sets from city to city to avoid the Nazi censors, Carné managed to make one of the great French masterpieces, while helping to fight with the resistance.

It was an example that any artist in an age of upheaval might be drawn to, and although Dylan had long since moved on from writing political songs, he seemed to appreciate the film, lingering afterward in Robbie's kitchen while Sara Dylan, Dominique Robertson, and Albert Grossman's wife, Sally, dished out a wonderful bouillabaisse served with a Chardonnay from a small California winery called Stags' Leap that Albert had brought back from his latest visit to Janis Joplin in San Francisco. I was coming to see that the way the artist resists the dominant culture can take multiple forms. There is the resistance of a song like "Masters of War," calling us to struggle; there is the resistance of Carné's *Children of Paradise*, a subtler move against a hostile power; and finally there was the sort of assertion of self—"How does it feel to be on your own?"—which Bob Dylan had been drawn to. They all seem like forms of the same thing. The idea that each artist was going to have to choose his form of resistance was just entering our consciousness at this moment.

And there was another resistance on the horizon. The incredible women who stood by the artists were not content to just play the muse role that had been dropped in their laps. They rejected the idea that they stay home with the kids while their husbands were out gallivanting around the world, hanging with John Lennon and Allen Ginsberg and who knows what gorgeous twenty-two-year-old model. For Sally Grossman, who had no children, her resistance took the form of regular explorations to the most exotic parts of the world. She was a fearless traveler and would regularly light out for Oaxaca, Mexico, in her Mercedes-Benz convertible coupe, like some latter-day Georgia O'Keefe. There she found Native tribes who would let her into their peyote rituals. I remember one December a group of singers from Calcutta called the Bauls of Bengal were Sally's houseguests. Albert had called them an Indian Blues band, and they were a fair distance from the classical asceticism of Ravi Shankar's music. Before they played for us they ingested a lot of a wild combination of pot, yogurt, and honey.

But for Dominique and Sara, the negotiation was more complex. Both Bob and Robbie had been on the road consistently since 1960, and the mythology of Jack Kerouac was ever present. But their wives weren't just hangers-on—they were two of the smartest women I ever met—and between them and their husbands there was a dialectic, as neither woman wanted to be in the harsh spotlight that fell on their husbands whenever they ventured into public. Eventually the contradictions became too intense, and by the mid-1970s both couples had split.

But that summer night of 1969, we were all still together, and Albert, who was thinking of opening a restaurant in Bearsville, was holding forth on the virtues of the new California wines. Dominique, with all of her French reserve, was arguing for the continued primacy of the French whites she liked. I remember Sally Grossman looking as chic as always, ever a style icon and a brilliant conversationalist able to hold her own in any company, and never fazed by the hypermasculine bent of the rock-and-roll business. You know her from the cover of Dylan's *Bringing It All Back Home* album—that's her with the cool gaze on the chaise lounge in the Grossmans' Gramercy Park townhouse, surrounded by symbols of the moment: a fallout shelter sign, Lyndon Johnson on the *Time* magazine cover, and album covers from Eric Von Schmidt, Lotte Lenya, and Robert Johnson. It's like Bob wanted you to know what he was thinking about at that very moment.

Levon Helm's first house in Woodstock was not so refined as the Grossman or Robertson aeries. Out on a road toward the town of Shady, it appeared to be a close approximation of the Arkansas shack he had grown up in. An old pickup and a new Corvette were parked on the weedy dirt that surrounded the cabin. I would usually find Levon in the early afternoon sitting on a porch in one of two metal chairs, next to which a mangy dog was tied up. Even in winter the dog stayed outside, but inside, a blaze almost as big as a bonfire would be roaring in the old stone fireplace. It would get so hot you would have to step out occasionally to join the mutt.

Levon's girlfriend was Libby Titus. She was like a character from Scott Fitzgerald's *Tender Is the Night*, keeping her beautiful face and body out of the sun under big hats and long silk dresses. She talked with a sophisticated New England inflection that inclined always toward the sarcastic. She might have been the wittiest girl I had ever met, and the contrast between her 1920s demeanor and Levon's good-ol'-boy mannerisms couldn't have been more stark. But sex makes up for a lot of differences, and somehow Libby and Levon stayed together through thick and thin.

I was welcome at their place, but I knew never to show up before noon, because Levon liked Valium and he could sleep through a hurricane. On those mornings when we had to hit the road on tour, this presented a problem. More than once I found myself facing the drummer in his underwear brandishing the Bowie knife he kept next to his bed. By the spring of 1970 I had recruited my college buddy Lindsay Holland to work with me on the Band road crew, and waking Levon became his responsibility.

But late at night after a concert, when Rick, Levon, and Richard would be playing for some friends on mandolin and guitars in a hotel suite, Levon was the soul of gentleness. He would tell tales of the early days on the road with Ronnie Hawkins when the bar crowd was so rough that they put up chicken wire in front of the bandstand to protect the musicians from knife fights and flying beer bottles. I think he felt he was pretty lucky to have escaped the dirt-farmer existence of his parents, and yet he was never going to forget where he came from. "The Night They Drove Old Dixie Down" is as much about Levon's pride as about the Civil War.

I remember the approach of my birthday three months after I had graduated from college. The possibility of being drafted loomed over me. On the morning of July 20, two days after my twenty-second birthday, a notice from the Cleveland Draft Board arrived telling me I had been classified 1-Y, which meant that I would not be called up unless they ran out of all other possible recruits. I had suffered from very bad allergies most of my life, and my allergist happened to be opposed to the war. Evidently his letter to my draft board was serious enough to get me the medical deferment. When Richard Manuel heard that I had gotten out of the draft, he suggested we should celebrate. And so around four in the afternoon, he and Andy Yarrow (Peter Yarrow's younger brother) showed up at my house with three tabs of Owsley acid.

I had dropped acid once before, in the summer of 1966. This time, as Richard and Andy were wandering about, I was listening to Jimi Hendrix's album *Are You Experienced* on headphones, and even when I wasn't on drugs, the way he would pan his guitar solos around my head almost made me dizzy, even if I was sitting down. I could imagine how people I would describe as "control freaks" might have a very hard time on LSD. Nothing seems like it is in your charge, and you simply have to go with the flow or risk sliding into a panic. The ego disappeared. I could see why when Leary was at Harvard he was using LSD to treat severe alcoholics.

But I was not prepared for Richard Manuel's idea of an acid trip. Two hours into the trip, just as the Owsley was really kicking in, Richard suggested we go for cocktails at his favorite bar, Deanie's. It also happened to be the local police hangout, but that didn't bother Richard a bit. The cops all knew Richard well and they occasionally would drive him home when he had had one too many. He seemed totally at ease in this bizarre setting, while Andy Yarrow and I were trying to keep our paranoia at bay. Finally we convinced Richard to go back to his house, and as night fell we found ourselves mesmerized by the television, waiting for Neil Armstrong to step out of the lunar landing vehicle he had piloted onto the Sea of Tranquility. Mason Hoffenberg, Richard's neighbor, wandered over and spent the evening laughing at us and debunking the idea that the pictures were really being relayed from the moon. Hoffenberg, short and stout and with the barrel stomach of a voluptuary, was a first-class cynic who had lived off the royalties of his book *Candy*, which he had co-written with Terry Southern. He was a stone junkie, so most of the money went into his veins, and although he still retained his sense of humor, the smack kept him from any productive work.

They had just made a movie of *Candy* starring Marlon Brando, Richard Burton, James Coburn, Walter Matthau, and Ringo Starr, and so Mason was set up for another few years and didn't need to make excuses for not writing. I watched the pudgy little addict carefully while trying not to stare as you might when sitting across from a dangerous character in a subway car. He seemed vicious and out of sync with my harmonic mood, and I wanted him to disappear and leave us to trip with Neil Armstrong on the dusty moon. When his whiny voice and the electronic crackle from the moonwalk started to overwhelm my senses, I wandered outside into the quiet of the evening and stared up at the moon in some vague hope I could see the orbiter that would be Armstrong's lifeline back to Earth. Soon my powers of concentration settled on the intricate patterns the moonlight made on the big maple leaves pulsing with life as the fireflies flew close to them in the humid night air.

Despite my blissed-out state I had argued with Mason that the moon landing was just the kind of big idea that America loved. JFK had said we would go to the moon in ten years, and we did! And the massive project was funded and coordinated by the government, the only investor willing to take such a risk. The payoff to the whole society in terms of technological improvement proved that the investment was worth it. It was so in tune with the optimism I was still clinging to despite the three assassinations that had killed my political heroes. And even though the LSD had momentarily peeled away my own protective layer of cynicism, Mason's wised-up, ironic knowingness became the model for the decades to come, and my sentimental idealism became as unfashionable as bell-bottom pants. If I could have looked into the future, I might have seen that the air of passionless detachment that the age of irony was about to bring upon us would render most of my generation and the one to follow politically impotent.

The next week, the country was still buzzing about going to the moon. TWA announced it was going to take reservations for flights to the moon starting in 1990, and optimism of this sort provided a brief respite in the midst of the bad news out of Vietnam. In retrospect, the outrageous ambition of the whole moonshot was symbolic of the 1960s. There was impatience in the air, a sense that, if we could only get out of the soul-draining swamp of Vietnam, there were better days ahead and those days would be brought to us by the technological miracles that were not just moving humans to the moon but were appearing on the streets here on Earth.

It took a long time for us to realize the folly of this notion, but in 1969 the music business was just beginning to explore the boundaries of these new technologies—and learning how to wrestle with them—and the public was eagerly embracing advancements like 8-track and cassette players for cars. The idea that you could program the music in your car was so novel that I don't think anyone could have imagined where it would lead us, and especially not, several decades later, into the death of radio as we knew it. No one was thinking that technology would profoundly affect the music business, because it had not really changed much since the 1920s, when radio first became a mass-market product.

Amidst the impatience to push technology to its limit, there was also a generational gulf widening between the generation of teens and young adults and the people in charge. We felt it in the hostile stares at our long hair from maître d's in good restaurants. We felt it when we tried to check in a whole rock-and-roll band to a Hilton in Chicago, when we talked to our parents about their reaction to a film like *Easy Rider*. In San Francisco the stance of our generation was to "fly your freak flag," put it in their face, but the feeling in Woodstock was a little less confrontational. (The Band had just put out *Music from Big Pink*, which featured a group photo with all of their parents on the back of the album cover.) I remember Levon trying to explain to Dennis Hopper that the South was not as simple as portrayed in *Easy Rider*. There was a stoned exchange in the movie between Billy (played by Hopper) and George (Jack Nicholson) that pissed off Levon.

> Billy: What the hell is wrong with freedom? That's what it's all about.
>
> George: Oh, yeah, that's right. That's what it's all about, all right. But talkin' about it and bein' it, that's two different things. I mean, it's real hard to be free when you are bought and sold in the marketplace. Of course, don't ever tell anybody that they're not free, 'cause then

they're gonna get real busy killin' and maimin' to prove to you that they are. Oh, yeah, they're gonna talk to you, and talk to you, and talk to you about individual freedom. But they see a free individual, it's gonna scare 'em.

Billy: Well, it don't make 'em runnin' scared.

George: No, it makes 'em dangerous.

Hopper, who had also directed the film, had originally come to the Band to do all the music for the movie, but after an early rough-cut screening Levon said he would take a pass. For him, Hopper's depiction of the Southern crackers was beyond a cliché—it was totally offensive. Levon knew that his own daddy, a hardworking farmer, had some of the prejudices that flowed through Arkansas, and yet he was able to love the music of Muddy Waters and offer a meal to Sonny Boy Williamson. To Levon, *Easy Rider* was as full of stereotypes as *Li'l Abner*. Robbie later agreed to let Hopper use the song "The Weight," but even that decision caused some tension within the group.

Two nights after my acid trip, my girlfriend Wanda threw me a real birthday party and all of our local musician friends showed up. I had met Wanda in Princeton when she had broken up with Peter Kaminsky in a rage. She was beautiful in a kind of Irish country girl manner, and she had a biting sense of humor, but not enough confidence in her own instincts. As much as I aspired to be with a woman like Dominique Robertson, I was too young to know how to get there, and so I will confess that sex was my main attraction. Wanda and her girlfriend Britt were dangerous, both in the bedroom and out. Our house sat up on a hill and across the narrow valley where the mountains rose up behind the town of Shady. When it was really hot we would go swimming in Cooper Lake, taking a bottle of Beaujolais and a good goat cheese we could get from a local farmer up in Shady. The girls would strip off their tight Levi's and dive into the frigid lake and their nipples would be as hard as pebbles and the mystery of young sex would be upon us.

My birthday party was filled with local musicians, both old friends and new. Geoff and Maria Muldaur, who had given me my first job as a road manager for the Kweskin Jug Band, had moved in next to Garth, overlooking the Ashokan Reservoir, and they led the music for the evening. They were probably the two best white blues singers in those days, and even Dylan would end up singing harmony while they took the lead. The blues had a curious hold on all of us. We had invited the filmmaker Les Blank, who brought a 16mm projector and his latest film, *The Blues Accordin' to Lightnin' Hopkins*. Les was an underappreciated genius who made documentaries that were part music and part anthropology, and in that film you could experience the music as played in back rooms and small clubs. You could almost smell the barbecue that smoked outside the roadhouses. What Alan Lomax had done in the 1930s recording the sounds of old-timey music, Les took and then added this wonderful fly-on-the-wall visual element, which made for a much richer portrait of both the people and their culture. I hope the Library of Congress has all of Les's films in their collection.

When my birthday broke up at midnight, Bob asked me to give him a ride home. In the quiet of that July night, both of us a little drunk, it was clear how much his life had changed. Three kids and a fourth on the way with a loving wife, plus his painting and music, all made with a calm sense of humor and joy that had been missing in the angry years of '65 and '66. No more being booed around the world, he seemed fulfilled. If you had told me then that he would still feel the need to be in front of audiences forty years later, I would have questioned your sanity. Looking back, though, I remember he sang a George Jones song that night with Bob Neuwirth, and of course old George was still on the road at age seventy-five, so maybe that was Bob's idea of a life well lived.

Four days after Neil Armstrong's moonwalk, I had to go down to New York City to do some business. Albert Grossman's office was on 55th Street just west of Park Avenue. In the summer of 1969, it felt like the center of the music universe. Because he represented Dylan, the Band, Janis Joplin, Paul Butterfield, Richie Havens, Peter, Paul and Mary, and others, every record company in the world was visiting. He had arrived on the scene at the very moment when the music business was becoming a real business. Robbie Robertson and Levon Helm's early experience with the industry had taken place a few blocks west in the Brill Building on Broadway, where the young songwriters like Doc Pomus, Carole King, and Jerry Leiber and Mike Stoller mixed with the mobbed-up record kings like Morris Levy.

Robbie and Levon had always assumed that the business was crooked. Albert Grossman, who had come out of the Chicago nightclub scene, had observed Black artists like Muddy Waters and Little Walter getting screwed by the notorious Chess Brothers, Leonard and Phil, who had risen from running liquor stores to nightclubs to record companies. It's important to understand that many of the white men who ran both the record companies and the clubs Black artists worked for had mob roots. So there was always the notion that they were "offering you a deal you couldn't refuse." Albert, however, had from the start operated on the proposition that the artist had to earn more money and the record company less. His genius was to assume that any contract an artist had signed with a record company could be renegotiated if the artist was successful. This put him in direct confrontation with a few growing media conglomerates that were beginning to control more and more record companies.

The first two media conglomerates, the Music Corporation of America (MCA) and Warner Communications (now WarnerMedia), both had their beginnings in the music business. Although both companies started on a shoestring, their early survival can probably be attributed to one man: Meyer Lansky. While Lansky's involvement with the Las Vegas and Havana casino businesses of the forties and fifties is well known, his connection to the two original media conglomerates is less recognized. What Lansky understood in a way that his Italian American partners never could was that the key to wealth was to funnel the incredible cash flow from illegal business into legitimate business. The second thing Lansky understood was to keep a low profile and have lawyers do all the front work. No John Gotti act for him. At some point, Lansky knew, the only way to take money out of those legitimate businesses was to get them "public," and that required managers who had a clean record and could talk to Wall Street.

In 1969 the two managers that fit that bill were Jules Stein of MCA and Steve Ross of Warner. MCA, started in Chicago in 1924 by Stein, was originally in the business of booking bands into nightclubs. Since the mafia controlled both the nightclubs and the unions (including the musicians union), Stein found it easier to let the mob be a silent partner than to endure constant pressure from both labor and speakeasy owners. Steve Ross, a young man on the make in the go-go sixties, had married into the funeral home business. He then had merged his funeral home operation with a parking lot company, Kinney National Services, a classic Jersey mob front. After expanding into the janitorial business, Kinney went public and Ross used Kinney stock to buy out Warner Bros.-Seven Arts from Frank Sinatra and some old associates of Meyer Lansky—Louis Chesler and Mac Schwebel—allowing them to "get liquid."

In buying Warner, Ross really got a record company more than a movie studio. Jack Warner had run the studio into near bankruptcy, but an extraordinary former accountant named Mo Ostin had begun to build a record business around Sinatra and Warner's Reprise label. In the course of four years Ross, with Ostin's help, purchased several important independent record companies, including Atlantic, Elektra, Nonesuch, and Asylum. By consolidating the distribution functions in one company, they were able to make significant cost savings by cutting out the middleman and achieving increased promotional power with both radio stations and retail chains. Most importantly, Steve Ross understood that the key to success was artist relations. By allowing his senior managers like Ostin, Ahmet Ertegun, Joe Smith, Jac Holzman, and David Geffen the freedom to sign who they wanted, he enabled the various labels to keep their individual identities. The sense that an Atlantic record would be different from an Elektra record or a Reprise record is all gone now, but at the time it was important. Grossman signed both the Kweskin Jug Band and Peter, Paul and Mary to Reprise and began a long and profitable relationship with Mo Ostin.

The unusual autonomy the Warner Music executives retained was solely based on the faith Steve Ross had in them. The basis for all the early success of Warner Communications was in music, and Ross kept trust with men like Mo Ostin and David Geffen. When Ross got prostate cancer in the early 1990s, his control began to slip, and when he died in 1992, the era of freedom for the label heads ended. Most of them quit within the year, and the golden age of Warner Music was over.

Though Albert had his share of run-ins with the Chicago mafia and the mobbed-up characters five blocks west in the Brill Building, he represented a clear break from a record business that exploited artists. Just how much the world had changed since the days when the Chess Brothers ruled was clarified when a few of us in the Grossman office went over to the garden of the Museum of Modern Art, where Muddy Waters was going to play a concert. New York in 1969 was such a laboratory for "high-low," the notion that high culture and low (or popular) culture were mixing, so it was only fitting that Muddy Waters should be performing at the Museum of Modern Art, the temple of Rockefeller high culture. Tom Wolfe had mocked a different version of this in his magazine article "Radical Chic and Mau-Mauing the Flak Catchers," in which he depicted a cocktail party held at composer Leonard Bernstein's Dakota apartment for the Black

Panthers. Slumming was not new to the beautiful people of Manhattan whose parents had probably ventured up to the Cotton Club in Harlem when it was still a speakeasy in the twenties to hear Duke Ellington play and see the beautiful tall dancers with skin like coffee and cream. But now there was no need to go to "dangerous" places to experience Black musical culture; society mavens like Ahmet Ertegun's wife, Mica, would bring it to your fancy apartment or the garden of your favorite museum.

Muddy was the real thing, and despite being surrounded by Giacometti sculptures, he wasn't going to change his act. I had first seen him at the Newport Folk Festival in 1965 and, in the context of the country blues revival that featured Son House and Skip James, Muddy seemed like the rural cousin who went north and got electricity. He still played in a raw Robert Johnson slide-guitar style, even though he had a band of six players behind him. The most important of his sidemen was Pinetop Perkins, the legendary piano player, by then in his mid-fifties. Pinetop had started out playing guitar in his twenties, but he had to switch instruments following an incident that had resulted in a slashed tendon on his chording hand. As he told the *Chicago Tribune* in 1990, "This woman stabbed me, we was at this place drinkin', and she went to the washroom, and I closed the door. Then her husband put barrels of coal ashes in front of the door and she couldn't get out for a couple hours. I was the last one she seen shut that door, so when she got out, she lit in on me with that knife." When Pinetop recovered, he couldn't hold a guitar chord but he could still play piano, and willing to risk the perils of the juke joints, he accepted that he was born to play the blues, and he ended up backing Sonny Boy

Williamson for a while before he joined Muddy's band.

For a culture obsessed with youth, it was fun to see these fifty-year-old men strutting their stuff. Muddy sang all his classics like "Rollin' and Tumblin'" and "Hoochie Coochie Man," and his promise in "Mannish Boy" to satisfy "all you little girls" in "five minutes time" brought squeals of laughter and joy from the sophisticated crowd. What we all sensed was a direct connection to those Mississippi roots of the blues that had come to this crowd through the circuitous route of young London musicians like Keith Richards and Eric Clapton, who had heard Muddy in London, where he had exiled himself in 1959, unappreciated in his own country. Now he was back. The Rolling Stones had named their band after his most famous tune, and the slim young girls with chopped hair and miniskirts were quivering in an ecstatic dance in front of his bandstand while he proclaimed, "I just want to make love to you."

It could be argued that the blues is the most American of music forms. It flows out of both slave work songs and gospel music. But more than anything, its twelve-bar structure allows for the concept of improvisation. B.B. King could push the envelope on his guitar solos because everyone in the band understood where the tune was going. The very lyrical notion of "the blues"— that deep sadness when you know your love is dying—is somewhat universal. The pain is usually that of the man who realizes he is on his way out. Two wonderful examples:

Bobby "Blue" Bland, "Who Will the Next Fool Be"

After all is said and done

Girl, you wouldn't be satisfied with anyone

So when you get rid of me

Who will the next fool be?

Junior Wells, "Little by Little"

I tried to tail you last night sitting in my car

But I was scared that I would see what I was looking for

Little by little, I'm losing you, I can see

Bit by bit, your love is drifting away from me.

8. The Woodstock Festival

1969

On Saturday, August 17, the members of the Band and I woke up in the real Woodstock (as opposed to Max Yasgur's Bethel farm, which was now filled with three hundred thousand hippies) and read the *New York Times*'s hysterical coverage of the first day of the Woodstock Festival: "3 Days of Peace and Music." If one could believe the paper, there was no food or water, and the sanitation was so bad that a cholera epidemic seemed to be on the way. I never liked helicopters, but Michael Lang, who was running the Woodstock Festival, had told us that it was the only way we were going to get there in time to play. I called down to Lang and he assured us "everything is groovy."

That was typical Michael. He had lived in Woodstock for a couple of years and, with two partners, had dreamed up the idea of taking the Monterey Pop concept to the next level. But in the two years that had passed since Monterey Pop, the music business had gotten very commercial, and so every band wanted a lot of money to show up. My own experience of the past three years was a microcosm of the price inflation that had transformed the industry. In 1967, the Jug Band took home $15,000 for two nights at the Fillmore. By 1968, Judy Collins was earning $20,000 a night for a big concert. By 1969, bands were regularly selling out large arenas and taking home $75,000 (tickets were usually $10) for a single night's work. Somehow, Michael had managed to get the money together and the Band had already gotten a healthy 50 percent down payment on its fee for Woodstock.

Obviously Michael's "everything is groovy" philosophy had not grappled with the fact that three hundred thousand kids might show up in the space of four hours to a pasture in the Catskills. The citizens of Woodstock proper had made it clear they wanted nothing to do with the festival from the start, and so Michael had settled on a farm in Bethel, fifty miles south of Woodstock. But when the New York State Police reported a huge traffic jam one hundred miles north of Manhattan at noon on a Friday, they knew something strange was happening. Michael Lang's eight-foot-tall chain-link fence around the twenty-acre pasture was the first thing to go as the first fifty thousand kids tried to get through the five entrance gates. By 3 p.m. on Friday afternoon, the festival was officially free to all.

On Sunday at 1 p.m. the helicopter sent by the festival landed in my backyard in Woodstock. The Band and I piled in and within twenty minutes were coming up over a ridge in Bethel, which revealed a sea of humanity dancing in the field below to Sly and the Family Stone. It was a stunning, almost biblical sight. There was a sense that Youth Culture had reached some sort of critical mass. The notion that being young was a blessed state was a relatively new phenomenon in the world. Looking back at *Life* magazine from the forties and fifties you can see that all of the commercial messages and most of the editorial ones are pitched at people older than thirty. But somehow, around the time that James Dean and Elvis Presley emerged as symbolic teenagers, kids had an image of something wholly their own to connect to. This was not the teens of the swing era trying to dress and look like sophisticated grown-ups while bopping to Benny Goodman. This was an image of youth in all of its painful glory and rebellion. But it wasn't necessarily a political rebellion so much as a desire to be able to act with a kind of autonomy that had been missing before. But the notion that pleasure was an answer to social discord, not merely a diversion from it, was a sort of collective hallucination.

As the culture progressed from the fifties into the sixties, a universe of symbols grew up around this youth autonomy: long hair, Levi's, teen movies, books like *Catcher in the Rye*, pot, and most of all rock and roll. The fact that three hundred thousand kids were camped out in the mud below us in order to celebrate their culture, with no regard to the responsibilities of adulthood, must have opened the eyes to the advertising executives that read the morning paper over the weekend. If there was a single point at which the symbols of rebellion got co-opted by Madison Avenue, it was those three days in August. And for thirty years we've lived with the inauthenticity of that decision.

Think about the early Chuck Berry. Was his work "safe" or "cute" or acceptable to polite society? It was not. It was as dangerous as the Southern sheriffs who constantly harassed Berry for winking at white girls in his audience thought it was. Here we return to Pete Townshend's "massive question" to his fellow artists (from a 2019 *New York Times* interview): "Who are we? What is our function? What is our worth? Are we disenfranchised, or are we able to take society over and guide it? Are we against the establishment? Are we being used by it? Are we artists, or are we entertainers?" Woodstock would not answer these questions but only complicate them.

Our helicopter slowly settled behind the Woodstock festival stage and we jumped out to be met by Michael Lang. Lurking just behind him was Barry Imhoff, Bill Graham's majordomo. Barry suggested that we could "camp out" with him while we were waiting to go onstage. He ushered us to the largest motor-home I had ever seen, which he had parked behind the stage. Evidently Bill Graham, though not involved with the Woodstock Festival, was determined to do some major artist-relations work at the site. Despite the *New York Times* report that the crowd was running out of food at the festival, Barry had two refrigerators filled with prime steaks, a major barbecue grill set up on his patio, and several cases of red wine. Barry was not going to do without, and neither were his friends.

We settled in and partied with Crosby, Stills, Nash & Young until they had to go onstage. I had known Stephen Stills back when he was in love with Judy Collins and had been a Buffalo Springfield fanatic. By adding Neil Young to the sweet harmonies of the three original members of the band, they created something of real power and substance. Woodstock was their first concert as a quartet (plus backup musicians) and they really rose to the occasion. With Neil's long, searing guitar solos, their act was perfect for the vast expanse of Woodstock. I didn't realize it at the time, but the whole nature of playing to three hundred thousand people (or even fifty thousand in a stadium) requires a certain kind of attack. The guitar solo is probably the most effective weapon, because even if you are five hundred yards away from the stage you can still see the lone player in the spotlight and viscerally hear and *feel* the output. That's how Neil Young brought CSNY up another level.

When they finally came offstage, it was the Band's turn. Unfortunately, it was night by then, and there was something about playing into the vast void of darkness that didn't suit the music that Robbie and his compatriots made. It wasn't as flashy as Sly's or CSNY's, and so that night the Band never quite reached the audience in the same way some of the other acts did. But for the musicians in attendance, the Band was an important force. At one point in the middle of the set I looked behind me in the wings of the vast stage. There, lined up, were Janis Joplin, CSNY, Jimi Hendrix, Country Joe McDonald, and Richie Havens, all spellbound by "The Weight."

The week after the Woodstock Festival, Albert Grossman announced that some English promoters had offered Dylan and the Band $150,000 for a twelve-song set to be performed at a pop festival on the Isle of Wight. This was a big paycheck, and Bob, who had been on a three-year hiatus, decided to accept the offer. I got the promoters to rent Bob a big manor house on the island and we went over to England a week early to rehearse. The Band stayed in a big old seaside hotel that had a beach of stones. Old English couples were sitting in lawn chairs under umbrellas on the stony beach. Weird. On the first day at the hotel, Levon got into a fight with the drummer from the Jimi Hendrix Experience. His name was Mitch Mitchell and he had the exact same haircut as Libby Titus. Somehow he felt that this entitled him to flirt rather boldly with her in the restaurant, but Levon put an immediate stop to it by threatening to cut off Mitch's hair with the steak knife he was holding.

Around three in the afternoon on the day before the concert, a young man named Bill Oakes, dressed in impeccable Savile Row style, showed up at the manor house saying the Beatles would be appearing in the next half hour. Behind the house he found a suitably large field and set down a landing sign, and then within forty-five minutes a relatively large helicopter appeared and out stepped John, George, and Ringo with their wives. (Paul was home with Linda and their newborn daughter Mary.) It was just like in the movies. We all had dinner together and then went out to the barn to play some music. Bob insisted that the rehearsal of the set take precedence before we devolved into jamming. He was clearly focused on the importance of his return to the stage after a three-year absence. Ringo kept things light, calling for "more drums" in the monitor mix. At the breaks, George and John would pick up their guitars and play a bit, with Rick and Levon as rhythm section.

Whenever musicians from very different backgrounds gather, there needs to be common ground. That night, the common ground was the Deep South—that mystical land that gave birth to Muddy Waters, Elvis Presley, Little Richard, Jerry Lee Lewis, Johnny Cash, and Bo Diddley. All of the musicians in the room had grown up on that music, and both the Band and the Beatles had played it in their early bar-band careers.

To try to understand just what it was about the Mississippi Delta that created such amazing music from both Black and white musicians is something of a mystery. Levon's theory was that the "medicine shows" of the late 1940s might have had a hand in birthing the music called rhythm and blues. There was already a blues tradition in the bar scene, but the medicine show was sort of an adjunct to the traveling carnivals of the time. After 10 p.m. on a Saturday night, when all of the churchgoing public had left the carnival grounds, a medicine show would start in one of the tents. The events were supposedly for men only, and you had to be eighteen years old to get in. Once inside, the hoochie-coochie dancers started moving. And to make the dancing more interesting, some promoters hired local musicians. Putting drums and bass behind the basic twelve-bar blues shuffle helped the dancers move a little more seductively, and eventually the music became an important part of the medicine show.

For myself, I was convinced that the gospel church music was a critical part of the movement from blues to R&B, though whatever the roots of the music, John Lennon knew all of the tunes. But Bob was all business that evening, and since it was clear that he intimidated both John and George, the session never took off in the creative direction it might have gone.

The concert itself was glorious. Bob and the Band played brilliantly, and the one hundred fifty thousand fans (including the three Beatles) got two encores. The last time Dylan and the Band had played together in England had been the end of the epic 1966 tour. There had been such resistance to the music then, so much truly hateful booing and shouts of "traitor." It was hard for Bob and Robbie to understand then, because they knew they were making magnificent music and yet the audience was acting as if it was terrible. I imagine for Bob the sense of risk in returning to the stage was especially palpable. After all, the Band had recovered and had been on the road for the last three months, but while Bob had shown up as a "secret guest player" on a couple of occasions, *this* was *his* show. And now they were playing some of the same tunes that had caused such outrage in 1966—and presenting them with the same fury—and the audience was ecstatic.

When it was over, George Harrison asked Robbie and me if we wanted to spend a couple of days at his estate in Henley-on-Thames, about forty miles outside of London. The next morning we took a private hovercraft from the island to a dock near London, where we were met by George's driver. We arrived at Friar Park around lunchtime, and Pattie Harrison had set out a beautiful meal in one of the gardens of the vast estate. Henry Ernest Milner, who had done garden design for Queen Victoria, had designed and built the extensive gardens at Friar Park. Milner was a bit of an eccentric, and George was convinced that he was an opium smoker like many of his contemporaries of the period. One of the gardens was a maze punctuated with small pedestals in which were embedded intentionally broken sundials and quotes from Blake about timelessness—the combination serving as a kind of surreal parlor game. In another spot you could sit in a small alpine hut and look out at a replica of the Matterhorn. The rock was only about two hundred feet tall, but the trick of perspective made it look just like the famous Swiss peak. George was having it covered with chalk, as the original plans had specified, and it looked like winter was arriving on the mountain.

George and Pattie Harrison seemed like the most ideal couple in the world. Born Patricia Anne Boyd, she had modeled in London and met George during the filming of *A Hard Day's Night*. She seemed to be incredibly grounded and was full of humorous stories about life with the Beatles. George was equally centered. He had clearly taken the Beatles' early attraction to Indian mysticism to a much deeper level, practicing a daily one-hour meditation, eating no meat, and bringing a sense of joy to every room, a power that clearly came from a place of inner contentment. When I first visited Friar Park they were doing construction in the manor, and so George and Pattie were living in a guesthouse on the property. One piece of art in the house struck me as slightly odd: the cover painting for *Layla and Other Assorted Love Songs*, the album Eric Clapton had recorded with Derek and the Dominos, was hung over George and Pattie's bed. The meaning behind that gift from Eric to Pattie would become apparent only in 1975, when Pattie left George to live with (and then marry) Eric.

George live much of his life on a spiritual plane, but he indulged in his share of earthly pleasures. Aside from the sprawling Friar Park, he had one of the few twelve-cylinder Mercedes-Benz 350 four-door sedans that I had ever seen. One night at 2 a.m., traveling on the M4 out of London, George took the car up to 140 kilometers per hour. As I sat there contemplating all the laws we were probably breaking, it seemed to me that the Beatles lived in a cocoon in London and were as protected as the royal family. While various members of the Rolling Stones had been busted for drugs, no one ever laid a hand on the Beatles. I got the impression that George had been given a friendly warning about speeding from more than one constable, but that clearly wasn't deterring him from his joyrides.

And yet, slowly but surely, the Beatles were withdrawing from the harsh public spotlight they had lived in since 1964. They had been playing live gigs since 1960, but now they were using only the recording studio to get their work to the fans. It must have been frustrating. And George let me in on another secret, which was that the constraints of being a Beatle were beginning to wear on his own sense of autonomy.

How to account for Beatlemania? Today, we talk of "world music" and mean an amalgam of styles from around the globe, but the first truly world music—music that reached unprecedented numbers of people—was the Beatles. These days, I couldn't tell you what the number-one hit is in London, Rome, or Buenos Aires, but in 1965, you could pretty much guarantee that the top hit in any city was a Beatles record. As John Lennon's voice got more political, he understood that the weight of America's culture warriors could affect even a band that was "more popular than Jesus," but he didn't let that change the way he interacted with the world. The mainstream outrage at Lennon's remarks were not new—the popular artist had often bit the hand that fed it—and the Beatles showed time and again how artists could control their own destiny. They had their own record company, Apple, and it was a model for what was to come.

That said, they were somewhat constrained by the power commerce had over art—and even more so when their whole output was reduced to what came from the recording studio rather than interaction with live audiences. In the fact of this limitation, they retreated from the world, and their public presence was noticeably missing during the uproar that was the mid-sixties. John Lennon would later return to politics with Yoko, after the Beatles' split, but in the critical years between their last tour in 1966 and the 1970 breakup, they left a void.

9. On the Road with the Band

1970

Two years of constant touring with the Band was beginning to wear on my dream of personal autonomy. A tour manager is forever at the beck and call of each of the members of the group, and my guys were not always easy to deal with. Richard Manuel would regularly crash cars in a drunken stupor. Rick Danko had a tendency to snort up copious amounts of any white powder put in front of him—cocaine or heroin, he was not a discriminating user. Levon Helm was partial to Valium and heroin, and getting him up in the morning when we were on the road was a constant struggle. Only Robbie and Garth lived what one might call normal lives. And yet in the swirl of this chaos, somehow the Band had entered the elite cultural conversation. In January of 1970 they were on the cover of *Time* magazine. The distinction doesn't mean that much today, but in 1970 it was everything. Why was it so important then, and how did they manage it? I think the public image of these country folk, making music with real stories, appealed to the intelligentsia in a way the psychedelic bands did not. The picture of them standing in my backyard looking at the dog Hamlet tells the story. Good timing.

As good as the music usually was at the concerts, all the drama in the other twenty-two hours of the day began to wear on me during this time. I longed for some kind of work where I would not get 2 a.m. phone calls that meant only trouble. I realized that I wanted my own life, and though it seemed like I was surrounded by rock stars enjoying their existence as free individuals, I knew from reading Kant at Princeton that this wasn't really true. The great moral philosopher defined personal autonomy as "the ability of the agent to act in accordance with objective morality rather than under the influence of desires." But Levon, Richard, and Rick were in constant thrall of desire, whether sex or drugs, and maybe even rock and roll.

Pete Townshend (in his *Times* interview) had addressed this Epicurean question of autonomy and philosophy:

> Well, I wrote "Won't Get Fooled Again," which was essentially saying to the audience: "Just fuck off. I'm not going to be your tool." It led to the question, If you're going to say "fuck off" to revolutionary thinking, then what it is that you *are* going to do?

The change in the landscape of drugs during this time was perhaps symbolic of the larger cultural malaise. In 1965, among the musicians I knew, pot was the only drug. Sure, Dylan had become a major amphetamine user during the 1966 tour, and even in 1969 the members of his band would occasionally take Dexedrine to get up for a show, but it didn't cause major problems. Once cocaine and heroin entered the picture, though, everything got ugly fast.

Personally, I felt that I was "losing my religion" in the midst of everything. Somehow I had always connected the counterculture that I inhabited with not only the wider political struggle but also the internal struggle to live a life filled with meaningful work and some sort of philosophy of what was right and good. Epicurus said that freedom from fear was the key to happiness, and while Bob Dylan seemed to have that, even he had become fearful after John Kennedy was assassinated. In December of 1963, about ten days after the assassination, Dylan was given an award at the Emergency Civil Liberties Committee banquet, and in front of the assembled crowd he gave a meandering (and some say drunken) speech in which he called out most of the liberals in the room and ended by saying that he "understood" Lee Harvey Oswald—not that he would have shot the president but that he *identified* with Oswald. Dylan was booed off the stage and in remorse sent a long poem to the Union the next morning. This was part of it:

> my life is lived out daily in the places I feel
> most comfortable in. these places are places where
> I am unknown an unstared at. I perform rarely, an
> when I do, there is a constant commotion burnin
> at my body an at my mind because of the attention
> aimed at me. instincts fight my emotions an fears
> fight my instincts . . .

If even the most brave and autonomous artist can be afraid, then who could I look toward to inspire me to keep moving forward in my pursuit of Epicurus's ideal life? I had found a group of good friends. I had work that satisfied, though I was a long way from feeling autonomy in it. What had gone missing in the wake of the multiple assassinations was faith. I had believed deeply in Dr. King's own faith in the power of love, and I was afraid my own faith was now gone.

I want to be clear in what I mean by the word faith here. The Zen philosopher Alan Watts, in his book *The Wisdom of Insecurity*, most clearly modeled what I think about faith:

> We must here make a clear distinction between belief and faith, because, in general practice, belief has come to mean a state of mind, which is almost the opposite of faith. Belief, as I use the word here, is the insistence that the truth is what one would "lief" or wish it to be. The believer will open his mind to the truth on the condition that it fits in with his preconceived ideas and wishes. Faith, on the other hand, is an unreserved opening of the mind to the truth, whatever it may turn out to be. Faith has no preconceptions; it is a plunge into the unknown. Belief clings, but faith lets go. In this sense of the word, faith is the essential virtue of science, and likewise of any religion that is not self-deception.

So it was that in my disgust with electoral politics I had lost faith in the liberal vision of progress that had defined my life to that point. The philosopher Richard Rorty believed that the key dividing line between the left and the right in America was about whether the government has a responsibility to ensure a moral and socially desirable distribution of wealth—"to protect the weak from the strong." The right rejected this proposition, the left embraced it. He called this tradition "the Reformist Left." When Rorty spoke those words in a 1997 lecture, America was on its way to becoming a plutocracy in which the top 1 percent controls about 21 percent of American wealth. Today they control 37 percent of the wealth, while the bottom 90 percent controls only 26 percent.

Rorty points out that as the Reformist Left fell apart in the late 1960s (after the deaths of Dr. King and Bobby Kennedy), a Cultural Left took its place.

> If you turn out to be living in an evil empire (rather than, as you had been told, a democracy fighting an evil empire), then you have no responsibility to your country; you are accountable only to humanity. If what your government and your teachers are saying is all part of the same Orwellian monologue—if the differences between the Harvard faculty and the military–industrial complex, or between Lyndon Johnson and Barry Goldwater—are negligible, then you have a responsibility to make a revolution.

To believe that there was nothing worth saving about America often meant totally abandoning electoral politics. And that of course left the playing field to the greedheads and the generals. That was the great mistake of 1968.

The Cultural Left continued the march forward, and the year 1969 served as a marker to their ascendancy to a place of power in the business world. Woodstock Nation may have become a

Madison Avenue marketing trope, but in the halls of power in Hollywood (now the nexus of both the music and the film business), it was real. As the *New York Times* critic Jon Pareles wrote in 2019, "Most importantly, the scale of Woodstock showed people who had considered themselves 'freaks' that they weren't as small a minority as they had thought." That sense of cultural clout among the former outlaws was pretty heady. The irony was that former SDS officials were now running movie studios and record companies.

> *Say a prayer for the Pretender*
>
> *Who started out so young and strong*
>
> *Only to surrender.*

The display of wealth has always been a part of rock-stardom, ever since Elvis bought his first Cadillac. That search for prosperity existed in the sixties too, and now it was more openly connected to a vision of something beyond pure materialism. The Diggers in San Francisco were trying to convince bands like the Grateful Dead that they could move beyond the self-centered claims of rock privilege to a more united future. Some listened but many didn't.

What was real at the Woodstock Festival was that for three long days the transactional side of life in America seemed to disappear. While the *New York Times* was writing on Saturday morning of food and medicine shortages, and sanitation and security problems, for the people at the festival these issues did not actually exist, or they didn't matter. There was food served up by the Hog Farm commune, and doctors and nurses who were attending the festival organized tents to bandage wounds and bring down bad acid trippers. What happened at Woodstock *worked*, and yet it was just a moment in time; by December of 1969, the violence of Charles Manson and his Family plus the tragedy at Altamont had obliterated the hippie ideal. And it was easy to turn on the hippies, perhaps in part because, in the mass media at least, Woodstock Nation was little more than a marketing hook, not far removed from the advertising-industry brainchild that was the concept of the Pepsi Generation. Richard Nixon, always attuned to marketing possibilities, seized on the anti-hippie fervor and produced millions of bumper stickers reading "Acid, Amnesty, and Abortion"—his version of the future of America should he be defeated in 1972.

But despite the efforts of many people (including most recently Quentin Tarantino in his 2019 film *Once Upon a Time in Hollywood*) to paint a whole movement with the insanity of Manson, the cultural revolution that began in the 1960s was rich and deep, and it didn't disappear under the attacks of critics. The counterculture narrative of the movies and music of that time was extremely popular, and because there were fewer sources of media and we were not yet locked away in our own balkanized media world, everyone was exposed to fairly revolutionary music like the Rolling Stones' "Street Fighting Man" and the Beatles' "All You Need Is Love."

If the political revolution had failed with the election of Nixon, luckily for me and my friends the cultural revolution had managed to oust the old guard from the seats of power in music and movies. A younger generation of executives held on to dreams of a new kind of future that opened up space for popular artists to take big risks and be heard. In 1996 the *New York Times* film critic Janet Maslin summarized the change in Hollywood:

> When Hollywood opened its floodgates at the start of the 1970's, it unleashed an astonishing wave of creativity and experimentation. Whether the films of that era conveyed profound thoughtfulness or just suggested that the inmates were running the asylum (both were often true), they had a blazing, headstrong individuality that Hollywood's blockbuster mentality would all but destroy.

I realize now that, as I watched the Band's decline, I could not have seen that death would come for both Richard and Rick so soon. Even in 1971 they both seemed so full of life and good humor. The last truly great moment with the Band for me was a week of performances at New York's Academy of Music at the end of December. Robbie and I had planned the concerts as a way to record a live album that might capture some of the amazing energy we were experiencing in the Band's concerts but that never seemed to be captured on their studio albums.

Robbie had written a song called "Life Is a Carnival" for the *Cahoots* album and had engaged the New Orleans legend Allen Toussaint to write horn charts for the tune. The song continued Robbie's fascination with the life of the "carny"—the flimflam man who took advantage of the marks when a carnival drifted through town. Perhaps it had started with Carné's *Children of Paradise*, perhaps it was a buried connection to his birth father, a gambler who had been killed just before Robbie was born, but whatever the reason, it had grown into a near obsession, and the New Orleans horns were a perfect addition to transform Robbie's vision for the Band's sound. Robbie decided to have Allen write charts for eleven of the Band's older tunes, and the four days of taping (including an epic New Year's Eve concert) were some of the best music the group had ever made.

Because every night was being recorded, Richard, Levon, and Rick stayed on their best behavior, and the audience in the three-thousand-seat hall was incredibly enthusiastic. One of the highlights was an old Marvin Gaye tune, "Baby Don't Do It," sung by Levon with harmonies by Rick and Richard. We had been using it as an encore for about six months, and it never failed to bring down the house. It showed the Band as a world-class R&B unit and allowed Robbie to get off one of the best guitar solos of his career. For a band whose roots were in playing bars, Robbie and the others had been reluctant to "show off," even though flashiness had been in the DNA of rock since Jerry Lee Lewis kicked the piano bench over. Had the Band so set its image in opposition to Led Zeppelin and Cream, both known for their extended guitar solos, that they had trapped themselves within a sort of puritan destiny? Maybe, for at least one brief four-minute moment, "Baby Don't Do It" allowed them to shed the hair shirt and let it rip.

For me, it was time to move on, and for all the years that have come after I have held those magic nights at the Academy of Music in my heart as evidence of what the Band could achieve. The Band slowed down their touring for a while after the Academy of Music gig, and I went my own way, eventually moving to Los Angeles. I joined them once, in the summer of 1973, for a music festival at Watkins Glen, New York, that attracted six hundred thousand fans to see the Grateful Dead, the Allman Brothers, and the Band. I was no longer responsible for the show, as I had turned my tour managing duties over to Lindsay Holland. The whole day is a psychic blur in my mind, in part because the Dead's sound mixer, Owsley Stanley, gave me MDMA (later called Ecstasy) just before the Dead went onstage. He assured me the drug was "very gentle," but at one point I wandered out into the massive crowd and found myself consumed with paranoia. The day was incredibly hot and muggy, but instead of handing out water to the crowd, the greedy promoters engaged the local fire brigade to spray water on them indiscriminately. The effect was not gentle at all—closer to Bull Connor's Birmingham crowd control. I retreated quickly and hid behind the Dead's four-story-high sound system, powered by 25,000 watts of amplifiers. It was perhaps the beginning of the hearing loss I suffer from now.

The Dead set seemed to go on forever, and the humidity was rising. Finally the Band got to go on, but the four hours of waiting in a trailer full of booze had rendered Richard Manuel almost unconscious. He managed to fake it for twenty-five minutes until, mercifully, the clouds opened up and delivered the real rain that the fire department had been faking. All of the Band except Garth retreated backstage, and we plied Richard with coffee while Garth entertained the drenched fans with an organ concert that ranged across many musical genres. Eventually the downpour subsided and the concert resumed with a somewhat refreshed Richard.

I felt a deep sadness after that concert. It wasn't just that the dreams of the Woodstock Festival had been bastardized by a couple of greedy promoters. I couldn't lose my MDMA-fueled vision that I had been trapped in a vast concentration camp with complimentary musical accompaniment, but the sadness also flowed from the reality that the thrilling authenticity of *Music from Big Pink* was dying. As George Harrison had made clear to me, bands are hard to keep going after the first magic wears off and it becomes just another job.

I retreated to my house in California. Robbie Robertson followed a month later, and by the end of October the whole group had moved out to Malibu. I secretly hoped that the move to California would represent a step away from the darkness and gloom that loomed over Woodstock for at least six months a year. California had worked for Dylan and was working for me. There were still mountains to climb for the Band—Dylan's 1974 tour and *The Last Waltz*—but some end was in sight.

10. The Concert for Bangladesh

1971

Although the Beatles' last live performance was in August of 1966, the pressure had never ceased for them to perform live again. George Harrison had described to me the touring scene in 1966 as a nightmare in which you were trapped for hours on end in a hotel only to be brought to some vast stadium in an armored van. Once you got up onstage the screams from the crowd were so loud that you couldn't hear yourself play and weren't even sure your voice was on key.

In late 1968, John Lennon had hired an inventor who went by the name of "Magic Alex." His first job was to build a new sound studio in the basement of the Apple headquarters on Savile Row in London. Fueled with Beatles millions, Alex dreamed big and eventually came to the band with his solution for the live-appearance problem. Alex would build twenty stage sets of drums and amplifiers that would be 15 percent larger than normal. The Beatles would rent twenty stadiums and Alex would project holograms of the band (blown up by 15 percent) onto the stage sets and the Beatles would play twenty simultaneous live shows without ever leaving the comfort of their London studio.

Unfortunately, like the model of Stonehenge in *This Is Spinal Tap*, the vision failed, as Magic Alex was never able to project a holographic Beatle taller than six inches. Needless to say, this crackpot idea never progressed further than the first demonstration with Peter Brown, the manager of Apple, and so it was decided to do a film on a soundstage instead. The plan was to film the recording of the new album, *Let It Be*, and release the film simultaneously around the world. But unlike our magic night in the manor on the Isle of Wight, the musicians weren't gelling, and the presence of the cameras just brought out all of the simmering tensions between John Lennon and Paul McCartney. John, with Yoko in tow, and Paul, with Linda hovering just offstage, were at each other's throats. As Paul's music got more sentimental, John's got harder and more political. For George Harrison, it was an opportunity to step away for a while. He had for the last five albums been given his allocation of one or two cuts, while John and Paul wrote most of the tunes. He felt he could do more on his own and still stay a member of the band, and so he began spending time away from London.

In the late fall of 1970 he called and asked if he could stay at my house in Woodstock for a couple of days. He visited with Bob Dylan and Robbie Robertson, but the mood was kind of blue and he soon returned to New York City to keep recording. We were all in a kind of quiet wake for Janis Joplin, who had died in a motel in L.A. a month before. For Albert Grossman, it was an especially bitter blow. Dylan had left him in anger a year before, and now Janis, his favorite client, was dead from what seemed to be an accidental overdose. Albert stopped going into New York

City and spent more time in his garden and building a restaurant in Bearsville, near his house.

In this context, George Harrison's return to Woodstock in the spring of 1971 was a lifeline. When George arrived, we spent the day visiting with Robbie and trading songs. He played demo versions of some new songs he was working on, and it was clear he was itching to prove something to the rest of the Beatles. But he also mentioned that he had been spending some time with Ravi Shankar and that he was looking for a way to support Ravi and an emerging crisis. In March of 1971, East Pakistan had declared its independence under the name of Bangladesh. Almost immediately, the world became aware of the famine conditions in the new country, and Ravi Shankar set out to try to do something about the crisis. He enlisted George Harrison, who in turn asked me to help him organize a benefit concert for Bangladesh.

Our first meeting was in the New York office of Allen Klein, who had been hired to administer Apple. Klein had been John Lennon's idea, but the rest of the band went along with it. Mick Jagger had boasted to Lennon about the huge amount of back royalties Klein had collected on behalf of the Stones from their American record distributor, and the general impression in London was that most American record companies were run by crooks who would steal from you whenever possible. Jagger's solution was that you should hire your own American mafia enforcer who would know where to look for the thievery. Having spent some time with the Apple executives in London, the notion of this mobbed-up Damon Runyon character from the Brill Building running the Beatles' company was somewhat puzzling. In London, men like Neil Aspinall, Derek Taylor, and Peter Brown, who had worked for the Beatles for many years, were straight shooters—witty, cultured, and smart. George, however, had made his peace with Klein and so it was not my job to comment on his choice of executive talent.

Klein's right-hand man was named Pete Bennett (shortened from Benedetto), and he was a real Mr. Five by Five. Pete was one of the earliest "promo men" in the record business, and he dressed like a member of the Gambino Family. He was about five-foot-two and 260 pounds, with a twenty-inch neck. Pete knew *everyone*, and as a joke Derek Taylor had made a book called "Who's That Man with Pete Bennett?" that consisted of fifty black-and-white stills (all real in the pre-Photoshop days) of most of the major celebrities in the known universe standing next to Pete in the exact same pose, with Pete's arm around their shoulder in a modified bear hug. There was Elvis Presley and President Nixon, Mick Jagger and the Pope, John Lennon and Frank Sinatra, all grinning stupidly for Pete's ubiquitous photographer. Although Pete was still convinced that Bobby Darin was "the world's greatest entertainer," he was willing to work for the Beatles even though he confessed to me that rock and roll wasn't really his thing. The more I got to know Allen Klein's operation, the more I realized that the mob had always been part of the music business.

The early planning of the Concert for Bangladesh went smoothly. The basic band was to be Ringo and session musician Jim Keltner on drums, Klaus Voormann (a friend of the Beatles from the Hamburg days) on bass, Eric Clapton and George Harrison on guitar, Beatles regular Billy Preston on organ, and Leon

Russell, another favorite session musician, on piano. Leon had been one of the few musicians to survive the ill-fated Joe Cocker tour for *Mad Dogs and Englishmen*, and he told me he owed all to God. The Cocker tour had started in 1970, just a month after President Nixon had announced a deal with Mexico to spray all of the marijuana crops with a herbicide called paraquat. Now, the idea of a rock-and-roll tour in 1970 without pot was pretty unthinkable, and so some fiendish greedhead had come up with a substitute for the band called "angel dust." It was essentially elephant tranquilizer sprayed onto oregano leaves and smoked like pot. Joe and most of the band (along with some poor hangers-on including the actor Michael J. Pollard of *Bonnie and Clyde* fame) smoked the angel dust for the four months of the tour and slowly fried their brains. When it was all over, Joe could hardly compose a sentence and Michael Pollard's movie career was finished. Leon, who was a somewhat religious man, knew there was something about this unnatural substance that bugged him, and so he never touched it.

I had the unfortunate opportunity to see the downside of angel dust a couple of years later. In 1976, in my new position as a film producer, I had hired the New York author Jean Stein to be an East Coast scout for movie material. Jean was the daughter of Jules Stein, the founder of MCA, and she lived in a grand apartment on Central Park West. One evening she had a party for Gore Vidal and I found myself in the foyer being introduced to Jackie Onassis. Just as I was establishing my credibility by mentioning that her half-brother Jamie had been a schoolmate, Michael Pollard walked in the door (having snuck in with Bobby Neuwirth), and he immediately started fawning over Jackie, babbling nonsense. She took one look at him and excused herself, rapidly retreating toward Vidal and his more cultured friends.

Before the Concert for Bangladesh, all of the musicians, including guest stars, agreed to show up in New York to rehearse at a studio I had rented above Carnegie Hall. On the afternoon before the first rehearsal day, I got a telex from Terry Doran at Apple in London saying that Eric Clapton was sick and would not be on the appointed flight. The next day we started rehearsals without Eric and it was clear that the basic band was tight and could play behind both the guest stars and Harrison. That afternoon a second telex from Terry Doran arrived saying he had driven out to Eric's home in Surrey and been met by his girlfriend at the door saying he was still sick and to come back the following day. After three days of this, George began to get worried. Meanwhile, the rumor mill must have been working overtime because a lot of famous guitar players started showing up uninvited at the Park Lane Hotel, where we all were staying.

Finally, in desperation George asked Jesse Ed Davis (Taj Mahal's guitar player) to substitute for Eric, and I sent Terry Doran a telex letting him know we had found a sub. He reported this to Eric's girlfriend, and within an hour Clapton had revived himself enough to travel to New York. At rehearsal that afternoon George asked me to accompany Pete Bennett to the airport to pick up his guitar player. He cautioned me that Eric might be a little rangy and that he wouldn't appreciate having his picture taken with Pete.

For Bennett, meeting English pop stars at the airport had become old hat. He'd been shepherding the Stones and the Beatles through immigration for years, and when we went into the international arrival terminal he whispered, "Stick close to me, kid," and then walked the wrong way through the doors into the customs area. Met by shouts of "Who's coming in today, Pete?" from the customs guys, it was obvious he was a celebrity in his own right.

We walked all the way out to the airplane and into first class as the doors opened. I introduced Pete to Eric and his girlfriend and then we took them off the plane quickly. Inside again, we went through a door and were greeted by a single immigration official who knew Pete well. One quick look at the two passports and we were out a back door to a waiting limo. Eric seemed slightly dazed at the ease with which he had entered the country, but his girlfriend had another point of view: "Why did we have to leave all of our stuff in England if it was going to be this easy?" Pete had no idea what she was talking about, but George's caution about a "rangy" Clapton now made sense to me.

By the time I put them in the room next to mine, Eric was asking to see George as soon as possible. George came back from rehearsal and went up to Eric's room, and about ten minutes later he came out and asked me to find Phil Spector, who was going to produce the album of the concert. It became clear that Phil was the only person George knew who might know how to score some heroin for Clapton and his girlfriend. Within a couple of hours, however, it became evident to me that Phil's "stuff" wasn't up to the standards of Eric's girlfriend, as through the walls of my room I could hear her howling at Eric, "This is shit! It does nothing for me!" Eventually, New York somehow provided for Eric like it had for Billie Holiday and Charlie Parker, and within a couple of hours I was able to get Eric in the car to Madison

Square Garden so he could fulfill his promise to George. An hour later, as the pulled notes of "While My Guitar Gently Weeps" sang from Eric's guitar, the promise had been fulfilled. When the concert was over, I took Robbie Robertson and Rick Danko back to see Eric at the hotel. Robbie was harsh: "Don't be living in some blues fantasy, man. We watched Sonny Boy Williamson spit blood in a bucket trying to play three weeks before he died."

The Bangladesh show was a triumph on many levels. It was the first rock concert to use celebrity drawing power to help a worthy charitable cause—the birth of the idea that artists had a higher calling. It also proved to George that he could have a public life and career after the Beatles. As for me, I began to feel like we were nearing the end of an era. The Beatles had broken up. Dylan still didn't want to tour, the Band were in hibernation, Richard Manuel was drinking really hard, and players like Eric Clapton were too strung out to play. I realized that these scenes come and go. Here was just another moment in time in the way that, as cultural historian Jacques Barzun has noted, Michelangelo, Leonardo, Raphael, Donatello, and Botticelli were all working within walking distance from each other's studios in Florence from 1495 to 1525. Most historians believe the High Renaissance was over by 1535. Such scenes begin with boldness and innovation and often end in dissipation. That's just the way it is. I mentioned to Garth Hudson how sad I was that drink and drugs were getting in the way of the music. Garth stroked his beard and told me to sit down and he would tell me a story of his favorite music, jazz, and how it had survived dissipation and exile.

In October of 1939 the itinerant saxophone player Coleman Hawkins, who had played with Louis Armstrong in Fletcher Henderson's band, returned to New York from five years in European expat exile and went into the studio to record. Something must have happened to free Hawkins's concept of melody in those years on the Left Bank of Paris, for almost as an afterthought he decided to do a version of "Body and Soul" that moved so far away from the Benny Goodman hit as to be almost unrecognizable. What is remarkable is that Hawkins ignores almost all of the melody, stating only the first four bars in an identifiable fashion. What he does with the harmonic structure, the liberties he takes, make the recording another break point, equivalent to Armstrong's "West End Blues." Hawkins's bold exploration would presage a new genre called bebop and lead to the rise of an extraordinary partnership between saxophonist Charlie Parker and trumpet player Dizzy Gillespie.

The story of bebop is the story of a wartime interregnum—a city left to the hepcats who avoided the draft and to a recording business silenced by a musicians' strike over the issue of payments for radio broadcast of music. What began to transpire in the New York jazz community during the strike would not, however, be heard at this time outside the confines of a few New York clubs and a couple of after-hours Harlem hangouts called Minton's and Monroe's. As Miles Davis said in his autobiography, "The music wasn't being documented. If you didn't hear bebop in the clubs then you forgot it."

The most important figure in the birth of bebop was Charlie Parker, who learned his chops in the vibrant Kansas City music scene. John Hammond wrote in a 1936 *DownBeat* column, "In

Kansas City there are no less than 854 spots with night life of some kind. Descriptions of the place as the hotbed of American music are in every way justified." Parker had started playing saxophone at age eleven and committed himself to a rigorous practice schedule. He used to memorize all of the great sax solos from every player of note. He would then transpose them into every key. Gary Giddins (in Ken Burns's documentary *Jazz*) notes Parker's great breakthrough in 1938, when he was eighteen: "He would take a piece of music like 'Cherokee' and play it, hundreds and hundreds of times every night. That was the piece that he had his great breakthrough on all of a sudden. He broke through the basic chord system that was common in jazz, started playing on the upper intervals, and brought a whole new spontaneity and melodic vocabulary to the music."

In 1939, after a year on the road with Jay McShann's Kansas City band, Parker came to New York, where he picked up some odd jobs, worked washing dishes at Jimmy's Chicken Shack, where Art Tatum played every night, and eventually got a job with the Earl Hines Orchestra. Parker had been a junkie since getting into a serious auto accident at the age of sixteen, and his ability to score in New York was as much a part of what drew him to the city as his desire to make it in what musicians were calling "The Big Apple." While playing with Hines he met a young trumpet player named Dizzy Gillespie, who was also trying to break out of the straightjacket that swing music was becoming. Gillespie had probably heard Parker in Kansas City when he'd traveled there with Cab Calloway's band, but their bond was not sealed until they were both playing for Hines.

Gillespie was not only a trumpet virtuoso but also the

original hipster. He spoke in his own hepcat patois ("I'm gonna split") and was visually unique with his stylish suits, horn-rimmed spectacles, and beret. His puffed-out cheeks blowing into a trumpet with a bent bell seemed to reach for the spot-lights. Frank Tirro, in his book *Jazz: A History*, defined (with tongue in cheek) the hipster: "He is amoral, anarchistic, gen-tle, and overcivilized to the point of decadence. He is always ten steps ahead of the game because of his awareness, an example of which might be meeting a girl and rejecting her, because he knows they will date, hold hands, kiss, neck, pet, fornicate, per-haps marry, divorce—so why start the whole thing? He knows the hypocrisy of bureaucracy, the hatred implicit in religions—so what values are left for him?—except to go through life avoid-ing pain, keep his emotions in check, and after that, 'be cool,' and look for kicks. He is looking for something that transcends all this bullshit and finds it in jazz."

That was Dizzy, and in a way the music he and Charlie Parker would invent was a way to separate the hepcats from the squares or, as in the pianist Thelonious Monk's phrase, "We wanted a music that they couldn't play." "They" (the squares) was not meant as a racial distinction, and among the white men the bebop insiders considered hip were trombone player Jack Tea-garden, piano player Al Haig, and singer Bing Crosby. Perhaps it was the preference for reefer as the social lubricant of choice that partially separated the hip from the square.

In 1942 Earl Hines's band was playing fairly straightfor-ward swing, and so when the regular gig was over, Gillespie and Parker would go uptown to Monroe's on West 134th Street and jam with Monk, drummer Kenny Clarke, bassist Curley Russell, and sometimes the guitarist Charlie Christian. What transpired in those sessions was a kind of free negotiation anchored only by the drums and bass (the latter of which was crucial to the bebop sound). Parker was the driving force and, as Giddins said, his genius was "just inexplicable and wonderful." Describing Parker's influence, he wrote, "It's a magical thing and it's only happened relatively few times in the history of western civilization where a musician comes along and can completely transmute the music."

All of this wonderful music made between 1942 and 1945 was never recorded because of the musicians' strike. Then, in June of 1945, when we were still battling the Japanese in the Pacific, Dizzy Gillespie and Charlie Parker played a concert at New York's Town Hall with Al Haig on piano, Curley Russell on bass, and Max Roach on drums—and someone recorded it. The tapes of the concert were not discovered until 2004 by a jazz collector, and they are remarkably good considering they're a live recording taped off the PA board. Listening to what Dizzy and Charlie were doing in 1945 is like having a window directly into the past that created what jazz would become.

The concert opens with "Symphony Sid" Torin, the MC, noting that even though they are late getting started, Charlie Parker hasn't shown up yet. The image of Bird wandering the streets of Harlem still looking to score a half hour after a gig was supposed to start was not uncommon in those days. Parker eventually strolls on the stage, and by the second number, a tune appropriately called "Groovin' High," he is in fine form. The tune starts with Parker and Gillespie playing the signature riff in very fast, fluid harmony over Russell, Haig, and Roach's solid rhythm, and then Bird takes off on a solo that just soars over the vamping of the piano and the ride cymbal. Dizzy then takes his turn and throws off a torrent of notes that show he can keep up with Bird in this new frontier. Haig then does a wonderful piano solo over the driving bass and drums, making anyone wonder why he was not more famous at the time. Parker and Gillespie then rejoin the ensemble, restating the intricate harmony theme and then taking it out to a stunning climax.

What brings about such periods of genius and innovation? Maybe the fact that Dizzy and Bird could invent this music outside of the spotlight is what helped them to tap into the "flow" that is so evident on the Town Hall recording. (I certainly experienced this phenomenon on first hearing Dylan's *Basement Tapes* with the Band right after they were done in 1968.) If Dizzy and Bird had been recording their early experiments in 1943, they might have faced a backlash from the music business and abandoned the effort. More importantly, it's clear that the interplay between the two musicians drove them to a level of excellence they could not have found on their own. Listen to Dizzy's studio recording of "Groovin' High" and it pales in comparison to the live recording with Parker at Town Hall. What it comes back to again is that we have periods of cultural experimentation that free geniuses like Parker, Clapton, and Dylan. And then we have periods of cultural consolidation, in which we find formulas and repeat them endlessly. The question is, Does the spotlight of success somehow stifle the willingness to innovate? In its most brutal form, too much early fame leads to death—we saw that with Hendrix, Morrison, and Joplin, and, more recently, innovative young rappers Lil Peep and Juice WRLD.

The economic historian David Galenson has argued that there are two kinds of creative innovation. On the one hand, Experimental Innovators work slowly, by trial and error, and often take most of their lives to arrive at their greatest work. Cézanne, who flourished in his sixties, is such an artist. And then there are the Conceptual Innovators, who more often make extraordinary breakthroughs early in life. Dylan and Picasso are examples of this type. The harder question here is just what role the public, including feedback from critics, plays in these modes of creation. James Joyce's answer to this question was definitive—for him the best way to create was "as freely as I can" and while defending himself with "silence, exile and cunning"— but it's clear that other artists consider the public, both fans and foes, just another force that pushes them toward greatness.

11. The Rolling Stones in Exile
1972

By September of 1971 I was back in Woodstock, and most of the artists I cared about had decided to stop touring. Dylan and the Band were holed up in Woodstock, the Beatles had officially called it quits, George Harrison was so exhausted by the Concert for Bangladesh that he had no interest in touring, and his friend Eric Clapton was too strung out to think about going on the road. The one big touring act of the early seventies who could afford my services was Alice Cooper, but the idea of spending four months on the road listening to music I didn't like was out of the question. And so I decided it was time to try something new.

I told my friend Jay Cocks that I was going to move to California. Jay was a writer and film critic for *Time* magazine and had written the cover story on the Band that had been our first major national media break. Jay suggested that when I got to Los Angeles I should look up his friend Marty Scorsese, a young film editor who had worked on the Woodstock movie. He said Marty was a music fanatic and we would get along.

I went over to Albert Grossman's house to tell him I was

going to go out to California. Albert was in a dark mood, enveloped in a deep sadness over both Janis's death and Dylan's exodus. He had been working hard for twenty-five years, and things like food and architecture were now attracting his attention. It was an Indian summer at Woodstock that year and the windows were all open.

Someone turned up the stereo in the next room and Marvin Gaye's *What's Going On* filled the air. We walked into the living room and found our wives and girlfriends all dancing in the wisps of smoke flowing from the passed-around joint, their long skirts wrapping sinuously around their legs, and we remembered that the torch is passed often to a new generation.

Though Marvin Gaye is the same age as Smokey Robinson, who had been on the scene for years, he identified with a younger generation. *What's Going On* was a work of genius and was as politically symbolic as track star John Carlos's raised fist at the 1968 Olympics. Marvin Gaye came up through the Motown studio system, which looked very much like the Hollywood system of the late 1930s. There were not just songwriters but choreographers on staff, and wardrobe consultants to hone the stage looks of each of the acts, including the Supremes, the Four Tops, the Temptations, Martha and the Vandellas, Smokey Robinson and the Miracles—the list goes on. But early in his career Gaye rebelled against the Motown system, quitting the "grooming school" run by Maxine Powell.

By 1962 Gaye began to put out a string of hits, including "Can I Get a Witness," "Stubborn Kind of Fellow," and "Pride and Joy," but his true break from the paternalism of Berry Gordy's Motown management style came at a time of a personal tragedy.

Marvin had been paired with singer Tammi Terrell on a series of number-one hits, but in the midst of a concert in late 1967, Terrell collapsed in Marvin's arms and was rushed to the hospital. She was diagnosed with a brain tumor and died in March of 1970. Gaye went into a severe depression and decided to quit show business, going so far as to try out for the Detroit Lions football team.

Then, a chance encounter with two close friends on the Motown roster, songwriter Al Cleveland and Obie Benson of the Four Tops, changed his career. The two were working on a political song they called "What's Going On," written from the point of view of a Black vet returning from Vietnam. They asked Marvin to help them with the song, and Gaye later told *Rolling Stone*, "I began to re-evaluate my whole concept of what I wanted my music to say . . . . I was very much affected by letters my brother was sending me from Vietnam, as well as the social situation here at home. I realized that I had to put my own fantasies behind me if I wanted to write songs that would reach the souls of people. I wanted them to take a look at what was happening in the world."

In June they went into the studio and recorded "What's Going On," along with Gaye's own tune "God Is Love," which reflected the increased spirituality of Marvin's personal quest. The three were pleased with the session and brought the finished mixes to Berry Gordy to release as a single. Gordy refused, calling the song "the worst record I ever heard." Gordy's fears that it was too political and too "far out" musically for the core Motown audience did not sway Marvin Gaye, however. He essentially went on strike through the fall of 1970, and in January of 1971 Gordy relented and released "What's Going On." The song became the fastest selling single in Motown history and rocketed to the top of the charts. Marvin then left Detroit for California and wrote the rest of the song cycle that would comprise the *What's Going On* album, the whole thing told from the same point of view of the vet, who has come back from the war only to be disappointed by the life in the ghetto he has returned to.

Marvin Gaye moved to Los Angeles because he wanted to be part of a different scene—a new set of players. If you were on tour in the early 1970s, as I was, the localism of the music was quite astounding, and that meant that finding a new sound often started by moving to a new city. The sound of the Sir Douglas Quintet in San Antonio, Texas, was completely different from the Austin sound of Willie Nelson, and San Francisco's Jefferson Airplane was different from Los Angeles's Beach Boys. I will never forget when the Band was playing in New Orleans in 1970 and I met Mac Rebennack for the first time. His stage name was Dr. John the Night Tripper, and he shuffled into our dressing room like some kind of voodoo priest come to give the pre-concert blessing. Mac could only have been encountered in New Orleans, and he spoke a patois that almost required a translator, but Levon had spent enough time in the bayou that he filled in the missing details. After the concert, we were taken in a long limo to a curious house in the Garden District—probably owned by some drug dealer—and Richard and I had our first encounter with a water bong, which did not go well. I had to carry Richard to the limo later. Dr. John took it all in stride.

Detroit, Memphis, New Orleans, Chicago, and Muscle Shoals, Alabama, all had a different flavor of rhythm and blues, and each city had progressive FM radio stations that were playing local music. But all of that would end in a few years when a single corporation, Clear Channel, was given the go-ahead by the Reagan administration to buy up thousands of local radio stations and convert them to a centrally programmed format for the whole country. Sure, it was more efficient, but something important was lost.

Watching Sally Grossman dance across the floor as the *What's Going On* song cycle continued, I wondered if Marvin Gaye was ever going back on the road from his self-imposed exile in the hills of L.A. For many artists like Marvin, the comfort and intimacy of the recording studio was all they needed, but other bands craved the thrill of the big crowds. Which type was Marvin? The answer to the question came when Jo Bergman called.

Jo was Mick Jagger's majordomo and she was calling from the South of France, where the Rolling Stones were holed up. They had left London partially to avoid police harassment about drugs, but more importantly to avoid UK taxes. Jo said that the Stones were going to do a tour of the United States and asked if I would be interested in managing the tour. I said yes, and the next day a round-trip ticket to Nice showed up at my New York hotel.

Two days later, in early November, I left the bitter cold of the city for the Côte d'Azur with a sense of excitement and mystery. Because I had been a blues fan from the start, the Stones' early work covering tunes like Solomon Burke's "Everybody Needs Somebody to Love" put them above the Beatles, whose work seemed softer in my eyes. Along with every other hormonal seventeen-year-old, "Satisfaction" had become my anthem for the summer of '64. Strangely enough, it was the Beatles' two films, *A Hard Day's Night* and *Help!*, that totally won me over to their wry humor, and by the time *Rubber Soul* was released in late 1965, I was totally in the Beatles camp. As the Beatles' work matured, the Stones seemed to become somewhat lost in the psychedelic era. They hit a low point for me with *Their Satanic Majesties Request*, which seemed like a very bad imitation of *Sgt. Pepper's Lonely Hearts Club Band*. It was clear that acid was not the Stones' drug of choice. It wasn't until I arrived in France that I discovered just what their drug was.

The reason I was on a plane to France at all was because in the late sixties, as the antiwar movement raged around us, the Stones had once again created an anthem—"Street Fighting Man"—that inspired people on a political level. In late 1971, the Rolling Stones were still seen as a political band, despite their wealth, and while the Beatles, the other big political band, refused to tour, Mick and the boys kept putting on a show. For that I was grateful. But I had also heard from George Harrison that Mick and Keith's relationship had some of the same tension that had torn John and Paul apart and had led to the end of the Beatles. Beyond that, the stain of the death at their Altamont concert in December 1969 still lingered over the Stones' tour plans. Whoever had decided to hire the Hells Angels motorcycle club for security had obviously been canned, and now it was Jo Bergman's job to make sure the tour for the summer of 1972 was properly managed.

When I got off the plane in Nice, Jo met me with a driver in a Citroën that was the closest thing the French had to a limo. We drove to a hotel in Cannes, where I left my bags, and then went out to Keith's villa in Saint-Jean-Cap-Ferrat for lunch with the band. I was well aware that I was being interviewed as much for my "sensitivity" to artists as for my production skills. Rick Danko had once written on the back of the road case that carried his bass amp "Don't bring the entertainer down," and that was a motto I tried to inculcate in myself and my crews. For me, the key to a great tour is making the technology fade into the background. The bass player should never worry about a hum in his amp because it wasn't grounded right. The drum kit should be set exactly the same way each night, the heads tightened to the same tone and the stool at exactly the same height. The lighting should not call attention to itself but just magically light up the soloist or singer a few seconds before he steps to the microphone. Most of all, don't rely on the local promoter to provide a good sound system. Bring your own. As the touring revenue got greater, the best way to keep musicians happy then became using a private jet. And no band traveled in more luxury than the Stones.

When we pulled into the long driveway of Keith's villa, I had a sense of entering the world of Scott Fitzgerald's expat crowd who gathered at Gerald and Sara Murphy's Villa America, which was probably just down the road. Unlike the artists of the twenties, however, the Stones were not escaping a world of Babbitts in search of a cheap place to write or paint. London in 1971 was probably cheaper than a two-acre villa on the Mediterranean, especially one with elaborate gardens, swimming pools, and speedboats tied up in a boathouse, so it was not about cost. The Stones' exile was simple: They didn't want to pay 86 percent of their income to Britain's Inland Revenue department.

That said, they were still expatriates and carried with them all of the emotional baggage that entails. To read Hemingway's account of Scott and Zelda Fitzgerald in *A Moveable Feast* is to get some sense of the displacement that even a rock-and-roll star might feel on permanent vacation in the South of France. Like Scott and Zelda's New York City in the twenties, Mick and Keith's London in the late sixties was the center of the universe, but it was the artists themselves who made the cities powerful, and so when the artists went into exile, the cities lost their magnetism.

Jo and I walked up the steps to the main foyer and were greeted by a butler who told us, "Mr. Richards is not awake yet." It was 1 p.m. We wandered into the main living room. Guitars and small amps sat in the corner, but otherwise it could have been the home of a tycoon the likes of James Goldsmith or Pierre Bergé, the property dripping with the kind of "luxe" style *Paris Match* liked to depict to prove that the French business world still mattered. Jo looked a little nonplussed that none of the band had managed to wake up for the interview lunch. As for me, I was a bit jetlagged and in no hurry to sell myself to the band. The winter midday light of the Riviera was captivating, and I took a coffee on the terrace, watching a huge yacht navigate the coast. By 2:30 Charlie Watts had strolled in and asked the butler for *"jus d'orange et café au lait."* It was going to be one of those slow-starting days if even Mr. Responsibility (Charlie was widely considered the sane one of the band) was having breakfast at 3 p.m. By 5, Mick had arrived and acted as if the meeting was scheduled for 5:30 and he was early. I could tell from Jo Bergman's body language that this was par for the course, and she said nothing to contradict the fearless leader.

The author (seated at center) as coxswain on the crew team at Brooks School, 1962. Courtesy of the Frank D. Ashburn Archives.

Yale University chaplain Reverend William Sloane Coffin, who was arrested during the Freedom Rides in Montgomery, Alabama, May 1961. Public domain.

The author (right) with (from left to right) first mate Theodoric, the author's father, and his brother Randy, in Greece, July 1963. Author's collection.

Sixth Form Brooksians March For Civil Rights

Dean and Taplin on the March.

Four Brooks students took part in the recent Roxbury-to-Boston civil rights march protesting de facto segregation in the Boston school system. The boys, Jon Taplin, Grey Ferris, Bob Dean, and James Auchincloss, were accompanied by Mrs. Wilder and later met Mrs. Waterston in Boston.

Bus To Roxbury

The group was transported to Carter playground, in the heart of the predominantly Negro section of Roxbury. They arrived in a chartered bus at 10 o'clock on the morning of April 23.

Marchers Cheered

The march, led by the well-known civil rights leaders, Dr. Martin Luther King, Ralph Abernathy of the Southern Christian Leadership Conference, and Virgil Wood, proceeded through the city to the historic Boston Common, with the Brooks boys walking thirty ranks back from the front. Negroes cheered as the marchers strode through the slums of Roxbury while elsewhere the crowds watched in silence.

(Continued on Page Four)

The author marching for civil rights. From the Brooks School newspaper, April 1965. Courtesy of the Frank D. Ashburn Archives.

Albert Grossman and Bob Dylan at
the Newport Folk Festival, July 1965.
Photo by David Gahr, courtesy of
Getty Images.

Concert poster for the Doors and the
Kweskin Jug Band at San Francisco's
Fillmore Auditorium, June 1967.

Bob Dylan and the Hawks at the Woody Guthrie Memorial Concert, January 1968. Photo © Elliott Landy.

The author with Janis Joplin at the Newport Folk Festival, July 1968. Author's collection.

The Band in Bearsville, fall 1968. Photo © Elliott Landy.

Janis Joplin and Albert Grossman, 1969. Photo © Elliott Landy.

The Band recording in Sammy Davis, Jr.'s pool house in Los Angeles, February 1969. Photo © Elliott Landy.

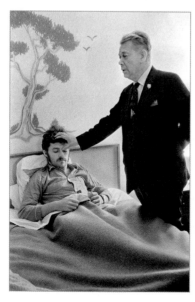

A hypnotist getting Robbie Robertson ready for the Band's Winterland debut, San Francisco, April 1969. Photo © Elliott Landy.

The author (center, black jacket) at Woodstock with the Band, Albert Grossman (far left), and Bob Neuwirth (center left), August 1969. Author's collection.

The author (far right) with Rick Danko, Janis Joplin, Jerry Garcia, and Ian Tyson on the Festival Express, July 1970. Photo © John Scheele.

The author (foreground, in glasses) on the set of *Mean Streets* with director Martin Scorsese, fall 1973. Author's collection.

The author with Bob Dylan in Chicago, January 1974. Photo by Charles Osgood, courtesy of the *Chicago Tribune*.

Martin Scorsese and Robert De Niro at the 1974 Cannes Film Festival. Photo by the author.

The author (left), making *Under Fire* in Oaxaca, Mexico, 1982. Author's collection.

The author with his children, Blythe, Daniela, and Nick, in Montecito, California, 1985. Author's collection.

The author with director Wim Wenders, making *Until the End of the World*, 1989. Author's collection.

The *Hollywood Reporter*'s depiction of the author's interaction with Harvey Weinstein at the Sundance Film Festival in January 1996. Illustration by Kyle Hinton.

Richard Avedon's portrait of the author (far right) and the Band, September 1969. Courtesy of the Avedon Foundation.

Mick and I sat down to talk. On the table was a plate of those silly English sandwiches with cucumbers and all the crust cut off. Jo and Charlie listened in, but it was clear that Mick was in charge. At 6:30, Keith was still missing in action and I could tell even Mick was beginning to be a bit peeved. He finally sent the butler up to roust his partner out of bed, and a half hour later Keith appeared looking like the proverbial forty miles of bad road. The first thing I noticed was that his teeth seemed in bad shape and both his cheeks and his eyes seemed like dark craters on the surface of his ravaged countenance. As Mick went on about what they wanted to do with the tour, Keith chain-smoked Gauloises and drank multiple espressos and didn't say a word. Occasionally I would spy him scratching his neck too, and all these warning signs put me on junkie alert and distracted me from Mick's businesslike manner.

Eventually the meeting came around to my work, and I talked about the Isle of Wight with Dylan and the Band (we had played to the largest crowd in English rock history), and also the Concert for Bangladesh and the Band's famous first appearance at Winterland. At some point, it was obvious that my bona fides were cool, and it also helped that George Harrison had vouched for my discretion. At this point, Mick began to sell *me* on the job. He played me a rough mix of "Tumbling Dice," which I loved, and we talked about Winterland, which he wanted to play in addition to all the big arenas they would inevitably have to do. At 10 p.m., "lunch" was served, and by midnight the band was ready to start recording again. I left at 1:30 a.m. and asked Jo if we could have breakfast at my hotel around 10:30 in the morning.

The next day was hard. I did like Mick a lot. He was smart,

cultured, and incredibly curious, and he asked great questions. But having just gone through the nightmare of Clapton's heroin habit on Bangladesh, I was in no mood for a rerun, worrying about Keith. I told Jo that I had to politely decline the invitation, even before the job was formally offered to me. She was wonderfully understanding but, like the den mother she was, she defended her boys and said it wasn't as tough as it seemed once they got on the road. I left with the understanding that we'd get together once the band arrived in L.A. to mix the album that was to be called *Exile on Main St.*

I flew home thinking of all the damage heroin had done to my friends in the last few years. I had watched Janis Joplin bounce between heroin and booze until she just wore herself out. One of my roadies had worked for Jimi Hendrix and told me of being awakened in Stockholm at three in the morning by Jimi, who was smacked out, his works still sitting on the bed in full view, and trying to get the armoire out of his window because he was feeling crowded and claustrophobic. And now, two of the musicians I cared about most, Eric Clapton and Keith Richards, had the monkey on their back.

It made me sad for them but also for the music. It didn't escape me that both Eric and Keith were more into the romantic tradition of the blues than any of their countrymen; for each of them it had started with an almost obsessive interest in the life of Robert Johnson, America's greatest bluesman. It was a life that fit the Thomas Hobbes phrase "nasty, brutish, and short," and although Johnson's influence was huge, he never got the chance to share all the music that was undoubtedly inside him. Everything we have ever heard from Johnson was cut in two days' worth of sessions in November 1936 and June 1937. The day before his first session, Johnson was arrested as a vagrant by the Dallas police and had to be bailed out by the producer Don Law, who gave him fifty cents for breakfast. A few hours later Johnson phoned Law in his hotel room, saying, "There is a lady here. She wants fifty cents and I lacks a nickel."

His life came to a premature end when he was poisoned by the jealous husband of a woman he began seeing during a gig at the Three Forks juke joint in Greenwood, Mississippi. The poisoning occurred on the night of August 13, 1938, and Johnson went through three days of hell before dying at the age of twenty-seven. I couldn't help think that the notion that all bluesmen lived a similarly brief time on this Earth contributed to the carelessness that Keith and Eric showed toward their health. Looking back thirty years later, it is a miracle that both men, now in their mid-seventies, are today among the healthiest artists of their generation. For Keith, the turnaround came courtesy of the love of a woman, Patti Hansen, who insisted he clean his act up. And for Eric, it was partially romantic love and most definitely the intense tragedy of his young son's death. His eventual sobriety was also probably due to the effects of age and wisdom.

By the end of January 1972, I was in a house in Los Angeles's Laurel Canyon, and Mick was ensconced in a rented mansion in Bel Air. One night, his assistant, Chris O'Dell, who was a close friend of mine, invited me to come up to Mick's house to talk about photographers for the album cover. Even though I had turned down the job to be their tour manager, there were no hard feelings between me and the Stones. Mick liked many of the album covers that Robbie Robertson and I had produced for the Band, and so Chris asked me to come prepared with suggestions. Leaving my house, I had what I thought was a brilliant idea. I did not, however, have a clue of how that idea would complicate my life for the next month.

Aside from music, my other big passion was photography, and I owned an original American edition of Robert Frank's *The Americans*. If any book of photographs can be thought of as an almost perfect art piece, it is *The Americans*. Frank took the pictures with a Leica with one lens during the course of a trip across the country in 1955. To a nation in the grip of Eisenhower normality, *The Americans* was a view of another, lonelier, more desperate America. As Jack Kerouac wrote in the book's introduction, "That crazy feeling in America when the sun is hot on the streets and the music comes out of the jukebox, that's what Robert Frank has captured."

I grabbed my copy of the book as I ran out the door to Mick's house at 10 p.m. When I got there, Bianca was leaving to go out and so it was just Mick, Chris O'Dell, and myself. We settled down with some nice Bordeaux and I showed Mick *The Americans*. As he started to leaf through the incredible pictures of Baptist preachers praying by the river and cowboys lit with the glow of saloon jukeboxes, I started my pitch: "Everybody knows what the Rolling Stones look like. Why do you even need your picture on the cover? Your album is bluesy and American, so why don't you just pick one of these iconic Robert Frank images and put it on the cover?"

I could see Mick wasn't really listening. He was too fascinated by the pictures themselves. He would look at an image for minutes and just sigh. Finally, after about ten minutes, he turned to me and said, "This is unbelievably good stuff."

"Thanks. I'm glad you like it as much as I do."

"Let's get him to take our picture."

I stopped short. This was not the idea. I knew that Frank had moved on from taking stills to making underground movies like *Pull My Daisy* with Allen Ginsberg and some of his beat pals, but that was ten years ago. I knew he hadn't done any significant photography since 1955, but I also had no idea where he lived or how to get in contact with him. I wasn't even sure he was still alive. But Mick was not to be dissuaded.

"Oh, come on, Jon, you can find him."

"I don't even know where to start."

"Put the word out that we'll pay him $20,000 to take our picture. He'll show up."

I left at midnight, promising to do my best.

The next morning, I was on the phone to the one person I knew in the underground film scene, Jonas Mekas. He recalled that Frank had been on welfare in the United States before moving up to Mabou, Nova Scotia, with his daughter about three years earlier. I figured I'd try directory assistance for the town, but I soon discovered that it was so far in the boonies that it still had a party line with a central operator for the whole town. When I finally reached the central operator and told her I was calling from Los Angeles for Robert Frank, she just chuckled and said it was impossible.

"Well, we had a big storm last week and the lines are down out to their place."

"When will they be back up?"

"In a couple of months when the storms stop."

"Well, this is kind of an emergency. Isn't there any way I can get through to him?"

"You could write him a letter. His daughter comes in twice a month for mail and supplies."

I could just imagine my telling Mick that maybe in the next *month* we might be in touch with the object of his *idée fixe*. So I tried another tack.

"Is there anyone I could pay to go out there and tell him the Rolling Stones want to pay him a lot of money to take their picture?"

"Hold on for a second. Let me check at the General Store."

In a minute she came back on the line and told me I was in luck. Robert's daughter just happened to be in the store stocking up. She put Andrea on the line and I explained the whole story to her. She was slightly skeptical but promised to have her father call the next day. She was very concerned that he be able to call collect.

The next morning I was on the line with one of my artistic heroes. Frank's voice had the timbre of New York and Switzerland, but it had been softened by age and the long winters of Nova Scotia. Once he had determined that the $20,000 was for real and not some Jonas Mekas prank, he agreed to come to L.A.

"I'll have to go down to New York to see if I can borrow a camera from someone. Send me a ticket to New York and then on to L.A. a couple of days later," he said.

The idea of paying $20,000 to a photographer who didn't even own a camera was a bit odd, but from my point of view this would be Robert's reward for his "years of service." Five days later I met him at the Los Angeles airport. This small, beautiful man walked off the plane with a Super 8 movie camera up to his eye and no sign of any other photographic equipment. I figured maybe he had a borrowed Leica in his checked bag.

The limo driver who seemed to be on twenty-four-hour call for the Stones drove us to the Beverly Hills Hotel, and when the room clerk asked Robert if he had stayed with them before, he replied, "Yes, in 1955." The clerk smiled and said the records didn't go back that far and had him sign a new form. We moved him into a small bungalow and it became clear to me that Jagger was treating Frank like minor art royalty.

That evening we were invited up to Mick's for dinner. Robert brought his little home movie camera and was the perfect dinner guest, regaling Mick with stories of Kerouac, Ginsberg, Burroughs, and the other beat heroes that any London School of Economics grad might have heard of. Occasionally he would bring the camera up to his eye and shoot little ten-second bursts of film. After that first dinner, the meals at Mick's house became a nightly affair and it soon became clear that Jagger had a true affection for this seminal American artist. Every evening after dinner, Mick would drag Robert to the recording studio, where Keith, Charlie, and the producers were mixing *Exile on Main St.* Here again, Robert's only accessory was the Super 8 movie camera. One night when Mick had invited some other guests, I went into his study and found Robert rummaging in the trashcan. He put some pieces of paper in his pocket without explanation. I didn't say a word.

After a week of this, the head of the Rolling Stones Record

Company, Marshall Chess (son and nephew of Chicago's Chess Brothers) began to get irritated. The Beverly Hills Hotel bill was getting serious and there was still no sign of a photo session. Marshall came to me and said that there had to be a photo session within forty-eight hours or he was "sending the old man home." I told Robert this and he asked me to get the Stones all down to the Grand Central Market on Broadway in downtown L.A. He also asked me to rent him a camera. I was a bit worried. He hadn't even bothered to borrow a camera in New York. I tried to find an old Leica but failed.

By the time the whole band assembled, the light was fading. Robert fumbled with the unfamiliar camera and seemed pretty disorganized. Marshall Chess began to rant about "incompetence." Keith looked pissed, as if this was all Mick's folly. Robert reverted to shooting Super 8 of Chess's rant, and the whole session ended badly. Chess called Mick and me over to the side and said he was sending Robert back to Canada in the morning and the whole thing had been a waste of their precious time. The album art had to be camera-ready in two weeks, and now they would have to start again with a new photographer. Chess was so angry he didn't even want to pay Frank.

"Hell, we gave him a ten-day vacation at the Beverly Hills Hotel."

But Mick was firm. "Pay him the $20,000, Marshall."

"Mick, you're crazy."

"Pay him today!"

It was settled. I went with Robert to the airport in the morning. He had his check, his Super 8 camera, and one roll of 35mm film from the aborted shoot on Broadway. I felt slightly awkward saying goodbye, as if somehow I had been responsible for this disaster. On a deeper level, though, at least the $20,000 would pay Robert's rent for the next two years, and if this was Mick's charity case, so be it. I asked him to stay in touch, but for a week I heard nothing. I assumed the worst.

Ten days later a package from New York arrived at the office of John Van Hamersveld, the Stones' album designer. It was from Robert Frank and was the complete camera-ready art for a deluxe two-album set for *Exile on Main St.* Robert had taken some of his old pictures, combined them with small strips of Super 8 film of the Stones at work, and added small scraps of paper on which Mick had jotted down lyrics and other leavings of the recording process. The cover is now considered one of the most iconic record covers ever.

Needless to say, Mick and I were overjoyed. Mick was so thrilled that when the tour started he invited Robert to make a documentary of it. Robert hung out with the band for six weeks on the road and shot everything. He called the finished film *Cocksucker Blues*, and when he showed it to the band and their business manager, Prince Rupert Loewenstein, there was near mass apoplexy. There on the big screen were scenes with heroin, blowjobs from groupies, and an occasional tune or two. Needless to say, the film was never distributed. But for Robert Frank, the whole adventure was a success. He had the money to get back into his work. He would never be on welfare again, and the public was once more interested in his art. Museums started to do retrospectives. Publishers brought out books of his photographs. He had a second artistic life instead of a cold, dark retirement on the Grand Banks of Nova Scotia.

12. Mean Streets

1973

I was lying by my pool in Laurel Canyon when Marty Scorsese and Barry Primus arrived in a 1957 Thunderbird. It was a brilliant summer day, eighty degrees and climbing. My girlfriend, Phyllis Major, was working on her tan, topless. Marty walked up the steps to the pool in a long black leather overcoat. The sweat was beading on his forehead and a slight wheeze issued from his asthmatic lungs. Barry followed him up the stairs and nodded respectfully to Phyllis. I offered them chairs under the umbrella and suggested to Marty that he take his coat off. He sat down but kept the coat on. As our conversation began he kept trying to reposition his chair so that Phyllis's amazing physique was out of his sight line. He took a quick hit from his inhaler and began his pitch about the movie he wanted to direct called *Season of the Witch*.

When I had packed up my things in Woodstock seven months earlier with the intention of moving to Los Angeles, my friend Jay Cocks had suggested that I look up a young film editor named Marty Scorsese. He had mentioned that Marty had edited part of the Woodstock movie and that we would be simpatico. Marty's friend and driver Barry Primus was a New York actor who had done one movie with Brian De Palma.

I had sold my house in Woodstock in December of 1972, after the Concert for Bangladesh, because it was a perfect conclusion to my concert production career and I was itching to see if I could produce films as well. It was the kind of naiveté that has blessed my life. I imagined that film production was easier than concerts because if something goes wrong you can always try it again tomorrow. On the concert stage, if something goes wrong you have thousands of impatient fans clapping in unison wanting the show to start. Although there was a certain logic to this reasoning, I might never have agreed to finance Marty's film if I had understood anything about Hollywood.

For his part, Marty talked faster than anyone I had ever met. I had spent a lot of time around laidback musicians, and with the exception of a couple of Dylan speed raps, I had never experienced anything like this little man in the Gestapo overcoat telling me why I should finance his movie. I listened. Phyllis got up and offered us all a drink. Marty seemed too nervous to look at her, but Barry coolly answered yes for both of them. After an hour-long meeting they left me with a script and an invitation to go to the William Morris office the next day to see Marty's student films.

I saw two shorts and a feature: *The Big Shave* (a surrealistic takeoff of Buñuel's *Un Chien Andalou*), *It's Not Just You, Murray!* (a wonderfully comic short about a New York hustler), and *Who's That Knocking at My Door* (his NYU film school feature). It was *Murray* that grabbed me. It was such a brilliant character piece that for some reason I just made the leap of faith. In telling the story of Murray, a gangster looking back at his life, Marty breaks the fourth wall, brings in a musical number, and borrows liberally from the French filmmakers he so admired. All the themes that would mark his later work are sketched lightly in this short from 1964.

That afternoon, I called Marty and told him I would finance his new film. The next day we met at an office where he was finishing a film for Roger Corman called *Boxcar Bertha*. He had called Jay Cocks with the news, and Jay had suggested that we change the title of our picture from *Season of the Witch* to *Mean Streets*, in reference to the old Raymond Chandler line. Marty pulled out four books of storyboards, and it was obvious that he had wanted to make the film for such a long time that he had literally drawn every single shot of the film on paper. Once we started production, these boards were to be our saving grace. I was able to raise $500,000 for the movie, but this meant a shooting schedule of only thirty days. The only thing that made it possible was Marty's uncanny ability to do thirty shots a day.

When I returned to my house, Phyllis expressed some skepticism about spending my hard-earned money and what was left of my inheritance on a movie. I had already convinced a boyhood friend, Lee Perry, to co-finance it with me, so I argued that it wasn't *all* on me. Phyllis was adamant, as if it was "our" money that I was spending. It was as if she had plans for our future that I had not been clued into yet.

I had first met her in 1966, when she was the girlfriend of Bob Neuwirth, Dylan's road manager. Neuwirth called her Tonto, and I assumed he was the Lone Ranger. She was one of the most stunning women I had ever met—tall, with an amazing body and beautiful long hair the color of winter wheat. She had a wicked sense of humor, which had probably been sharpened by hanging out with Neuwirth, the court jester of the Dylan circle. I had not pursued her, but somehow she made her way from New York to Los Angeles, showed up at my door in Laurel Canyon, and announced she had left Neuwirth and was starting a new life in California. I welcomed her in, and before I knew it, she had moved her few possessions into my house.

I think I was in a daze. I was enchanted, but underneath there was a sense of danger. In my mind I was still the awkward, shy prep school kid, but somehow one of the most beautiful women in the world was in my bed. I didn't question her motives, but I knew that life with Neuwirth had been fragile, so maybe I was a respite from all that. He was a painter and a drinker who had put off his own career ambitions to serve Bob Dylan, and he could be mean too, with stinging sarcasm. Later on, he went into AA and sobered up, restarted his art career, and found himself again, with the help of a great woman, Paula Batson. He has a good life now.

Phyllis and I lived together for six months before she began suggesting that if she was to have children, she needed to get started. (She was in her late twenties.) She suggested we go up and visit her mother in Northern California, but as we settled into the guest room in her mother's very modest home, I immediately began to sense that something was wrong. Over a long, boozy dinner, her mother disclosed that she had recently tried to kill herself by turning on the gas stove and shutting all the windows. The hitch was that there was a dog door that leaked gas out toward her neighbor's house, and the alarmed neighbor came to rescue her. She was sent to the hospital and then committed to the psych ward for a week before being sent home. The strangest part is that all of this seemed like new information to Phyllis, and yet she didn't process it in the way I would have expected. Instead of expressing shock or sympathy, she made a snarky comment about the stupid dog door. I came home worried but said nothing. (As you will see, my role in my relationships with beautiful women during this period was curiously passive. Phyllis was funny and good company, but she was controlling the terms of our relationship, and for the most part I let her have her way.)

When my mother came out to visit me in L.A., Phyllis did her best to please her. We all had dinner together, and the next day, while Phyllis was out, I was sitting at lunch with my mother when she made this frank statement: "You don't love that woman. You're just showing her off, hoping you won't have to get on with your real life." I realized she was right.

Things began to get edgy with Phyllis after that. Maybe she sensed I was getting shaky about her, especially about how much she wanted to get pregnant—treating me like I was a sperm donor. And then one night as I was coming in from an editing session on *Mean Streets* she announced that Warren Beatty had called her and said he was really depressed and needed to see her at his suite at the Beverly Wilshire Hotel. I said, "I know what you are doing," but she wheeled around and was out the door. Beatty had a reputation for getting any beautiful girl he wanted to come and "help him with his mood." While she was gone, I piled all of her clothes into her two suitcases and put them by the door. When she got home at 3 a.m. she stumbled over them, swearing like a sailor. I came out of the bedroom and found her on the floor crying. No words were exchanged and she moved out in the morning.

The postscript to this sad story was that within three weeks she had moved in with Jackson Browne, who lived down the street, and three months later she was pregnant. They had a boy named Ethan and got married in late 1975. In March of 1976, Phyllis committed suicide with a massive overdose of sleeping pills while Jackson was on tour.

The very fact that Marty and I were able to making a feature-length film for $500,000 is in part due to the groundwork laid by Dennis Hopper with *Easy Rider*. That film had come out the summer before, and by June of 1973 it was clear that the days of Old Hollywood were numbered; it was (and still is) a town that lived and died by the trend of the moment. After *The Sound of Music* became a hit in 1965, the studios went on a binge of big-budget musicals, all of which bombed. Then along came this movie about two hippies on motorcycles, made for $800,000, and it cleaned up at the box office. Next thing you knew, all the studio execs were wearing Nehru suits and taking supervised acid trips from personal gurus. (Now these same gurus are teaching yoga.)

At the same time that Marty Scorsese and I began making *Mean Streets*, Francis Coppola, George Lucas, Peter Bogdanovich, Steven Spielberg, Bill Friedkin, Bob Altman, Bob Rafelson, Dennis Hopper, Terry Malick, Hal Ashby, and a few others began making films outside the normal studio system.

Eventually, after the early success of some of their low-budget films, most of these filmmakers were welcomed into the studio system *because* of their youth, not in spite of it. For about eight years some wonderful movies got made: *The Godfather, American Graffiti, MASH, Nashville, Taxi Driver, Jaws, Five Easy Pieces, Shampoo, The Last Picture Show, The French Connection, Badlands,* and *Mean Streets,* to name just a few.

I owed a lot to the trail blazed by Bert Schneider, Bob Rafelson, and Steve Blauner, who called their company BBS Productions. Despite the success of their first three films (*Easy Rider, The Last Picture Show,* and *Five Easy Pieces*) they never sold out or tried to make what was popular; they believed in the authority of the filmmaker, a concept that was closer to France's auteur theory than to Hollywood's general distrust of the artist and worship of the box office. Jack Nicholson was the perfect actor for their ethos—the philosophical Southern hippie in *Easy Rider,* the alienated wanderer in *Five Easy Pieces.*

I think Bert Schneider in particular was deeply frustrated by the inability of art to essentially change politics. Although he had his successes, including making a searing documentary about the Vietnam War that won an Oscar in 1975, even that triumph was short-lived, as he got booed by the John Wayne crowd when he sent greetings from the North Vietnamese people in his acceptance speech. In the 1970s he began to quietly fund Huey Newton and the Black Panther Party—he probably bought them a bunch of guns—and when the Panthers and the Weathermen helped spring Timothy Leary from prison, it was Bert who smuggled him out of the country to Eldridge Cleaver's exile redoubt in Algeria. Like many revolutionary fantasies, it would all end badly—too much cocaine, too much anger, too little humility.

When we started production on *Mean Streets*, however, it was clear that we would have to operate completely outside of the Hollywood system. We spent the first five days of shooting in New York in Marty's old neighborhood on Mott Street, pretending to be an NYU film school crew. We were afraid either the Teamsters or the IATSE (the film craft union) would find us. For Marty, it was a return to his former stomping grounds, and the local friends who served as our extras were glad to see him. The six-year distance from the asthmatic kid who said he was considering becoming a priest to this "real Hollywood director" seemed amazing to his old friends in the neighborhood.

For his semiautobiographical *Who's That Knocking at My Door*, Marty had cast Harvey Keitel in the lead role, and he used his doppelganger again for *Mean Streets*. The narrative followed the intensely personal story of a young Italian American Catholic torn between the Church and desire, and the voice of yearning and all of the chaos it represented was played by a newcomer named Robert De Niro. Bobby had done two films with Brian De Palma that had not really been seen beyond the Upper East Side of New York, but Marty was convinced that De Niro had a kind of anarchic spirit that the character of Johnny Boy required. The other three main roles were filled out by kids we had seen in Jon Voight's acting workshop: David Proval, Richard Romanus, and Amy Robinson. (This was before John Voight turned into a total rightwing nut job. In those days he was a classic Hollywood antiwar liberal.)

After ten days in New York, we moved out to L.A. to shoot most of the interiors using the kind of nonunion crews that

Marty had met working for Roger Corman. It was here that I got a sense for the detail that would distinguish many of Scorsese's films. We built a set for the apartment that Harvey Keitel's character, Charlie, would inhabit with his mother and father (played by Scorsese's parents), and despite our meager budget Marty insisted that the set have a real New York tin ceiling to match the apartment he had grown up in. Most sets don't have ceilings, and finding that kind of old tin ceiling in L.A. was not easy, but Marty was insistent. But now, in the very first scene in the film, when Charlie is getting up, you see the tin ceiling from a low-angle shot. For Marty, it sold the fact that this was a New York movie, not a Hollywood one.

The filming of *Mean Streets* went very easily. Everyone got the SAG scale wage, shared one small Winnebago as a dressing room, and showed up to work early and stayed late. Except for De Niro's tendency to remain in character off the set (and thereby psych out Richard Romanus), it was the last stress-free experience I ever had with actors for twenty years, at which point I saw Nicole Kidman throw herself into *To Die For* with the same abandon.

The casting of *Mean Streets* was done with the intent of creating an ensemble of totally unknown actors, which would gave the film the realism of the early postwar Italian films like *Shoeshine* and *Rome, Open City* that Marty and I had both savored in our teens. Laid on top of this neorealism were two elements that became signatures of Scorsese's work: the use of slow motion to create a dream state, and the use of rock and roll as underscore. On a shoestring budget, this was how Marty managed to create a kind of magic that changed filmmaking forever. The first entrance of Bob De Niro into the nightclub, bathed in red light and moving in slow motion to the Rolling Stones' "Jumpin' Jack Flash," is still one of the best moments in Marty's work, and in the entire 1970s film canon.

Getting that song in the film almost killed me. The Rolling Stones' catalog was controlled by their American manager, Allen Klein, with whom I had toiled on Bangladesh. Klein offered to let us license the song, but when the contract arrived it contained a clause that would let him pull the song out if he didn't approve of the final film. To say that Allen Klein was a good judge of film-making would be a stretch, and so I didn't sign the contract for months, hoping I could convince him to remove the approval clause. Lucky for us all, once the film found a distributor, Klein allowed me to remove that clause and the song was ours.

Marty is one of the most complex artists I have ever encountered. Much is rooted in his Catholic faith—the constant wrestling match with sin—and much also in his childhood battle with asthma—the literal inability to breathe. He and I sometimes had a contentious relationship. I was learning how to be a producer on the fly, and with *Mean Streets*, as with any shoestring indie production, it was not always clear if the finishing money would arrive. But arrive it did. Once in a fit of anger he showed me *The Bad and the Beautiful*, just to remind me of the dark side of Hollywood and why I should avoid falling into it. He never wanted to stay in L.A., and as soon as he got successful, he moved back to New York.

The anxiety really hit both Marty and me when it came time to try to sell the film. My lawyer had arranged a series of screenings of the picture over two days for most of the major studios.

In 1973, there was no Miramax, Fine Line, or Focus Features—companies set up to release independent films. Back then there were only the majors, and so on a Monday morning at 9 a.m. we showed up at the Alfred Hitchcock Theater on the Universal lot to screen the picture for Peter Saphier, VP of Acquisitions for Universal.

My lawyer had warned me that the studio execs might walk out in the middle of the screening if they didn't like the movie, but Peter sat through the whole film. When it was over, he respectfully told us that this was not the kind of movie that major studios would release, but he suggested that if we wanted to cut a half hour out of the film, he would be willing to take another look at it, but, quite frankly, the chances of Universal picking it up were "extremely remote." My heart sank. It had never occurred to me before that moment that the $500,000 a friend and I had put into the movie could all be lost. I had been so naively confident that the possibility that the film might never see the light of day never entered my mind.

Marty and I collected the two film canisters and, like two sad-sack salesmen, drove off to Warner Bros. for a lunchtime screening. We were met at a small screening room behind the executive offices by John Calley, head of production; Leo Greenfield, head of sales; and Dick Lederer, head of advertising. Ten minutes after the film started, a waiter walked into the screening room with a large tray of sandwiches and proceeded to stand in front of the projector while he doled out the pastrami on rye. Marty was dying, sinking slowly in his chair while his movie was projected onto the waiter. Eventually the man left and the three execs settled in and began to enjoy the film. Calley was seated down front, and I later realized that his New York Catholic upbringing gave him a special window into Marty's particular obsession.

About two-thirds of the way through the film, Calley abruptly got out of his seat and started up the aisle. My heart sank again as I figured we now had two rejections. Instead of walking out, though, he sat down next to me on the couch at the back of the room and whispered, "This is the best movie I've seen all year, but I've got to take a leak. Do you mind stopping it for a minute?" My heart soared as I frantically searched for the intercom to the projectionist. John went to the restroom and Marty popped a Valium. We grinned at each other as the visions of disaster retreated from the dark room. When the film was finally finished, Calley got up and, without consulting anyone, said that Warner would buy the film immediately.

By the time Marty and I had arrived in Beverly Hills for our 3 p.m. screening at Paramount, my lawyer had almost finished the deal with Frank Wells, the head of Business Affairs at Warners. Paramount had moved their executive offices from Hollywood into Beverly Hills as Charlie Bluhdorn, CEO of the parent company Gulf and Western, had sold the lot to an Italian real estate consortium that was then revealed to be a mafia front. We were met at the screening room by Peter Bart, who had written favorably for the *New York Times* about both Bluhdorn and Bob Evans, the head of production.

Peter was now vice president of production, and without delay he started the film. If Marty did have extra Valium on board, it was the right choice, because an hour into the film Bart signaled the projectionist to turn it off, then got up and thanked us for letting him see it. As he walked out of the room, he said it wasn't "Paramount quality." Two weeks later, however, Bob Evans started a meeting with Marty by asking why Paramount wasn't given a chance to buy *Mean Streets*. Marty relayed the Peter Bart story and left it at that. Although there is probably no connection, Bart left Paramount's employ a couple of months later.

Journalist and critic Peter Biskind called his book about this period in Hollywood *Easy Riders, Raging Bulls: How the Sex-Drugs-and Rock 'N Roll Generation Saved Hollywood*. That is a catchy title, but it doesn't really capture the serious nature of the artists that, for a few years at least, were given total creative control. History tells us that it is often the creative destruction of capitalism that unleashes new ideas, and certainly the economic downturn that hit all the major studios in the early 1970s opened the door to young artists who could work cheaply. At the moment we sold our film to Warners, 20th Century Fox was selling its backlot to a real estate developer to make the payroll. Paramount was doing the same. Warner Pictures was surviving because Warner Records was printing money. Embracing the young film school grads who could make pictures for $500,000 was not just trendy but imperative.

Marty seized the opportunity. Some call him a chronicler of damaged masculinity. Like the Johnny Boy character in *Mean Streets* that De Niro had so perfectly embodied, Marty's best characters are self-destructive: Jake LaMotta in *Raging Bull*, Henry Hill in *Goodfellas*, and even Rupert Pupkin in *The King of Comedy*. And for a time, especially when we were working together on *The Last Waltz*, Marty was himself Exhibit A for damaged masculinity. Drugs, women, cheating on your wife, almost dying—this was not a life, it was a suicide mission, and he had lots of enablers. I chose not to be one.

But like Eric Clapton and Robbie Robertson, when Marty hit the bottom, he picked himself up. He moved back to New York, quit drugs, became a caring father and a good boyfriend and finally a great husband to Helen Morris. I had to go through the same journey of pain and fear with wives and children, so I know a little about what it must have been like for him. Fortunately, I didn't also get caught up in the drug of choice in the late-1970s movie and music circles. Around coke, I was like the Woody Allen character who sneezes so badly when attempting to snort it that I'd send most of the drug onto the carpet. My allergies would go crazy, so I never could indulge, but when you are *not* partaking and the people you are working with are using A LOT OF COKE, it becomes a problem. Coke is a stupid drug because it makes you believe you are a lot smarter than you really are. Levon used to call it "philosopher's powder," and if you ever have experienced the aftermath of an all-night coke binge, you understand how it got that nickname. The artists would come in at noon with their "brilliant" ideas, but by 6 p.m. it was "never mind."

But as I say, Marty got better. And so did many of the artists who managed to survive the seventies. Although we lost Janis Joplin, Jimi Hendrix, and Jim Morrison in the first two years of the decade, I am delighted that Keith Richards and Eric Clapton are now healthier and happier than they were at any point back then. So are Marty and Robbie. As to Marty's characters . . . well, some of them come to some sort of peace. Marty is still spiritual enough to believe that "everybody's in," in the sense that, at least in Marty's world, Jake LaMotta is not going to hell. The last frame of *Raging Bull* ends with these lines from chapter 9 of the Gospel of John:

> "Whether or not he is a sinner, I do not know,"
> the man replied.
> "All I know is this: once I was blind and now I can see."

Faith plays a tricky role in the lives of artists. Both Eric Clapton and Marty have told me that their religion helped them out of the death spiral of drug addiction. As Eric wrote in his 2007 autobiography, "In the privacy of my room, I begged for help. I had no notion who I thought I was talking to, I just knew that I had come to the end of my tether . . . and, getting down on my knees, I surrendered."

13. Cannes Film Festival
1974

In early 1974 I was involved in an elaborate dance choreographed by David Geffen to get Bob Dylan signed to Geffen's Asylum Records label. David, knowing I was close to Robbie Robertson, invited me to a few parties at his Bel Air mansion. Warren Beatty, Jack Nicholson, Joni Mitchell, Jackson Browne—you get the picture. He then asked me to introduce him to Robbie, which I did. Once he had secured Robbie's friendship with a trip to Paris on his private jet for Robbie and his wife, along with David and his friend Joni Mitchell (an event later memorialized in Joni's song "Free Man in Paris"), I was no longer invited to the soirees. From Robbie, David secured a dinner with Bob Dylan, at which he pitched a tour, a live album with Dylan and the Band, and lots of money. Bob bit, and before anyone could have second thoughts, Bill Graham booked the tour, and Bob did a studio album for Asylum and ended his twenty-year relationship with Columbia Records.

Just before the tour got started I went to a party with most of the Band at Seymour Cassel's house on Kings Road above the Sunset Strip. Seymour had acted in a couple of John Cassavetes movies and was a huge fan of the Band. In my early days of coming to L.A., he also had the best pot—not the Mexican weed with all the seeds and stems but the good stuff, grown by some folks in Humboldt County. At Seymour's I was introduced to a stunning actress named Rosana DeSoto. She told me her story. She was from a family of nine kids, and both her mom and dad had come over from Mexico on the top of a freight car in the late 1940s and then settled in San Jose and become American citizens. Rosana had met the director Luis Valdez at San Jose State University and had worked with Valdez's El Teatro Campesino, which acted as the cultural arm of Cesar Chavez's United Farm Workers movement. The company would mount short plays on the back of a flatbed truck to show the plight of the country's migrant farmworkers. It was important stuff, and in Rosana I saw an artist who was still committed to politics, even if she was determined to break into Hollywood. We started dating and she took me up to her mom's house in San Jose. Her brothers and sisters were very amused at the tall, blond Anglo she had dragged home. The ultimate test was watching me eat menudo for breakfast one morning. Menudo, which Rosana's father swore was the greatest cure for a hangover, is cow stomach sautéed in a red chili pepper base. I passed the test but vowed this was a one-time-only experiment.

With Dylan now hooked up with Asylum, I helped get the tour started and then, because I had *Mean Streets* obligations, I passed the torch to Lindsay Holland, who managed the rest of Tour '74. But already in David Geffen I had seen the dark side of Hollywood that Marty Scorsese had warned me about when he showed me *The Bad and the Beautiful*. Some people just refuse to be denied what they want, and they will use anyone to get where they want to go. And those being used often have no clue until the deed has been done. It was that way for Bob Dylan too. As soon as the tour was over, he left Asylum and went back to Columbia Records. I don't know if he ever talked to David Geffen again. He realized David's main motivation in signing him was to screw Clive Davis, who ran Columbia. It was a classic Hollywood dick-measuring contest.

In February of 1974 Marty Scorsese and I were informed that *Mean Streets* had been chosen for the Cannes Film Festival, to be held that May. For both of us this was a high honor, and the fact that Marty's film paid homage to both the French New Wave and the Italian neorealist traditions made the honor from Europe extra special. Cannes loomed large in our imaginations because it was one of the original film festivals. The idea originated in 1938 at the Venice Film Festival after the jury changed its winner for best film an hour before the award ceremony under extreme pressure from Hitler and Mussolini. As the award was being given to German director Leni Riefenstahl's fascist documentary *Olympia*, the French delegation walked out and began planning a counter festival for the next year.

Before the first Cannes event happened, however, Hitler invaded Poland and the war was on. After the war, the first Cannes Film Festival was held in 1946, and by 1949, when Carol Reed's *The Third Man* won the grand prize, the festival was established as the place to launch auteur-driven pictures. In 1951 the French critic André Bazin started editing a film magazine called *Cahiers du cinema*, in which a young François Truffaut began writing about "la politique des auteurs." Truffaut advanced the theory that the director was the true author of a film and pointed not to the French tradition but to the genre films of America from directors like Alfred Hitchcock, Howard Hawks, Robert Aldrich, and Nicholas Ray. By 1960, when Federico Fellini's *La Dolce Vita* won the grand prize, the European auteurs from France, Italy, and Sweden were preeminent.

The films of Fellini meant so much to Marty that later in his career he personally paid to restore the print of *La Strada*, noting that Anthony Quinn's characterization of the brutish Zampanò influenced the De Niro characters in *Mean Streets*, *Taxi Driver*, and *Raging Bull*. When Marty and I arrived in Cannes in 1974, our friend Jay Cocks, a *Time* magazine film critic, announced that he had arranged an audience with Fellini in his suite at the Carlton hotel. We were midway though a half-hour talk with Fellini (he had not yet seen *Mean Streets*) when his wife, Giulietta Masina, blew in followed by Fellini's Italian distributor and three bellboys carrying huge bags emblazoned with the logos of Chanel and Yves Saint Laurent. The maestro went through a kind of comic opera performance, complaining about how his wife (and star) was spending all their money shopping on the Croisette. When things settled down, he introduced us to his distributor, saying, "This is Martin Scorsese, the American director. His new film is genius work. You must buy it today before it is shown in Cannes." What an extraordinary gesture of generosity from one veteran filmmaker to his young potential successor. Luckily for Fellini, *Mean Streets* was a great success in Italy and he never regretted his blind endorsement of Scorsese.

The night after the film was screened in Cannes, I took Marty and his girlfriend, Sandy Weintraub, along with De Niro and his girlfriend, Diahnne Abbott, and Rosana to the best restaurant in the South of France, Moulin des Mougins. It was here that Rosana really stepped up to save what could have been an awkward evening. It was an epic feast interrupted only by a classic De Niro moment: The soup course had just been served when a giant bumblebee began to buzz our table. Diahnne immediately began to freak out, saying she was allergic to bees, and I called the waiter over and pointed to the bee, which was circling Diahnne's soup. The waiter pulled the napkin off his arm and with exquisite aim snapped the bee, which proceeded to tumble *into* the soup. The waiter quickly removed the bowl, saying he would return in a moment with a replacement. But it was too late. Diahnne began to howl, "He killed the bee! He killed the bee!" and although Bobby told her to pipe down, she was unwilling to relent in her defense of the poor bee. At which point De Niro told her to shut up or leave. She immediately stood from the table in her very high heels and walked out of the room. I said to Bob, "I'll get her a taxi," to which he replied, "Don't move."

Rosana excused herself from the table to visit the powder room, but unbeknownst to us she was trying to convince Diahnne to come back. Diahnne's wounded pride was too strong, though, and she took off down the road toward Cannes. The meal went on for another hour as if nothing had happened, and afterward we piled into a taxi and started down the mountain road into town. About fifteen minutes into the ride we came across Diahnne, carrying her high heels as she walked along the street. Bob opened the door and said, "Get in." Diahnne complied and not another word was mentioned.

The next morning, Bob and Diahnne and Rosana and I were going to fly to Rome. Rosana, who had grown up in a house with four rambunctious brothers and learned early how to defend herself with her raucous wit, was also good at being the diplomat and was always able to defuse any tense situation. That, among many other things, so endeared me to her that I proposed in the fall of 1974. But back at Cannes that spring, Rosana was somehow able to get Bob De Niro's girlfriend Diahnne to laugh about how ridiculous she looked walking down to road from Mougins carrying her purse and her stiletto heels. Even Bob was appreciative of the effort and bought Diahnne a very expensive bottle of perfume at the airport as a peace offering.

De Niro was going to Rome to meet Bernardo Bertolucci about a film he was planning called *1900*. We had all seen Bertolucci's film *The Conformist*, and I personally thought he was the best director in the world at that time. We arrived in Rome on the evening of May 12, 1974, and Bertolucci had sent two limousines to the Excelsior hotel to pick up both us and *1900*'s other star, Gérard Depardieu, and bring us to his house for an elaborate dinner. As we were driving through the streets, most intersections were blocked by people celebrating the divorce referendum that had just that day decided in favor of keeping divorce legal in the country. Three years earlier the parliament had legalized divorce for the first time in Italian history, but the Catholic Church fought back and had a referendum to repeal the law placed on the ballot. That night the other side won and the right to divorce was retained.

The mood was festive overall, but the young people waving the red flags of the Communist Party in the streets did not take kindly to our huge Mercedes limos trying to make their way through the crowd. Young, seemingly drunk young men would pound on the hood and roof of our car. At one point they started rocking our car, and Diahnne was freaking out. The irony of trying to make our way to the home of the most communist-sympathizing director in Italy, while encased in a luxury limo from Germany, was lost on no one.

Bob De Niro is my generation's Brando. And like Brando he came into his political consciousness slowly. The son of a painter, he was always allied with the avant-garde, but he was not yet very political when he met Bernardo in Rome. My guess was that spending a few months making the epic *1900* had an effect on his connection between art and politics. In recent years he has been one of the most passionate voices in trying to fight the authoritarian urges of Trump.

The fact that before *Mean Streets* was even released De Niro was being sought after by both Francis Coppola (for *The Godfather Part II*) and Bernardo Bertolucci gives you a sense of the tight network of filmmakers in the early 1970s. The cultural historian Jacques Barzun described the competitive dynamic of the Italian renaissance as "the feverish interest, the opposition, and the rivalry among artists working, comparing, and arguing, generat[ing] the heat that raises performance beyond the norm." Something similar was happening among these filmmakers. When Marty had finished editing *Mean Streets* he took the first work print up to San Francisco with editor Marcia Lucas to show Francis Coppola. Francis loved the film and also loved De Niro's performance so much that he immediately proposed to Paramount that Bobby play the young Don Corleone in *The*

Godfather Part II. He also told Bertolucci about De Niro, which led to his casting in *1900*.

Bertolucci was a true original. I was able to maintain a good relationship with Bernardo for many years, and in some ways I think he gave more direction to what I would call the American New Wave than any other filmmaker. *The Conformist* directly influenced the work of Coppola and Scorsese, and you can see how that movie plugged Italian neorealism directly into the 1970s renaissance in the form of Hollywood New Wave. Look at Bertolucci's lighting and color palette and you will see it echoed in both *Godfather II* and *Taxi Driver*.

Bernardo understood the power of shadows. American filmmakers in the early fifties, shooting film noir in black-and-white, grasped it too, but once color came in, the Technicolor consultant on every Hollywood film was always pushing for "more light." But Bertolucci believed mood was much stronger with the darker hues. When Francis Coppola brought this same style to Hollywood with *The Godfather*, however, critics constantly carped that the film was too dark, and the cinematographer, Gordon Willis, was dubbed "the prince of darkness."

But there was another aspect of Bernardo's work that I truly admired—the political message. Both *The Conformist* and *1900* are essentially antifascist movies. Jean-Louis Trintignant's character in *The Conformist* is as perfect an exploration into the pathology of fascism as exists on film, even as it is submerged in a beautiful thriller filled with car chases, sex, and violence. The leading woman, Dominique Sanda, defined the sophisticated sexual power of that moment in time, and Bernardo explored the strange connection between male sexual insecurity and fascism. It is a masterpiece. For Bernardo, the fascism of the 1930s seemed to be relegated to history, yet he was aware that there was always a danger that it could return to contemporary politics.

The film that followed *The Conformist* was *1900,* and it is more complicated to make an assessment of that film. *1900* depicts the grand conflict between fascism and communism that gripped Italy in the first half of the twentieth century. The first cut was six hours long, and although the Italian distributor agreed to show it in two parts, the American distributor, Paramount, refused. They wanted Bernardo to deliver them a two-hour movie before they would pay their share of the production. At one point I organized with Blaine Novak and Russell Schwartz a company called the Film League, with the express purpose of getting the rights from Paramount to show Bernardo's film in two parts. We didn't succeed, and I regret it to this day because, for Bernardo, the failure to have his film seen as he had made it was a huge disappointment from which I'm not sure he ever recovered. Just as Orson Welles had lost control of his second film, *The Magnificent Ambersons*, and went on to a career of always fighting Hollywood (and mostly losing), so too was Bertolucci burned, and he never again reached the heights he had with *The Conformist* and *1900.*

In a strange way, those two films mark the end of a glorious era for European filmmaking. I believe that *Mean Streets* and *The Godfather* would not exist if it were not for the trail blazed by Fellini, De Sica, Godard, and Truffaut. The European films of the fifties and sixties were like school for Scorsese and Coppola. Just a few years earlier, at the Cannes Film Festival of 1968, Truffaut and Godard had successfully shut down the event in solidarity with the "événements de Mai," which saw students and workers striking all across France in protest of the De Gaulle regime and the autocratic powers the president was deploying against the students and the workers unions on the streets of Paris.

As entranced as I was about the political import of Bertolucci's films, I had come to wonder if that same power to make a statement had escaped the music business. If Woody Guthrie in 1935 was a starting point in the musical bond between artists and the real working class, and Bob Dylan in 1963 was the midpoint, the question then became where this union had run its course. Had the artists abandoned their solidarity with what Dylan called "the workingman's blues"?

In the fall of 1975, I got my answer. A friend of Peter Kaminsky's, Josh Feigenbaum, ran a radio syndication business called MJI Broadcasting, and he had been invited in August to the Bottom Line, a music club in Greenwich Village, to see Bruce Springsteen and the E Street Band. Bruce had put out a couple records that had not become hits, but a music critic we all respected named Jon Landau had seen the band at the Harvard Square Theater and had written, "I saw rock-and-roll future, and its name is Bruce Springsteen." Josh was a friend of Landau's and told me I had to see Springsteen.

In mid-October Bruce was booked at a small L.A. club on the Sunset Strip called the Roxy. My friend the film director Bobby Roth, who was close to Bruce's sister, Pamela, got some tickets and we went to the Roxy, knowing only that a song of his called "Thunder Road" was beginning to be played on the local alternative FM station.

What transpired that night renewed my faith in America's

ability to keep renewing its culture. When the band came on-stage the room was packed, and Jack Nicholson, Bob De Niro, Jackson Browne, and Carole King were in the audience. In a rather daring move, Bruce started the set with his new radio hit, "Thunder Road," but instead of simply recreating the recording, backed by a full band, he was accompanied only by Roy Bittan on piano, which was broken up with the occasional harmonica interlude from Bruce.

He had us from the get-go. As he sang "Don't turn me home again, I just can't face myself alone again," I felt an almost spiritual feeling come over me. I became a believer in the redemptive power of Bruce's work. He was only halfway through the set when he got to "Born to Run," and when he finished that one the room went crazy. The set ended with "Jungleland" and "Rosalita," two of his more complex compositions, and the audience was ecstatic. The band came back for an encore and, in a tribute to Carole King, played her song "Goin' Back," followed by Chuck Berry's "Carol." My first impression was that this was a *real* band, not just a frontman and some backup musicians. A great band has the ability to react to the moment—playing off each other so that each show is different—and the ability to stay together for decades, which the E Street Band has. But the more important insight I had that evening was that, in the midst of Bruce's blue-collar poetry, there was optimism—"Show a little faith, / There's magic in the night."

The evening after his four-night stand at the Roxy was over, I went to dinner with Bruce and Bobby Roth at a kosher Chinese food joint off the Sunset Strip called Roy's. Bruce was curious about everything—the movie business, politics, food—and I loved talking to him. He was such an anti-star, and as the years went on he only grew into his working-class-hero persona. I must have seen him perform about ten more times in the next decade, and he never disappointed. He was "the hardest working man in show business," with many concerts going on for four hours and only one intermission. But it wasn't "show business." I had seen Elvis in Las Vegas in the early 1970s, and *that* was show business. But because Bruce and his band were full of surprises, their shows always felt as authentic as anything Woody Guthrie ever did.

In January of 1975 Rosana and I got married in a ceremony at our Laurel Canyon home. Sara Dylan was a maid of honor and Bob and all of the Band came to the celebration, and by fall of 1975, Rosana was pregnant. The responsibilities of parenthood were scary for me, and I felt a new kind of pressure resting on my career. They say about the movie business that you can make a fortune but you can't make a living. It was in this unstable environment that I made a rookie mistake by being taken in by a Hollywood agent who represented the director Terry Malick. Malick had made a wonderful film called *Badlands* that had debuted at the same New York Film Festival at which we premiered *Mean Streets*. I was really anxious to work with him, and I know the agent sensed this.

The agent sent me Malick's new script, titled "The Gravy Train," about two young Southern boys who get in a lot of trouble in the big city. It was full of that classic Malick good-ol'-boy dialogue and had an action scene that ended with a giant wrecking ball killing one of the protagonists. The agent implied that Terry might direct it, but he was going to auction the script, so I had to move fast to tie it up. I bit and bought the script. I then found out Terry had no intention of directing the movie and had written it in three weeks because he was broke. What I had thought was an auteur project quickly turned into a job, and I laid it off on Roger Gimbel's company, Tomorrow Entertainment, to finance. Gimbel wanted to make it cheap, so we hired a journeyman director named Jack Starrett. Someone wrote about Starrett, "[His] work carries with it a palpable sense of danger, perhaps never more so than in the ruthlessly violent streak coloring this satire of American ambition."

I got a bunch of my friends (Stacy Keach, Frederic Forrest, Margot Kidder, and Barry Primus) to be in it. When we sneak-previewed the movie, the audience commented that they didn't know what the title "The Gravy Train" had to do with the movie. What had once been known as a colloquial term for hitting the jackpot had since become a dog food brand. They changed the title to *The Dion Brothers*.

The movie bombed, and I would not have thought about it again had a friend not sent me an article from *Esquire* in 2014. It turned out that in the batch of emails the North Koreans hacked from Sony Pictures was a correspondence between Sony president Amy Pascal and Quentin Tarantino about *The Dion Brothers*. Evidently Tarantino has his own print of the movie and was contemplating a remake. The *Esquire* writer ends his piece with, "We're just happy somebody's talking about this forgotten grindhouse masterpiece." It may be a cult favorite, but for me it was a bust.

Nothing was really happening in the movies because I was dependent on the success of *Mean Streets* for funds (another rookie assumption). Following *Mean Streets*, I hit a bit of a dry spell. I had no money coming in and needed *Mean Streets* to succeed if I hoped to continue making movies. It took almost four years for *Mean Streets* to start paying profits, but luckily it turned out to be a good investment. Marty, myself, and my financial partner Lee Perry still get a check from Warner Bros. every July—even forty years after the film was released. I had kept my hand in the music business as a way to pay the bills, but it was never a sure thing. This was all pretty stressful for Rosana, and she wanted her own career in the movies and was probably disappointed that I wasn't more helpful in getting her work. She had gotten a role on a TV show called *Barney Miller*, but it was somewhat haphazard as to how many episodes she would be in, and then the pregnancy put a stop to that.

They say that the arrival of a child often brings good fortune, and for me that turned out to be true. Our daughter, Daniela, was born in late June of 1976, and by early fall I was reunited with both Marty Scorsese and Robbie Robertson in one of the most satisfying moments of my career. I learned during this period that you often just have to move on from a project that doesn't work and never dwell on "if only"s. If you stay positive, good opportunities present themselves.

14. The Last Waltz

1976

When *Mean Streets* opened the New York Film Festival, Pauline Kael wrote an eight-page review celebrating the originality of the film. She pointed out one fact about Marty Scorsese that had turned out to be true for all time. She felt he was an original artist who would spend his life trying not to compromise his vision. Whether it was the dark anger of *Taxi Driver* or the anguished questioning of faith in *The Last Temptation of Christ*, Marty's movies always reflected the passion he had for getting them made, and he often spent years trying to get them produced in the way he envisioned them. The few times he did a "job" like *Cape Fear*, the results are far less satisfying.

For me the greatest example of his being willing to risk everything in pursuit of an obsession was *The Last Waltz*. In 1976 Robbie Robertson came to me with an idea: the Band wanted to call it quits and put on a final concert with all of their favorite musicians as guests, and they wanted to film the concert and put out an album. The question was how to raise the film above the level of an average concert documentary. I suggested that Marty Scorsese—both a fan of the Band and a student of the music film genre, having edited *Woodstock* and some documentaries on Elvis—might be interested in the concept. Robbie had already gotten Bill Graham to agree to put on the concert at Winterland in San Francisco on Thanksgiving night, and Eric Clapton, Van Morrison, Neil Young, Muddy Waters, Joni Mitchell, and Bob Dylan had agreed to perform. I knew that Marty was ten days into the shooting of *New York, New York,* his first big-budget movie, starring De Niro and Liza Minnelli, but I figured it was worth at least asking.

The chances of him being willing (or legally able) to shoot our documentary in the middle of his *New York, New York* production schedule were slim, but Robbie and I decided to give it a shot. I arranged a meeting with Marty at 9:30 the next night at his MGM Studios office. When we arrived, we were greeted by Stephen Prince, Marty's hangout guy and assistant. If you've seen *Taxi Driver*, Prince is the fast-talking gun dealer that sells De Niro the .44 Magnum pistol, and for Marty in real life he was bodyguard, driver, and coke connection all rolled into one.

Prince was quietly famous in Marty's circle for an incident that had occurred six months earlier, in the spring of 1976, while they were prepping *New York, New York*. One day while opening his mail, Marty had come across an envelope on which the address was constructed of letters and numbers cut from a newspaper. Thirty years of watching movies in which people get letters like that spooked him, and as he told me recently, he opened the letter "with a sinking feeling in my heart."

He took out the letter, which was also written with cut-out newsprint. It read:

> If little Jodie wins the Academy Award for what YOU made her do, You will DIE.

Marty freaked. Jodie Foster, who was fourteen years old, had just been nominated for an Academy Award for her portrayal of a teenage prostitute in *Taxi Driver*.

Stephen's solution was to call the FBI. He went to the couch, picked up the phone, and dialed a number. He had boasted several times about being connected to the FBI, but everyone had thought it was bullshit. But sure enough, he was soon talking to an agent he knew on a first-name basis, and we listened as he described the situation and then hung up.

"The FBI will be here in twenty minutes."

Marty cracked. "What! What about the coke in the office?"

"We'll get rid of it!" Then Stephen picked up the phone and dialed one of the editors. "Bring a large film can to Marty's office."

In a few minutes the editor was walking out with ten grams in a can just as the FBI agents walked in. They put on their surgical gloves and looked over the letter. Then they got very serious and turned toward Marty: "How many days until the Oscars?"

"Ten."

"Well, you're not going to have to worry, Mr. Scorsese. Stephen has explained to us how important a man you are. We'll assign an agent to be with you twenty-four hours a day. He'll be right next to you and nobody's gonna kill you. I'll have the first agent here in an hour."

When the agents left with the evidence, Marty's first reaction was his usual reaction to anything stressful: rage. He had torn so many phones out of the wall that the MGM phone guys had rigged a special cable that would just unplug when he yanked it, and Marty asked his staff to give him breakaway water glasses and breakaway chairs, just like the stuntmen use, for his periodic office rages.

"Prince, you idiot. Now I'm gonna have a goddam FBI agent on my ass twenty-four hours a day, even in the fuckin' toilet. I'm in preproduction on the biggest movie of my life. And I'm snorting a gram of coke a day. Where is this supposed to happen?"

Stephen cowered in the corner as the telephone hurtled his way. "I'll figure it out, Marty. I promise."

And figure it out he did. Even though the movie they were prepping was shot mostly on soundstages, Prince decided that they would need to do a lot of "location scouting." Marty and Stephen would go in one car, and the FBI guy would follow in another. For ten days they drove all over the place, hiding cocaine, and then Jodie didn't win and the dogs were called off.

The postscript was that it turned out that the letter had probably been sent by a man named John Hinckley, Jr. Eighteen months later, when Robbie and I were making *Carny* with Jodie Foster and Gary Busey, Hinckley showed up and tried to get hired as an extra. He had by that time sent so many letters to Jodie that her mother had a permanent security company working for them, and I had to throw Hinckley off the set three times before the police of Savannah, Georgia, threatened to lock him up and he left town. A few months later he turned his rage on Ronald Reagan, injuring him and several security personnel in a gun attack. I never did understand how his obsession with Jodie fit into that assassination attempt except as further evidence that Hinckley was not well.

The night I introduced Marty Scorsese to Robbie Robertson, a partnership was formed that has survived for more than forty years. That they should become both close friends and artistic collaborators was perhaps inevitable given their similar world-view. On a philosophical level, both men were grounded in a spiritual tradition (Marty wanted to be a priest, and Robbie felt close to the Six Nations spirituality) that they had abandoned in their teenage years and eventually come back to after a journey into the ninth circle of hell. But throughout their personal journeys of pain, both had survived their struggles and refused to let the past compromise their artistic vision. Robbie never tried to make a pop record, and Marty never tried to make a franchise film.

The crazy times weren't all behind them, though, and in the two years after they met, they went through a level of mutual madness that was pretty extreme. While we were editing *The Last Waltz*, they both lived in a house Marty owned on Mulholland Drive. All of the windows had blackout drapes, and they used to boast that they stayed up late enough to see the sunrise every morning before retiring to their separate bedrooms, where they would sleep until four in the afternoon. Steve Prince acted as projectionist on that project, and in a weird way he was almost like a contemporary version of the Erich von Stroheim character in *Sunset Boulevard*, screening a couple of movies every night after midnight for the boys and the various women who came to hang out.

When we finally had the rough cut of *The Last Waltz* ready, we decided to have a screening for our friends and the United Artists brass at the Cary Grant Theater on the MGM lot. It was the first time we had ever projected the film, and we were thrilled that the decision to shoot it in 35mm had created a sense of being on the stage that was at that time rarely seen in rock-and-roll documentaries. Everything was going beautifully, until we got to the Neil Young song "Helpless." I was sitting right behind Neil's manager Elliot Roberts, and by the end of the first verse of the song, the twenty-foot-high close-up of Neil revealed something we had never seen on the editing bench: a large piece of cocaine was slowly falling out of Neil's right nostril. The more he put his heart and soul into the song, the farther the rock of coke tumbled onto his mustache. Elliot began to slip lower in his seat until he seemed to disappear. The audience of cognoscenti began to titter, and by the time the tune was finished, people were in near hysterics. When the movie finished, Elliot turned to me and said we had to take Neil completely out of the movie, despite the beauty of his performance. I asked for a week to see what I could do.

The next morning, I showed up at Pacific Title, a first-rate film optical house, with the reel of Neil's song. They put it on the Moviola with a magnifying glass, and the fifty-eight-year-old dean of the house, Roy, looked at the film while I explained Mr. Young's embarrassment that a piece of snot had fallen out of his nose during his performance. He asked me to come back in two days while they addressed the problem. When I returned, Roy told me he had invented a "traveling booger mat" with which he would reshoot each and every frame by moving a small black dot over the offending spot. A week later we had our film back, with the coke rock magically erased. The bill was a mere $10,000. Needless to say, Elliot didn't think it was a recoupable expense from Neil's royalty account on the soundtrack, and I agreed to eat it.

Looking at *The Last Waltz* nearly a half a century later, it is an astonishing film that captures a group of musicians at the height of their craft. The Band never played better. Their songs—from "Up on Cripple Creek" to "The Night They Drove Old Dixie Down"—represent the realization of a hundred years of American folk, country, and rockabilly flowing through the vessel of four Canadians and a man from Arkansas. But just as importantly, their backing from players like Muddy Waters, Van Morrison, Eric Clapton, Bob Dylan, Neil Young, Joni Mitchell, and Dr. John also captured for posterity the very best music of a generation. It is a film for the time capsule, filled with truth and sorrow, but always based in the essential notion that this wonderful wellspring of American music that flowed from the churches and bars of the Mississippi Delta could be shared by musicians from Arkansas, Ontario, Ireland, England, Tennessee, Louisiana, and Vancouver. There was common ground.

15. Rolling Thunder and Beyond

1980

Although I had spent most of 1976 and 1977 working on *The Last Waltz*, the convergence of my two worlds of rock and movies seemed to be reaching a crescendo. Bob Dylan had embarked in late 1975 on a tour called the Rolling Thunder Revue and was also filming a movie of the tour, to be cut with other footage, called *Renaldo and Clara*. One of my best friends, T Bone Burnett, had assumed the role of bandleader for Rolling Thunder. I had met him in 1967 in Fort Worth, Texas, because he was a friend of my college roommate Lindsay Holland. T Bone's band used to play in a club in a Black neighborhood called the New Bluebird Nite Club. He was one of the few white acts to play there and had a really integrated following.

The supporting cast of Rolling Thunder was filled with friends, including Bob Neuwirth, Joni Mitchell, Sam Shepard, Steven Soles, and David Mansfield. T Bone equated the aggressive nature of Bob's music to an early punk rock tour. The tour was going well, but *Renaldo and Clara* wasn't very good, and many years later Marty Scorsese recut many of the music sequences and made a new film of Rolling Thunder, which came out on Netflix in 2019. It retains some of Bob's perpetual desire to blend truth and fiction; it is filled with tall tales and characters that were never there.

Neither version of the film makes mention of some of the real dramas that took place on the tour, like the tumultuous affair between Sam Shepard and Joni Mitchell, so beautifully portrayed in Joni's song "Coyote," with its lines "Now he's got a woman at home / He's got another woman down the hall / He seems to want me anyway." I think Joni writes better about contemporary life and love than any of her peers. Her self-description in "A Case of You" says it all:

> Oh, I am a lonely painter
> I live in a box of paints
> I'm frightened by the devil
> And I'm drawn to those ones that ain't afraid.

For T Bone, Soles, and Mansfield, Rolling Thunder was a giant step. When the tour ended they formed a group called the Alpha Band and asked me to be their manager. It turned out to be both extraordinary and frustrating. To try to get a record deal, we took a rather oblique route. We rented a house in the town of Tesuque, a few miles outside of Santa Fe, New Mexico, and as the Band had done at Big Pink, the guys would get up every morning and gather in the living room after breakfast to work on the new material. T Bone played lead guitar, Steven Soles played rhythm guitar, and David Mansfield played man-dolin, fiddle, guitar, and keyboards. They were backed by the rhythm section of Matt Betton and David Jackson.

After about three weeks of woodshedding, I booked them into a small club in Tesuque. Within a week, word had spread and it was standing room only in the club. I had never seen anything come together that quickly and totally catch fire. In the second week of the club engagement I called my friend Roger Birnbaum, who worked for Clive Davis at Arista Records. Roger took a chance and flew to Albuquerque and made it to the second show, on a Wednesday night. The band just killed it, and the crowd was going crazy. T Bone sang a song called "Interviews" behind a bass- and drum-heavy shuffle beat. The lyrics depict interviews with three characters that represent T Bone's view of contemporary capitalism: a wrestler, a gambler, and a carnival barker who "the people at the next table think . . . might be Russ Meyer." It was a brilliant mashup of blues, punk, Dylan-like lyrics, and a kind of pre-rap spoken word and singing delivery.

Roger found a payphone in a bar next door and called Clive at home, insisting he had to fly down immediately. Clive showed up in a blue blazer and gray flannels the next evening and by the end of the second set had convinced me and the band to sign with Arista for a pretty large advance.

We woke up the following morning with the arrogance of youth—this rock star stuff is not so hard. But of course it was, which is why you probably have never heard of the Alpha Band. We recorded the first album over three nights in August of 1976. When it was time to do the album cover, I got the great fashion photographer Deborah Turbeville to come to L.A. to do the photos. But in the spirit of T Bone's rather dark view of the future, he chose as the shooting location a building that had been destroyed in the L.A. riots and never restored. Then, in choosing the cover image, he insisted on a picture in which the band was so far in the background that the bombed-out building was all you could see. Both Clive and I believed that the artist should choose his cover art, so no one really complained. It was obvious that T Bone was not interested in being a rock star.

That became even more evident when the Alpha Band was booked as the opening act for the Doobie Brothers' arena tour. The Alpha proto-punk attitude did not fit too well with the Doobies' audience, and when the reaction was not great, T Bone took to playing the set with his back turned to the crowd. It went downhill from there. The concert wasn't a success, but that doesn't mean the band was no good. Sometimes breakthroughs are just a matter of timing. No one who saw the Alpha Band in that small club in New Mexico will deny that it was one of the most amazing shows they've ever experienced. Ask Roger Birnbaum. But somehow the transition from a club to a sixteen-thousand-seat arena is just too much. I'm partially responsible for thinking the band should have done that.

Quite often, business setbacks have an effect on one's home life, and that was certainly true for me. I was spending a fair amount of time and money developing screenplays, but like any independent producer, getting a studio to commit $10 million to a project was a heavy lift. I used to participate in a weekly poker game with some of the best young screenwriters and producers in town—people like Tony Bill, John Byrum, John Brower, Jeff Fiskin, Danilo Bach, Paul Schrader, and an amazing woman named Lizzie Gill, who could hold her own with any of the guys whose egos led them to believe they were Ben Hecht reborn. The games were excellent and amusing company, but you couldn't pay the rent on my measly poker winnings.

My wife, Rosana, had come into my orbit at a very high point. She met George and Pattie Harrison on our third date, and we flew first-class to New York and Cannes and to meet Fellini, Bertolucci, and other lions of the cinema. It was all pretty heady, but even I knew I couldn't sustain that glory forever. Perhaps she (as an actress) thought that her connection to me would naturally lead to roles, but eventually she figured out that producers can't give roles to actors—that's the director's job. As the financial strains increased, we took to arguing about money. Rosana came from a family in which people would fight and then make up and act as if nothing had happened. But I nursed the wounds from her sharp tongue for days. By early 1978, she and I had split. Later on she told our daughter that I "didn't fight for" her, and maybe that was true. She soon moved in with David Ward, who had won the Academy Award for Best Screenplay for *The Sting* in 1974 and was planning a directing career. Rosana and I parted on good terms and are friends to this day.

My home life had much to be desired, but I was surrounded by good friends, and there were two genuine rock stars whose company I enjoyed in the late 1970s. The first was Jackson Browne. Jackson, Jeff Fiskin, and I worked for about six months on a movie idea that we were never able to get made. We all took it in stride and realized the marriage of film and rock was not fully consummated. To me, Jackson's song "The Pretender" is the most perfect realization of how our dreams of the 1960s were fading as we rolled toward the age of Ronald Reagan.

> *I'm gonna find myself a girl*
>
> *Who can show me what laughter means*
>
> *And we'll fill in the missing colors*
>
> *In each other's paint-by-number dreams*
>
> *And then we'll put our dark glasses on*
>
> *And we'll make love until our strength is gone*
>
> *And when the morning light comes streaming in*
>
> *We'll get up and do it again*
>
> *Get it up again.*

Two years after the breakup of my marriage, I longed to find that girl who could show me what laughter means. In the summer of 1979 I found her sitting in a sushi bar at 2:30 in the afternoon. We were the only two people in the restaurant, and the sushi chef made us sit next to each other. Her name was Lesley Gilb, and she was gorgeous—tall and lean with a wicked sense of play. We hit it off immediately and she reminded me of the forthrightness of some of the girls I had met on the road in the sixties. She had been scraping by as a part-time assistant to a TV producer when we started dating, and within a month she told me she wasn't interested in fooling around. She was convinced we were meant to be together. Being the serial monogamist that I was, I asked her to move in with me.

After she moved into my house, I was introduced to one of

her girlfriends, an actress named Lois Chiles. Lois was from Texas and had a sarcastic wit. Lesley and Lois together kept everyone on their toes. Lois had been a model but done a only little acting before she got two big roles—as Robert Redford's college sweetheart in *The Way We Were* and as Jordan Baker in *The Great Gatsby* (again with Robert Redford). By the time I met her she had just finished filming her notorious role as Dr. Holly Goodhead in the James Bond film *Moonraker.* (1979 was long ago, but can you imagine a screenwriter using that name for a character today?)

Lois's boyfriend was Don Henley of the Eagles, and the four of us began to spend time together. They made an interesting pair—both Texans but from distinctly different social classes. Lois's family was from oil money, and she was probably at the country club most afternoons in the summer when she was growing up. Don, by contrast, was either working in his father's auto parts shop or hoeing the long rows of the family's cornfield. Living in the tiny East Texas town of Linden, Don learned to play the drums because he was unathletic and music was like a magic carpet that transported him up and away from the sometimes-suffocating small-town life. He was like Rick Danko and Levon Helm in that they had grown up in a place with no local radio stations, so they only had access to the big "clear channel" stations from Nashville and New Orleans. That was their musical education, and it was pretty eclectic.

Hotel California was one of the most important albums of the seventies, but by the time I started hanging out with Henley I sensed a certain exhaustion that I had seen in George Harrison in 1969 and Robbie Robertson in 1975. The road is a cruel mistress, and keeping a band together is an object lesson in the tension between the individual and the collective. The very fact of getting four or five artists to cooperate without letting ego get in the way kind of defies the reality of creative business. Can you imagine Picasso being in a band? Even Janis Joplin had to leave Big Brother and the Holding Company to thrive. The sad thing is that there should have been room (there certainly was money) for each of the Beatles to do their own solo projects without having to kill off the Beatles as a group. That said, even a manager is helpless to stop a band from breaking up if animus grows between the members. I recall talking to one of the managers of the Beatles about the period of making *Let It Be*, when Paul and John were at odds. When John would bring Yoko to the recording sessions and sit her right next to him in the studio, it would drive Paul crazy. And yet there was nothing the management team could do to solve the problem.

By 1980, when Don Henley and Lois Chiles visited Lesley and me on our honeymoon in Maui, he knew his band was going to break up. He later told me that it had him at loose ends, as "my whole identity, my sense of self was, unfortunately, wrapped up in that band." The great irony is that when the compact disc was introduced in 1981, everyone renewed their record collection, and by 1983 the Eagles' compilation *Their Greatest Hits (1971–1975)* became one of the two biggest sellers of all time. In addition, during the Eagles' fourteen-year hiatus, rock radio had continued to play their extensive catalog. Though various band members had solo success during the 1980s, none of them achieved the heights the band had reached in its heyday. The Eagles' long absence from the live concert scene had made the hearts of the fans grow fonder, and by 1994, the demand was so big that Don and his partner, Glenn Frey, had no choice but to put the band back together and go on the road playing stadium tours around the world. Their once-close relationship had unraveled in the late 1970s, but money and global adoration have a way of lubricating tension.

These days, though, it's not just about fortune and fame. They've had that, now, for almost fifty years. As Don told me recently, "It has become more gratifying, more soul-satisfying, with each passing year, to be able to get up on a stage and provide people with two and a half hours' worth of comfort and joy . . . an escape from the relentless, dread-inducing onslaught of the twenty-four-hour news cycle." But, beyond continuing to play for huge crowds around the world, Don has also kept faith with his fellow artists by being one of the most eloquent spokespersons for artists rights in the continuing battle with Google and YouTube.

The one band that seemed to be immune to the ego battles that plagued the Beatles, the Band, and the Eagles was U2. I saw them for the first time in March of 1982 at the L.A. Memorial Sports Arena, and the show almost instantly renewed my faith in rock and roll as an instrument of enlightenment and joy. Bono knew how to write inspirational hymns that then became a part of our collective awakening from the torpor of the Reagan era, and his three bandmates had an almost magical ability to make a huge sound (from only drums, guitar, and bass) that was perfect for getting fifteen thousand voices chanting in unison. The guitar player, Edge, had some real electronic tricks to his guitar sound that I never quite could conjure. It was genius.

Today's streaming scene has made even U2 change their approach. Back in 1987, the Edge would begin "Where the Streets Have No Name" with forty seconds of ambient noise. Then a guitar arpeggio enters and accelerates into the driving rhythm of the drums and bass, which arrive about a minute into the song. Nearly two minutes pass before Bono starts to sing. They still do this onstage, but services like Spotify have reshaped the music business—and pop songs. If the singing doesn't start immediately, users click to the next tune.

I come back to Pete Townshend's question of What it was that rock and roll tried to start and has failed to finish. When I posed Townshend's challenge to Bono, he wrote me back:

> U2 did all the dull things that change requires before it enters real life. Less revolution more evolution. We tried and succeeded to get actual change across the line by discovering the most forbidden word in the lexicon that was rock. The word was compromise.
>
> We set up the ONE Campaign [to fight poverty and disease] because you don't have to agree on everything to work with someone if the ONE thing you agree on is important enough.

If U2 was the last great band of the rock era, I think they succeeded in continuing what the Beatles had started. Whether rock's project is finished is an open question, but U2 has represented the notion that we can take all the anger and sadness flowing from war and assassination and turn it toward a mass celebration of hope and community. That's what a U2 or a

Springsteen concert feels like. The very act of rock is that bands are collectives that have come together and freed themselves from fear. It is *daring* to go out there in front of twenty thousand expectant fans and not let them down. That is why Robbie Robertson wrote "Stage Fright"—he hadn't yet freed himself from the fear. In the *Times* interview in which Pete Townshend asked his probing question, he addressed what he thought was rock's failure: "What we were hoping to do was to create a system by which we gathered in order to hear music that in some way served the spiritual needs of the audience. It didn't work out that way. We abandoned our parents' church, and we haven't replaced it with anything solid and substantial." I'm not sure what Pete said is true, and I do believe that both U2 and Springsteen have tried to fill the spiritual emptiness that is so much a part of our postmodern era. In that sense, they are the true heirs of Walt Whitman, who, as Richard Rorty wrote, "hoped that America would be the place where a religion of love would replace a religion of fear."

Over the years I have continued to see U2 whenever they come to L.A., and it has never gotten stale. And Bono has kept faith with all musicians. Once in 2016, after I had written an op-ed in the *New York Times* entitled "Do You Love Music? Silicon Valley Doesn't," I got a wonderful email from Bono asking how he could help the cause. I wrote him back with a couple of suggestions and included my phone number in case he wanted to talk further. A day later, as I was hiking in the Santa Monica mountains near my home, Bono called and we had a twenty-minute talk about steps he could take to try to help Google and YouTube understand they had to respect artists' rights. I suppose it is a tribute to the power and arrogance of the tech monopolists that we were no more successful in this effort than we have been in getting Facebook and YouTube to police the paid disinformation spread through their platforms.

16. Under Fire

1980

Rock and roll and movies continued to coexist in my life, and in the late 1970s and early 1980s there was still a liberal spirit in L.A. It allowed me to get my most political movie made.

In June 1979, Bill Stewart, an ABC News correspondent, was killed in Managua, Nicaragua, by a government soldier. Stewart had been covering the civil war between the government of longtime dictator Anastasio Somoza DeBayle and the Sandinista rebels. Stewart's soundman described his murder to the *New York Times* in 1979.

> I saw Bill on his knees with his hands raised. The guardsmen approached and motioned for them to lie face down. Then one guard walked over and kicked Bill in the side, and we realized there was a problem. He moved back, motioned like he wanted Bill to put his hands on his head, at least that's what it appeared like from where we were. Bill started to put his hands on his head but as he did so, the guard took one step forward, as I recall, and shot Bill once in the head with a rifle.

I had recently read *Dispatches* by Michael Herr, a riveting account of his life as a war correspondent in Vietnam, and I was drawn to the notion that the correspondents and photographers were a different breed—true action junkies. Herr describes the depression that enveloped him once he left the war zone, and the constant desire to find a new conflict to cover. And the action junkies weren't just men. Clare Hollingworth, Martha Gellhorn, and Lee Miller were in the trenches during World War II. In the Vietnam War, reporters including Kate Webb, Elizabeth Becker, Sylvana Foa, and Frances Fitzgerald served alongside nervy photojournalists like Catherine Leroy, Dickey Chapelle, and Françoise Demulder.

I decided to do a movie built around war correspondents in Central America, and I got a young writer named Clay Frohman to take a trip with me down to Guatemala and Nicaragua. After that journey we knew for sure that our sympathies lay with the rebels and not the corrupt government troops that had murdered Bill Stewart. Clay wrote a really good first draft of the script we called *Under Fire*.

A young British editor named Roger Spottiswoode was working at the studio I now owned, called Lion's Gate Films, which I had bought from Robert Altman in 1981. I got the script of *Under Fire* to Roger, and he came back and said he wanted to direct it. This was a bit of a risk, because he had only directed one film at that point, but I had developed a theory that editors (like Scorsese) make the best directors, because they can always figure out which setups are superfluous, especially when time pressures inevitably build.

Roger had a young writer friend named Ron Shelton who

had some wonderful ideas for heightening the drama. He and a war photographer friend, Matthew Naythons, took a quick trip to Managua, and in eight weeks we had a second draft. Roger had a mentor in Karel Reisz, who had directed both *The French Lieutenant's Woman* and, more importantly, *Who'll Stop the Rain* with Nick Nolte. Nick was perfect for the lead role of a cynical action-junkie photographer, and after he signed on, we took the script to Mike Medavoy, who had purchased *The Last Waltz* and had since left United Artists with his partners Arthur Krim and Eric Pleskow to form a new studio called Orion.

By the time Orion agreed to finance *Under Fire* for $8 million in late 1981, the Sandinistas had overthrown the Somoza government and were instituting a cultural revolution, partially with the help of $99 million in aid sent by the Carter administration. Jimmy Carter had strongly condemned the murder of Bill Stewart, and most of the Organization of American States had supported the Sandinistas, but by late 1981 the Reagan administration had decided that Nicaragua was the new Cuba and they started supporting a counterrevolutionary force called the Contras. All of this was just background for us, because we had centered our story on the killing of an American journalist right before the revolution. Gene Hackman signed on to play a fictional version of Bill Stewart, and Joanna Cassidy, whom we had all loved in *Blade Runner*, took the role of the fearless correspondent torn between two men.

We moved the *Under Fire* company to the town of Oaxaca, Mexico, which became our stand-in for Managua. We gave the art department a book of photographs that Susan Meiselas had taken in Managua during the revolution, and used them to transform a few blocks of Oaxaca with the distinct pastels of Nicaraguan houses. Our budget of $8 million was not a lot for a war movie, but we were aided by two factors. First was Roger's ability to shoot each setup with two cameras. Helping him with this was our extraordinary director of photography, John Alcott, who had shot most of Stanley Kubrick's films. John traveled with very few lights and used large scrims to bounce natural light into the set. He had a small crew of Englishmen who had been all over the world with him, augmented by an amazing Mexican crew of riggers, set dressers, and wardrobe, armorer, and special-effects men and women. Most of the Mexico crew had been making movies since the 1950s, when John Ford, Henry Hathaway, and John Wayne shot their Westerns in Durango. One old grip told me the story of going to church on the last week of a shoot and having the local priest say a blessing for their "Durango families" (including girlfriends and children) before they returned to their other families in Mexico City.

The second factor that saved our budget was pure luck. I had a good friend named Bernard Faucher who had lived all over Central and South America. He was working for me at Lion's Gate and was serving as a go-between with the Mexican army to secure our use of soldiers and tanks for the war scenes. We had long negotiations and knew that some of the money we were promising them might not make it into the government treasury, but we nevertheless finally signed a deal that guaranteed us a certain number of soldiers and tanks for twenty-five days for a fairly substantial number of pesos. Five days later the government drastically devalued the peso, which meant our whole army fee ended up being only around $15,000. Pure luck.

As it happened, I needed all the luck I could get, in part because Nick Nolte was in one of his wild-man phases. Cocaine and tequila were his lubricants of choice, and he never seemed to run out of either. He had a stuntman who was included in his contract for every movie, and I think part of his job was to make sure the stash was never empty. On the fourth day of the shoot, Nolte's driver showed up at the set saying that Nick was not in his hotel room. It turned out he had decided to take up residence at Oaxaca's finest whorehouse. His contract provided him a good per diem for hotel and food, and I figured how he spent it was his business.

We finished the film on time and under budget, and I was thrilled with Roger's first cut. I had given him a piece of temp music by the jazz guitarist Pat Metheny to underscore the Nolte-Cassidy love scene, and although we had hired the great composer Jerry Goldsmith to do the score, Roger had so fallen in love with the Metheny tune that he insisted Jerry work it into the score and have Pat play at the recording session. The score ended up getting nominated for an Academy Award.

Arthur Krim, the chairman of Orion, arranged for a preview screening of the film at the Motion Picture Association of America theater in Washington, D.C. Jack Valenti, who ran the MPAA, invited all the foreign-policy movers and shakers, including Reagan's secretary of state, Alexander Haig, and his three top deputies. In his memoir, Christopher Hitchens describes Haig as having a "usual engorged position of being crazy for anything that was militaristic, sadistic and butch in a uniform," so we figured he was unlikely to enjoy a film about a group of young guerillas overthrowing a brutal military dictatorship. About thirty minutes into the film, when it was obvious this was not *Back to Bataan* set in Central America, Haig and his deputies very noisily got up and left the screening. Pretty soon the nascent conservative movement too had the knives out for the sensibilities of our film. Luckily for us, Roger Ebert loved the film. He got the sense of ethical ambivalence we were all living with in the early Reagan years. In 1983 he wrote:

> There are, in fact, a lot of ethical stands not taken in this movie. It could almost have been written by Graham Greene; it exists in that half-world between exhaustion and exhilaration, between love and cynicism, between covering the war and getting yourself killed. This is tricky ground, and the wrong performances could have made it ridiculous.
>
> The actors in *Under Fire* never step wrong. Nolte is great to watch as the seedy photographer with the beer gut. Hackman never really convinced me that he could be an anchorman, but he did a better thing. He convinced me that he thought he could be one. Joanna Cassidy takes a role that could have been dismissed as "the girl" and fills it out as a fascinating, textured adult. *Under Fire* surrounds these performances with a vivid sense of place and becomes, somewhat surprisingly, one of the year's best films.

But Ebert was not enough to save the picture. The *New York Times* went so far as to have its UN correspondent write a political evaluation of the film. This paragraph tells you all you need to know:

Given the current situation in Latin America, it seems very likely that the choice made by the journalists will be hotly disputed by some who see the film. For one thing, there is the question of political judgment. The film portrays the Sandinistas—against whom the United States Government is supporting a guerrilla war—in a favorable light, as idealistic and handsome youths fighting for the cause of liberation, not hardbitten and ruthless Communists.

Perhaps we were naive in our depiction of the rebels. Daniel Ortega—leader of Nicaragua from 1979 to 1990, and now again since 2007—has, like all autocrats, become incredibly corrupt. Perhaps if Carter had won the 1980 election and the United States had continued to support the Sandinistas, the situation in Central America that now plagues us might have turned out differently. Reagan supported, with guns and money, not only the Contras but also dictators in Guatemala, El Salvador, and Honduras. His successors neglected the whole region, which then became a key transit point for the Colombian drug cartels and subsequently emerged as the most violent area on the planet. And now we wonder why so many families are fleeing to come to the United States for asylum?

I guess with *Under Fire* I tested the boundaries of corporate tolerance for dissent. Orion Pictures held up under the criticism and I am still proud of what we made together. Like many of my films, it did better in Europe, and in 1984 I stood on a stage in Rome and received the Italian version of an Academy Award (Ente David di Donatello) for Best Foreign Film from Bernardo

Bertolucci. I returned home to our small rented house in Santa Monica, now bursting at the seams with Lesley and our two children, Nicholas and Blythe. Coming off a movie that was a financial flop in the States, I had no idea how I was going to afford a bigger house. The answer came from the strangest of circumstances.

17. Saving Disney

1984

American capitalism had always run a boom-and-bust cycle, as any historian of the panics of 1837, 1857, 1869, 1873, 1893, 1903, 1907, 1929, and 2008 would tell you. By the late 1960s, economists had come to believe that fiscal and monetary policy had eliminated the extremes of the business cycle, but by the mid-1970s, after the Arab oil embargo, the American economy began to fall into a condition known as "stagflation"—a brutal combination of business stagnation and unemployment mixed with the inflation brought on by rapidly rising energy prices. The low return on equities left institutional investors dissatisfied until a financial Svengali by the name of Michael Milken arrived on the scene in late 1978 at the investment firm of Drexel Burnham Lambert. For Milken, the solution to the ailing American business economy was simple: What we needed was leverage—having much more debt to each dollar of equity would "juice" the returns. And since many of the companies Milken wanted to work his magic on were considered less than credit-worthy, Milken invented his own currency: the high-yield bond, or junk bond.

What followed was an orgy of corporate raids and leveraged buyouts, all financed by a circle of Savings and Loan CEOs who loved the 11 percent interest that the junk bonds were paying at the time and who were confident that Milken would always keep the market for the bonds liquid. Thus began the financialization of the American economy. Whereas the conventional capital structure of the American corporation had been relatively conservative, now any corporation that wasn't leveraged to the gills would find itself a target of Milken's raiders. This theory resonated in the media industries, which by 1984 were becoming an important part of the nation's economy.

It's hard to understand, but in 1963 movies and music did not constitute a large part of the American economy. In 1963 the total U.S. box office revenues for the year were $425 million, an amount that might now come in over the course of one week during the summer. In 2019 the total U.S. box office revenues were $11.45 billion. The biggest grossing movie of 1963 was *Cleopatra*, which made $56 million; by contrast, 2019's big seller was *Avengers: Endgame*, which took in more than $858 million. Even adjusting for inflation, the growth in entertainment revenues is stunning. In 1963, the number-one-selling music album was the soundtrack for the movie version of *West Side Story*, and the year's total recorded music sales were $698 million. Today, despite all the value destruction caused by Internet piracy, total music revenues are close to $10 billion.

By 1983, corporate forces were in control of the music and movie business. The era of the blockbuster had arrived. In 1983 George Lucas had created the first modern movie franchise, *Star Wars*, by opening a second and third chapter in what was to become at least a twelve-chapter story. But the scale of budgets had also grown exponentially. Whereas the first *Star Wars* movie had cost only $11 million, the third in the series, *Return of the Jedi*, had a budget of $32 million. The financier and distributor, 20th Century Fox, was not complaining, though. The opening weekend for *Star Wars* had taken in $1.5 million. The opening weekend of *Jedi* took in $23 million.

In music, the same blockbuster dynamic was taking hold. In 1983 Michael Jackson released *Thriller*, which has sold more than sixty million copies worldwide. Jackson then demanded an advance of $5 million per album plus a 25 percent royalty to renew his contract with Sony's Epic Records. This changed the economics of the music business radically. By contrast, in the 1970s the Band would get an advance of $75,000 per record and would earn royalties only after they sold fifty thousand albums.

Somehow, one of the great American entertainment companies was falling behind in this time of plenty. In the spring of 1984, I was working as an independent producer on the Walt Disney lot. I had grown up watching *Walt Disney's Disneyland*, and I remember Walt introducing guests as diverse as aerospace engineer Wernher von Braun and cartoon insect Jiminy Cricket. The show was a staple of our Sunday nights in the fifties. In 1984, with three kids under the age of eight, my thoughts about entertainment had turned to their needs. I had produced a kids' series for Showtime (run by Peter Chernin, who would go on to run Fox) with Shelley Duvall called *Faerie Tale Theater*, for which we had engaged major directors and actors in retelling classic fairy tales, and now I found myself developing movies for Disney. But the Walt Disney Company of 1984 was a different animal than my 1950s dream of Walt on TV. It lacked confidence in itself, and the specter of the deceased (but cryogenically frozen?) founder haunted the halls. The phrase heard constantly in the offices was "What would Walt do?"

The Animation Building, where my office was, had been designed by Walt to allow the maximum amount of natural light into small studios for the artists who had made the company what it was. Walt put his own office there to be near the creative center of activity, but as the studio grew a bureaucracy, more of the mid-level executives moved into the Animation Building to be near Walt, and by the time he died there was no room for the animators.

Equally symbolic of the company's decline was a distressing scene that took place every afternoon from 2 to 4 p.m. outside the executive dining room on the top floor of the Animation Building. Ron Miller, president of Disney (by virtue of his marriage to Walt's daughter Diane), would play poker for two hours every afternoon with three cronies he had "producing contracts" at the studio. Miller, a former second-string tight end for the Los Angeles Rams, seemed to have no clue that he was running an American icon into the ditch. He blithely concentrated on his poker game and his winery while Disney's market share plummeted to last place among the major studios.

At one point, after about two months on the lot, I got so irritated with Miller's Nero fiddling act that I took the most recent 10-K financial filing down to my friend Richard Rainwater, the manager of Bass Brothers Enterprises in Fort Worth, Texas. I had first met Richard two months after I had purchased the Lion's Gate Films studio from Robert Altman in 1981. Lion's

Gate (not to be confused with the more recent Lionsgate, producer of large-scale blockbusters) was housed in a big two-story building that had offices and the best sound-mixing stage in Los Angeles. We had done some very innovative sound work for Disney on the movie *Tron*, which was Disney's first attempt to modernize the studio. I had called Rainwater out of the blue to see if the Bass Brothers might put some money into Lion's Gate. Richard agreed to see me in Fort Worth, and I took my business plan down to the Bass headquarters, a twin tower structure of some forty stories each. As I walked in one of the buildings for a 10 a.m. meeting, it was very clear from the directory that only maybe eight out of the forty floors were occupied. The Basses were willing to bet early and big.

Bass Brothers Enterprises was two floors near the top of one tower. All the walls were stark white and punctuated with beautiful modern art. Every office had a glass wall looking into a central secretarial space. Only the conference rooms had solid walls—floor-to-ceiling whiteboards where Richard Rainwater, Al Checchi, and three of the four Bass Brothers (Ed, the rebel, was usually holed up in Santa Fe or some other hippie watering hole) would sit and map out incredibly complex transactions with floor-to-ceiling numbers. It was math at a very advanced level. Although Richard was from the poor side of Fort Worth, he had not met Sid Bass until they were classmates at Stanford Business School. From there, Richard went off to work at Goldman Sachs but was lured back to Fort Worth by Sid when his great-uncle, Sid Richardson, passed away and left the family oil fortune to nephew Perry Bass and his four sons. Rainwater was a wiry genius, a contrarian, and a disciple of Benjamin Graham's value-investing style. More than anything, Richard had a sense of openness and optimism that was infectious. Working with him was a joy and an education, and I believe a lot of his success was due to the loyalty he engendered among his circle of associates.

With Richard's help the Basses had grown a $100 million oil business into an investment pool of $1.5 billion that was diversified over many sectors. In years to come, his fame was slightly tempered by the fact that he rescued George W. Bush from business oblivion. Before Richard Rainwater entered George Bush's life, the young man from Andover and Yale was a complete failure. He had ridden two oil service companies into near bankruptcy, he had a little cocaine problem, and he was known throughout Texas as a hard drinker. But I can imagine Richard calling the son of the new president of the United States into his Fort Worth office, with its huge windows overlooking the Texas prairie, and preaching the gospel of wealth: "George, I'm going to buy the Texas Rangers baseball team. I'll choose the managers and raise the money, but I need you to be the frontman that goes to the government to give us tax breaks and pay for a new stadium. All you have to do for me is show up sober to meetings and we'll take it from there. And for that, I'll give you 10 percent of the upside as a promote." And George accepted the offer. The SEC was looking at Bush's business Harken Energy, and he needed to get out of the failing company before his reputation and his political future were ruined. This all took place in late 1988, the year Bush says he found Jesus and stopped drinking and doing drugs.

It is a story that tells you a lot about the ethics of Texas business and the go-go years of the 1980s. Richard Rainwater was

Machiavelli in this story. He needed a big name to help him navigate the tricky world of corporate welfare, and by extricating Bush from Harken, he had his man. In the same way that Dick Cheney and Don Rumsfeld were, when the Republicans were out of power, good frontmen for businesses like Halliburton, which relied on government subsidies (i.e., corporate welfare), so Rainwater saw that a sober George Bush could be helpful to the cause of getting someone else to put up money for a stadium. And if he provided the incentive for Bush to join Alcoholics Anonymous, more power to him.

As I sat in his office explaining my business plan for Lion's Gate in 1982, Richard fielded calls on the speakerphone from every major investment bank in the world. After an hour of questioning me about the nature of the movie business, he got to the bottom line: "It takes just as much work to do a $2 million deal as a $200 million deal. Why don't you come back to me with a $200 million deal?"

With that in mind, a year later I had brought down all of the Disney financials and showed Richard that the company fit his model of a classically undervalued asset that was badly managed. The whole film library was carried on the balance sheet at $70 million. There were hundreds of undeveloped acres in Orlando, Florida, carried at a value of another $10 million. Most importantly, Disney, despite the mismanagement, still had the only "brand" in the entertainment business. Big Media has spent millions of dollars convincing Wall Street and Main Street that their value was in their brands, but this was a Big Lie. Universal Records is the largest record company in the world, but it is not a *brand*. Most people buying music have no idea who the artists are signed with. But for children between the ages of four and twelve (and their parents), Disney was a brand. That would give it an advantage in reselling its older products. Both Richard and I understood that if you applied X dollars of advertising on one end and had video cassettes of *Pinocchio* and *Winnie the Pooh* in every Walmart, you could expect Y dollars to flow out the other end.

Richard spent three hours quizzing me on Disney's management and poring over the numbers. He finally pointed to his Quotron screen (the stock-tracking computer of the day), on which was sitting a hat with the Texaco label. "Jon, this is a fabulous deal. There is only one problem. We own 9 percent of Texaco and are in a beef with the management. They want to buy Getty Oil, and we don't want them to. We may have to buy up to 25 percent of the company in order to get our way. Even for the Bass family, a couple of billion is a lot. We can't do two deals of that size." I said I understood, and he made me vow to keep in touch: "You never know what can happen in this business."

Eight weeks later, all hell broke loose on the staid campus of the Walt Disney Company. Saul Steinberg had announced that he was going to take over Disney, and Mike Milken had provided one of his famous "highly confident" letters saying that Drexel Burnham Lambert would raise the needed junk-bond financing to acquire the company. Steinberg is a fascinating character, maybe even an evil genius. In 1961, fresh out of Wharton Business School at twenty-two, Steinberg had a simple but brilliant idea. IBM was charging companies very high rates to lease their computers, and Steinberg discovered that he could offer computer leases that would undercut IBM's prices and still obtain bank financing for the entire purchase price of the computers by using the signed leases as collateral with lenders—thus, the first real use of leverage to create a startup. Prior to that, it was generally assumed that companies were built on venture capital purchasing equity, not on bank debt.

Steinberg was one of the original Mike Milken corporate raiders, and because one of the companies he had acquired during that time was Reliance Insurance, he could invest their premiums in Milken's junk-bond inventory. The circular nature of Milken's scheme was obvious: "You buy my junk bonds, I'll finance your corporate raids." In Steinberg and Milken's Disney raid, in order for the junk bond to be paid off Disney would have to be broken up, and Steinberg was already shopping the various parts (theme parks, movies, consumer products, TV, games). That would have been the end of the company, and Steinberg and Milken would have made out like bandits.

In 1984, Drexel Burnham Lambert was the most feared investment bank in corporate America. By inventing a whole new currency (junk bonds), by being the major market-maker in the currency, and being the biggest holder of the currency, they cornered the market for five years running. The partners in the firm made obscene amounts of money. Mike Milken, who invented the whole idea, made $600 million in salary in one year! Milken then teamed up with a new class of financier, a raider, and created a self-fulfilling prophecy. The raider would buy about 5 percent of a public company and file a disclosure form saying he wanted to "increase shareholder value." Milken would then write a letter to the raider saying that Drexel was "highly confident" it could sell enough junk bonds to buy all of the stock in the company and take it private, thereby paying off the junk bonds with the acquired assets. The stock inevitably went up on such an announcement, and for the executives wanting to keep their jobs, the payment of "greenmail" to the raider (buying his 5 percent at a much higher price) was a "prudent use" of corporate funds. Often the target company would look for a "white knight" who would let them become a division of a larger company and still keep their jobs.

For Ron Miller and his executives, the Steinberg raid was the height of apostasy. The dark little undercurrent of their anger was the fact that Disney was the last bastion of WASP power in Hollywood. In his days, Walt had kept a distance from the Jewish families that ran MGM, Warners, Paramount, Columbia, and Universal. The notion that Disney was about to be acquired and broken up by Saul Steinberg left Miller and his cronies in disbelief. At this point, Steinberg owned less than 10 percent of Disney's stock, but Milken was going to make it possible for him to formulate a public offer for *all* the stock.

In order to stave off this outcome, they sought out a White Knight and came to the rather remarkable conclusion that Auggie Busch of Anheuser-Busch was to be their Protestant savior. Their rationale for this was that Auggie also owned theme parks, although Busch Gardens wasn't quite in the league with the Magic Kingdom. Amidst the rather Alice in Wonderland notion of America's beer baron owning the family-friendly Disney empire, there was one voice of sanity: chairman of the board Ray Watson. Ray had been a real estate developer and was one of the few people at Disney not interested in channeling Walt for a living. At ten one morning I received a call from Richard Rainwater and Sid Bass.

"Jon, we just sold all of our Texaco stock. We're ready to save the Mouse."

"You're kidding me."

"Nope. We've got the perfect transaction that will put enough stock in friendly hands to block Steinberg. We will sell our Orlando real estate company, Arvida, to Disney for new stock worth $200 million. Between our holdings and the Disney family we would have 25 percent, and Steinberg could never finish the transaction. Unless he can buy it all, the Drexel junk bonds are useless."

"I think Ray Watson would understand this deal. He comes out of real estate."

Sid chimed in, "You tell him we'll send a plane to pick him up tomorrow. If we get him down here in Fort Worth, I'm sure a deal can be made."

I called to Watson's office on the second floor and asked if I could come down to see him for a few minutes. His secretary said he was about to leave for St. Louis. I knew the Anheuser-Busch's Budweiser headquarters were in that city. He agreed to see me, and I told him that the Basses were ready to help Disney stay independent and whole. He knew of the Arvida project, respected the Basses for their acumen and taste, and agreed to delay his trip to St. Louis in order to visit Fort Worth.

It took about five working days to get the transaction done, and when it was all over, Richard's prediction came true. Steinberg and Milken surrendered and Disney stayed independent. The Basses paid me as their investment advisor, and I made more money in five days than I had made in five years. But Richard did me another favor as well. He called Ken Miller, managing director of Merrill Lynch's mergers and acquisition group, and suggested he hire me. I went to see Ken and found in him an amazingly simpatico Harvard grad steeped in the same sixties activism I was and married to the daughter of Paul Sweezy, one of America's great socialist intellectuals. We hit it off famously and I started work as a vice president at Merrill Lynch working on media M&A transactions.

Ken and his wife, Lybess Sweezy, are extraordinary examples of 1960s radicals who traded in their bullhorns for Armani suits. This is hard to understand, but many sixties radicals burned out and quit the movement, even if they never really abandoned their leftist views. They still support left-leaning candidates and policies, but they are no longer on the ground or in the streets in the way they used to be. What someone like Ken, or like Mark Rosenberg (who ran Warner Bros. Feature Production in the 1980s), both of whom came out of SDS in the 1960s, knew was how to organize people. And being able to organize people is at least 75 percent of what it means to have good management skills.

For myself, the civil rights movement had come straight from the heart—building out of a deep emotional attachment to fairness. By contrast, the pivot to the antiwar movement was, for many of my age, a rational response—from the brain—to the possibility of being sent off to a senseless war. Once that existential threat was removed, for many people the urgency of being in the streets went away. There were many more counterculture battles to be fought over, including women's and gay rights, environmentalism, and consumerism. The political reform was abandoned to what Rorty called the Cultural Left.

Becoming an investment banker was certainly a "sellout" in the eyes of my wife, Lesley. She considered herself a hippie, and the idea that she was now married to a banker was beyond the pale. No rationalizations on my part about our family's financial security would placate her. She refused all invitations to business dinners and would regularly retreat to Mill Valley, just across the Golden Gate Bridge from San Francisco, where she could hang out with her real hippie friends, leaving me and our full-time nanny to take care of our two children, in our big new house in Santa Monica. At one point she moved the kids up to Mill Valley. When she was home she was relentless. "These are hollow men you are working with," she said. "If you are not careful, you'll become one yourself." I refused to argue and went off to my study to smoke a joint.

One of the "hollow men" I was dealing with was Sid Bass, who appreciated my rock-and-roll chops and Ken Miller's radical background. Sid liked talent, and he didn't care how weird a person was. His circle in Fort Worth and New York included its share of pot-smoking musicians and drunken painters of real note, and he had a deep affection for art of all kinds. He loved the Fort Worth rhythm-and-blues clubs, and he was the major patron of the American Ballet Theatre. When he was a little high, he was a great storyteller, and he was loyal to a fault to his friends. He took his responsibilities on Disney's board of directors very seriously and felt he was the steward of an American institution. Lesley was wrong: There was nothing hollow about Sid Bass.

For Richard Rainwater and Sid, stopping Saul Steinberg was just the start of "saving the Mouse." Job one was to replace

Ron Miller with a world-class manager. Almost immediately two names moved to the head of the list: Michael Eisner and Frank Wells. Both were men of extraordinary experience in the motion picture business, and both had been maneuvered out of running a studio within the last couple of years. Stanley Gold, who played the Rainwater role for Roy Disney (the last remaining family member on the board), was convinced that Eisner was the right man. I didn't know Eisner, but I had dealt with Frank Wells when I had sold *Mean Streets* to Warners and thought he was the most honest man in the film business. Something about Sid Bass told me that he would take to Frank Wells. Sid was soft-spoken and impeccably dressed but had a sense of adventure and mischief in his soul. Frank had similar qualities, and so Richard and Sid decided to meet with Wells in addition to Eisner.

They reported back to me that both men wanted the top job and there seemed no way to get them to work together. Stan Gold seemed adamant about making Eisner the CEO, and I think Frank knew that and figured Eisner had the "creative" reputation while he merely had a platinum business resume. Given that Disney desperately needed creative resuscitation, it looked like Eisner was going to win. I happened to be in Rainwater's office in Fort Worth the afternoon he reported that it looked like Wells was out of the picture. I asked Richard if we could take one last try to get Frank to work under Michael. I really believed he would provide balance to the team.

We called Wells at his home in Los Angeles. "I'm just booking the Sherpas for another Everest trip. I'm leaving for Nepal in five days." Wells was one of the few people at the time attempting to climb all seven of the tallest mountains in the world. He had made it to the top of every one but Everest, and he was determined to go back and try again. For a half hour Richard and I pleaded with him to reconsider working as president and COO under Eisner's CEO. As Richard preached his gospel of wealth accumulation through true ownership, it began to sink in to Frank that the Basses were serious about giving top management a real stake in the upside of Disney's potential future. Finally Frank agreed to have a meeting with Eisner to see if they could work together.

Ultimately, Eisner and Wells made one of the best partnerships that the entertainment business ever saw. The Basses kept their word and made both men incredibly rich through cheap options. Michael brought in a great creative team of Jeff Katzenberg, Rich Frank, and Bill Mechanic to revive the studio, and Frank did all the hard work to make the parks business grow at a record-breaking rate, all the while keeping peace among the various egos at the company. When Frank died tragically at age sixty-two while helicopter skiing with my friend the cinematographer Mike Hoover, a lot of the glue that held things together disappeared. Subsequently, most of the great creative talent left, and Disney was unable to sustain the remarkable 20 percent yearly growth curve that marked the first ten years after the deal.

At the end of the day, the success of Eisner and company in the first ten years of his leadership came out of the one small line item on the balance sheet that I had pointed out to Rainwater during our first Disney meeting: the film library. All of the classic animated films had been fully written off over the course of forty years, but when the home video craze hit in 1986, Disney was able to sell millions of units of classics such as *Snow White* through every imaginable outlet around the world. And every single dollar of that dropped to the bottom line.

As for Mike Milken, his Disney defeat did not stop his ambition, and he ended up changing the American media landscape in a far more significant way. The line from the rise of Mike Milken to the rise of Donald Trump takes a few twists and turns, but it never breaks. In 1982, Trump tried to get financing from Milken for his move into Atlantic City, coming to Los Angeles with Drexel's casino consultant Daniel Lee to "kiss the ring" of the junk bond king at 6 a.m. Although they never made a deal, Milken would go on to aid Trump's career in ways neither man could have imagined back then.

Milken had two important clients in the media business: Rupert Murdoch and Lowry Mays, a conservative Texan who owned a small radio company called Clear Channel. Mays and Milken used Reagan-era media deregulation and Drexel junk bonds to buy up thirteen hundred radio stations and essentially invent rightwing talk radio. Clear Channel created and distributed both the Rush Limbaugh and Sean Hannity radio shows. Murdoch's sole U.S. media property when he met Mike Milken was the *New York Post*. The whole rise of Fox News and rightwing TV was funded with Drexel junk bonds.

It would be a mistake to underestimate the influence of Mike Milken in the 1980s. Some have compared it to the dominance of J. P. Morgan's economic philosophy at the end of the nineteenth century. Milken found an ally in Newt Gingrich and the New Right, and much of the intellectual justification for Ronald Reagan's strenuous efforts to deregulate most of American business came out of their mid-1970s funding of the Heritage

Foundation and the American Enterprise Institute (along with some help from the *Wall Street Journal*'s editorial page). But it was Milken's cash that financed much of the lobbying for deregulation. By the time Milken was indicted in 1989 on ninety-eight counts of racketeering and securities fraud, he had transformed the landscape of American business. And even though he was sent to prison (for a short two years in "Club Fed") and paid a massive fine, he emerged from jail in 1993 with at least $2 billion in his bank account, and his beliefs in debt and deregulation were unchanged. It would take another fifteen years to prove that his prescription for the American economy was poisonous.

One of the most significant acts of Republican deregulation was to eliminate the "fairness doctrine" of the United States Federal Communications Commission. Even though the Supreme Court in 1969 had upheld the FCC's right to enforce the law, which required broadcasters to provide time for opposing viewpoints on controversial issues, Reagan's FCC eliminated this policy in 1987, a move that made possible the rise of the rightwing media empire, funded by Milken. The control of talk radio and Fox News led to another kind of loss in the years after the contested election of 2000. Essentially a vast swath of the public airwaves became a propaganda apparatus for the ruling Republican Party. At the time all of this was going on, I was among those who had no foresight into the long-term implications of these political and economic transformations. The mergers and acquisitions business is as Darwinian in practice as it is often depicted in theory. We could not see that the ways in which Milken had transformed the media landscape would lead to the election of Donald Trump, who could control a 24/7 propaganda machine fronted by Rush Limbaugh and Fox News. But of course Donald Trump understood how important Milken was and gave him a federal pardon in 2020.

I worked for Ken Miller at Merrill Lynch for four years. What had started out as an adventure, with lots of money flowing into my bank account, turned out to be (for me) a soul-killing death march. In 1987, we had successfully helped Sumner Redstone do a leveraged buyout of Viacom and so had moved into competition with Mike Milken when it came to media takeovers. One morning in New York, Ken and I were asked to go see Ivan Boesky, the king of merger arbitrage. Boesky had easy access to information from Milken (partially why Milken and Boesky went to prison), and so I figured he was going to try to pump us for what we were working on. We arrived at 8 a.m. in a gaudy office featuring green marble on every surface. Boesky immediately started boasting on what a good deal he had gotten on the offices, since the former owner, trader Marc Rich, had fled to Switzerland to avoid jail. He sat us down at a huge conference table and an assistant put a tiny croissant on a paper plate in front of each of us and then proceeded to bring us each a styrofoam cup of lukewarm coffee.

Ken Miller was having none of Boesky's phony charm offensive. No matter how Boesky probed, nothing was coming out of Ken's mouth. After twenty minutes we left. Boesky didn't even show us to the door. I went back to my hotel room and took a shower. I knew I had to get out of that business and that Lesley had been right. Ivan Boesky was a hollow man.

18. Until the End of the World

1989

In terms of my personal happiness, the summer of 1985 was a high point of that decade. Lesley and I had bought a big house in Santa Monica and were renting a small summer house in Montecito, a beautiful beach town outside of Santa Barbara. I treasure a photograph from that time of me and my three young children walking down a country lane in the woods. The afternoon light is casting shadows, and Daniela and Nicholas are walking confidently ahead as Blythe, the youngest, seems to be trying to explain something of great importance to her dad.

My new career as an investment banker meant that money was no longer a worry, but at the time I was not aware of how leaving behind my dreams of art and politics to "struggle for the legal tender" would disrupt my life, and especially my marriage. That's partly why I hold on to that moment in the photograph. Lesley had made the case that being the wife of an investment banker was not what she had signed up for—every counter-cultural bone in her body said that this was the devil's work and she would have no part of it—but for me it was an opportunity worth exploring. As much as I explained that a career in movie production was unstable and would always be a feast-or-famine existence, she said she would rather starve than be seen in the company of plutocrats.

It would take a German director named Wim Wenders and his crazy idea to make the ultimate road movie—a science fiction epic called *Until the End of the World*—to rescue me from the soulless universe of investment banking. In 1989, I went back to making movies. It was too late to save my marriage, but not too late to save my humanity.

I had first met Wim Wenders in 1978 at a screening of *The American Friend*, adapted from the Patricia Highsmith novel *Ripley's Game*. In a sense it was an homage to Hitchcock, but even though it starred the very American Dennis Hopper, it was far more stylistically European than Hitchcock's movie. At the time, I had an overall deal at MGM and I was preparing a thriller called *Trapdoor*, written by Tim Hunter and Charlie Haas. It was an imaginative early computer-crime movie, much in the Cary Grant *North by Northwest* mold, and MGM had signed Chris Reeve right off of the first *Superman* movie to play the Grant role. I took a chance and showed David Begelman, then head of MGM, the Wenders film, hoping Wim could direct *Trapdoor*. Begelman didn't get the film at all, but Wim and I stayed in touch.

As it happened, the script never got made, but Chris "borrowed" the basic plot for the fourth of his Superman movies. I know Charlie and Tim were pissed, but, like good Hollywood soldiers, they never said a thing to Warners. In 1989, when I was despairing for my soul in the investment banking business, Wim called and asked if I wanted to come to Cannes, where he was scheduled to be president of the festival jury. For years he had told me about a science fiction film he wanted to make that would be set in the year 1999, and I got the sense that he was ready to try to get it in the works. He had made two European hits in a row, *Paris, Texas* and *Wings of Desire*, and he clearly was the most important filmmaker in Europe at the end of the eighties. Although the film he wanted to make, *Until the End of the World*, was clearly more expensive and more ambitious than anything he had ever made, I was totally confident in his ability to pull it off. I think in some way I was looking for an out from being a suit, and so the idea of spending two years working all over the world with Wim was the equivalent of joining the French Foreign Legion. I was probably running away from my failing marriage. Wim told the *London Times* in 2003,

> My greatest hope and my entire passion for traveling
> is to lose myself. Or better yet, to get lost, to not know
> where I will be the next day. Turn the corner and see
> something you've never seen before. Look at a map, find
> a place with a name that attracts you, and just drive
> there. In a way, I never believed that it was me who
> found the places I photographed, but rather that the
> opposite is true. Those places called to me.

The experience of location scouting with him in the vast Outback of Australia, the rain forest of Cameroon, and the Dordogne of France was enchanting. In a way it brought me back to my earliest days on the road with the Band—a sense of brotherhood in pursuit of a common objective.

Scouting locations with Wim, we were like a United Nations

team roaming the globe. Wim was German; our cinematographer, Robby Müller, was Dutch; our art director, Thierry Flamand, and our first AD, Marc Jenny, were French; our composer and screenwriter were Australian; our video artist was Japanese; and I was American. The actors were from the United States, France, Germany, Australia, Italy, Japan, and Sweden. We shot the movie on four continents and sixteen countries, and the sense that we were making a movie in 1989 that was set in 1999 was spooky. In the script (written in 1982), the Berlin Wall comes down on the eve of the millennium, but while we were scouting in the Australian desert we pulled into a town called Coober Pedy that had one TV in the whole community, and there on the screen was a shot of Berliners on top of the wall, tearing it down. We changed the script so that our new version of 1999 would have the United Nations move to Berlin, as the United States had left the organization by then.

A few months earlier, when we were in Germany doing the special effects for the film, we often had to go into East Berlin because the only big soundstages in the country were at the Babelsberg Studio. I remember sitting in the cafeteria at the end of the day and noticing as it filled up with all the young East German film workers, who would hang out half the night drinking beer and watching TV. The favorite station was MTV Europe, which they were only able to see because Babelsberg Studio was a media facility and therefore had a satellite dish. Seeing the East Germans soak up the music and culture the government had denied the people made it so clear to me that the concept of a wall between East and West was tenuous at best. What I didn't comprehend was that it was so tenuous that it would be in rubble in five months.

And around the world in the decades after the American cultural explosion of the sixties, it was this same spirit of rebellion that was admired and imitated by leaders like Czechoslovakia's Václav Havel. What the politicians of the right didn't understand was that the Berlin Wall came down not because Reagan was any smarter or tougher than Gorbachev but because the world itself had changed. Bruce Springsteen, George Lucas, and Marvin Gaye had broken through the wall years before; Gorbachev was just smart enough to finally accept that a wall wasn't going to keep his people from the type of freedom they were seeing on MTV Europe and listening to on pirated American music CDs. He let it fall without a fight—later called a "velvet revolution." As the critic Adam Gopnik wrote in the *New Yorker*, the sixties "ended, perhaps, in 1989 with the fall of the Berlin Wall to the sound of rock and roll." Following Czechoslovakia's Velvet Revolution, the first person that newly elected President Havel asked to visit him in his country's White House was the American musician Frank Zappa. Zappa had inspired the Czechoslovakian band the Plastic People of the Universe, who themselves had been the foundation of the democracy movement Havel built around Charter 77, a group dedicated to human rights.

Havel understood something the late writer Toni Morrison said (in a conversation in 2016 with Ta-Nehisi Coates at the Stella Adler Studio): "The history of art, whether it's in music or written or what have you, has always been bloody, because dictators and people in office and people who want to control and deceive know *exactly* the people who will disturb their plans.

And those people are artists. They're the ones that sing the truth. And that is something that society has got to protect." The great irony is that while some American pundits hailed the fall of the Berlin Wall as "the End of History," everyone else was heralding an emergent globalist world that would take on some of the best values of America. Others, however, glimpsed the dire risk of the opposite: that the values of the kleptocrats would become America's own. Perhaps that grim vision—the age of autocrats— is even now nearing fruition.

I suppose Wim's fascination with the near future is that it allows us to play with the dystopian problems we see in the present. Part of the subtext of *Until the End of the World* was that globalization and technology had a distinct downside, especially for the United States. The idea explored in the movie that all manufacturing would, by 1999, be done in China was not as far-fetched as we thought. Today the U.S. is going through a "jobless recovery" due to the fact that most manufacturers are moving their factories to Mexico, China, or Taiwan. Even high-tech service jobs are being outsourced to India, where the cost of running a call center is one-tenth of what it is in the States. That in the U.S. all of those $18-per-hour factory jobs are being replaced by $10-per-hour retail service jobs makes for a depressing future. The most prescient central metaphor of our 1991 film was that we would get addicted to our screens.

It was no coincidence that Wim and I were thinking about these ideas related to the cost of globalization while we were in Berlin. Sixty years earlier, in that very city, an earlier experimentation with globalization was coming to a bad end as Germans had to carry wheelbarrows full of Deutsche Marks just to buy a loaf of bread. The crash of the world economy in 1929 led to different responses in different parts of the world. Historian Thom Hartmann, in a 2003 essay called "When German Democracy Failed," explained how Germany and the United States went in different directions:

> Germany's response was to use government to empower corporations and reward the society's richest individuals, privatize much of the commons, stifle dissent, strip people of constitutional rights, and create an illusion of prosperity through continual and ever-expanding war. America passed minimum wage laws to raise the middle class, enforced anti-trust laws to diminish the power of corporations, increased taxes on corporations and the wealthiest individuals, created Social Security, and became the employer of last resort through programs to build national infrastructure, promote the arts, and replant forests.

To talk to a German like Wim, who had been born just after the war, was to wonder how fascism had ever raised its head in a country that produced such a sensitive soul. Wim was as open and unprejudiced a person as one would ever want to meet, and yet "the sins of the fathers" seemed to be the cross the young German intellectuals had to bear. But they have borne it well and come out better as a result. As Susan Neiman wrote in her 2019 book *Learning from the Germans: Race and the Memory of Evil*, the postwar German populace worked to "acknowledge the evils their nation committed." There are no heroic statues to

Nazi generals but rather official memorials to the victims of the Holocaust. Neiman draws a direct contrast to the multiple statues of Confederate generals that occupy town squares across the American South. Perhaps the events of summer 2020 may start to right this wrong.

The *American Heritage Dictionary* defines fascism as "a system of government that exercises a dictatorship of the extreme right, typically through the merging of state and business leadership, together with belligerent nationalism." Wim's analysis of what happened in his country was that when things started to go badly in the German economy, the young Hitler was able to get the middle class to believe that their problems stemmed from the working class, their unions, and the Jewish radicals who were often allied with the unions. At that very moment, the big German corporate bosses at Krupp and other companies were lining their pockets at the expense of both the middle class and the workers. Hitler, by having allies in the media that would constantly attack anyone who dissented from the ultra-right point of view, and by using his armed Brownshirt thugs to break up rallies by leftist dissidents, was able to create a uniformity of thought in a few short years. Mussolini had similar success in Italy, and by 1936 he was able to declare, "Fascism should more appropriately be called Corporatism because it is a merger of State and corporate power." As we toured the world scouting filming locations in 1989, this notion of rightwing nationalism seemed the stuff of history. Neither Wim nor I could have imagined it taking root in the soil of America in 2016.

Working all over the world with Wim taught me four important lessons. The first was that international cultural pride was a coming force. Wim was a German director and proud of it. Until this scouting trip, I didn't really appreciate that, once a director had won the Palme d'Or (the grand prize) at Cannes—as Wim had in 1984—his or her reputation would spread to every corner of the world where cinema was celebrated. In Tokyo, we were treated to grand dinners with elaborate ceremony and even more exotic food. They would go on for hours, and every word that Wim uttered would be treated like a pronouncement from a modern oracle.

Because Wim viewed himself as a citizen of the world, he went out of his way to soak up the local music wherever we went. What we discovered was that what's selling in Brazil is Brazilian, what's selling in Nigeria is Nigerian, and what's selling in England is English. The days of Michael Jackson selling tens of millions of albums worldwide were gone (and the CD format is a casualty of the streaming revolution). Even before George Bush and Donald Trump started pissing off the rest of the planet, the days of American cultural imperialism were numbered. A couple of years ago, a friend who used to run an international culture section of the Ford Foundation told me of a wonderful program they had of funding radio stations in Africa. In Rwanda a station they fund that plays half Hutu music and half Tutsi music has become the most popular station in the country. The notion of American cultural imperialism (which is still taught at universities around the world) has been fading for years, and American companies better be ready for the change.

When we were in Coober Pedy, deep in the Outback, we came upon an Aboriginal Australian artist who was reimagining the traditional "message stick" that was traditionally carried between some tribes for communication. At one point I casually used the term "walkabout," and the artist let me know I had misunderstood the term, erroneously using it to mean a casual stroll. He clarified that "walkabout" was the word for the journey some indigenous Australian boys took during adolescence to mark their spiritual and traditional transition into manhood. It wasn't just a walk but an excursion into the Outback wilderness, where the boy would live for sometimes as long as six months. As with the country blues players like Son House whom I had encountered in 1963 and who were trying to preserve a dying culture, the Aboriginal Australians were keenly interested in preserve their traditional art, and I think Wim bought twenty of the paintings that we encountered in our month-long journey through the desert.

The second thing Wim taught me was that technology could be a mixed blessing. Wim was always the first to own the newest Sony camcorder, and *Until the End of the World* (made in 1989) is filled with tech that foreshadowed our future: wireless devices, easily searchable electronic tracks, voice-activated word processing, video faxes, and a precursor to GPS maps. But in the second half of the film, the key device—one that Max von Sydow's character has invented to allow his blind wife (Jeanne Moreau) to see—gets misused to record people's dreams. And then the addictive habits of the characters take over. They begin to want to live only in the dream world, like an opium smoker who retreats into his drug-induced stupor. The little screens become their addiction, and it's not hard to guess how that's mirrored in today's culture. In 1989, however, we could not yet see the other danger of those little screens: social media.

The binary nature of digital technology—it's either a 1 or a

0, a yes or a no—tries to pretend that there are no gray areas in our life. But if the previous chapters of this book have shown you anything, it is that this is a lie. The algorithms that filter what news you see on social media are making thousands of yes/no choices per hour to determine what you will see, and this is fundamentally different than being able to make my own choices when I peruse my morning newspaper, which is (hopefully) filled with content that might not fit the binary profile Facebook has of me. Despite our belief that we are still a country of rugged individualists chasing Jefferson's dream of "life, liberty, and the pursuit of happiness," the algorithms are transforming the lives of everyone. In mistaking convenience for freedom, we are willingly submitting to a surveillance economy, and because only a few firms control most of the consumer data, we have created new types of monopoly that even our regulators don't fully understand. Both monopolies and the surveillance economy have also fueled economic inequality on a level we could never have imagined in the 1970s. In 1978 (according to Deutsche Bank Research) the bottom 90 percent of American households held 37 percent of the nation's wealth, while the top 1 percent held 21 percent of wealth. Today, it's almost the opposite. The top 1 percent control 37 percent of America's wealth, while the bottom 90 percent control 26 percent.

When I first started questioning the effects that the Internet monopolists like Facebook's Mark Zuckerberg and Google's Larry Page were having on our democracy, the monopolists themselves were in denial. Today, they are at least recognizing there may be a problem, and while it's not enough, it's at least a step in the right direction. Zuckerberg recently wrote, "One of the most painful lessons I've learned is that when you connect two billion people, you will see all the beauty and ugliness of humanity." The problem is that while Zuckerberg acknowledges that Facebook has fundamentally changed the nature of communication, he doesn't see this as fundamentally detrimental to society. He wrote, "People having the power to express themselves at scale is a new kind of force in the world—a Fifth Estate alongside the other power structures of society." He is arguing that his new "Fifth Estate" has essentially replaced the old Fourth Estate—journalism—and while he may be right, I would argue that this is not necessarily a good thing. New research from Penn State suggests that the collection of rightwing conspiracy sites on YouTube are far from fringe; they're the new mainstream, and have recently surpassed the big three U.S. cable news networks in terms of viewership. Added on to the shocking power of YouTube, Zuckerberg's refusal to fact-check political advertising means we are about to experience the most massive political disinformation campaign in history, and it will come to us across multiple platforms.

The third thing I learned from Wim is that an artist has to keep creating and cannot become dependent on one source of work or funding. And this brings us back to Epicurus's notion of autonomy. American directors sometimes go three years trying to get the green light on a movie. Is this freedom? I would argue it is not, because they are trapped in a system not of their own making. Wim showed me that one antidote to feeling trapped is refusing to sit still. When he wasn't making a feature, he'd grab his video camera and make a documentary. When we were starting our film, he was just finishing a doc on the Japanese fashion designer Yohji

Yamamoto called *Notebook on Cities and Clothes* that has taught me more about Tokyo than probably any film I've ever seen. A couple of years later he went down to Havana with his friend Ry Cooder and made *Buena Vista Social Club* in twenty days.

In 2019, Criterion released the five-hour version of *Until the End of the World* on DVD. It was the film that Wim wanted to make from the start, and it's full of heart and faith and wonderful music. The original film (which ran to two hours and thirty-eight minutes) never made its money back, but a reviewer from the *Guardian* who saw the long version made me feel like I had succeeded in what I had set out to do.

> Watching it now, even with its dull patches, it seems like a miracle. Today, a director of evocative arthouse cinema would never be given such a wide canvas to make such a sprawling and undefinable film. But 1991, as this portrait of 1999 shows us, was a different time.

The fourth thing Wim taught me was that, in the postmodern world, we cannot underestimate the importance of faith. Wim's masterpiece, *Wings of Desire*, is probably the most significant meditation on that subject in modern cinema. After we had finished *Until the End of the World* in 1990, I separated from Lesley, my wife of eleven years. It was an extremely painful separation, especially because it involved our two wonderful kids, Nick and Blythe, and it stopped me in my tracks. My parting from Lesley was full of anger and recriminations, and for me it was more anguishing than I could have imagined. Looking back now from the point of view of twenty-one years in a happy marriage to my wife Maggie Smith, I realize that with Phyllis, Rosana, and Lesley, I had made the same mistake over and over. I had played the white knight to what I saw as a beautiful damsel in distress, and that is clearly not the basis for a good marriage.

At the depth of my depression over my divorce from Lesley, I went to visit my mother. On Sunday she suggested I accompany her to church. I had grown up in the Episcopal Church but, like many, I had stopped attending around seventeen and had lost touch with both the ritual and the concept of justice inherent in the church's teaching. The sermon that day was on a passage in 2 Corinthians in which Jesus says, "My Grace is sufficient for you, for my power is made perfect in weakness." The notion that we can grow from hardship and weakness was so counter to the Hollywood survival-of-the-fittest mentality I had been living in. Somehow, on that Sunday morning on my knees next to my mother, I began to reconnect with my faith. Perhaps what was different that day was that I at last grasped Alan Watts's description of faith as the "plunge into the unknown," which also describes the journey of the great artist. Occasionally, faith and art intersect.

I experienced that intersection when I came back to L.A. The director Sydney Pollack (I had written a script for him in 1988) asked me to come over to Warner Bros. to look at some documentary footage he was working on. In January of 1972 Aretha Franklin went down to the New Temple Missionary Baptist Church in Los Angeles to record an album of gospel songs. She had been raised in the church by her father, the Reverend C. L. Franklin, and the church setting and the amazing choir of the Reverend James Cleveland brought Aretha to a level of artistry that could make anyone a believer. Fortunately, Warner Bros. had hired Sydney Pollack to film the concert, and the thirty minutes of footage Sydney showed me moved me beyond belief.

There is a moment in the song "Precious Memories"—one of those tunes that teaches you the power of slow—when the bass and drums seem to hold back the beat to unbearable levels of tension, letting Aretha fill in the spaces. In the film, you can see her being transported into a spiritual ecstasy that almost lifts her off the ground. Sweat is pouring off her brow, and she is hitting high notes and almost scat singing as if she is not in control of her own instrument. The audience is going crazy, and there is a mystery in the room. It is magnificent. Ironically, Aretha refused to let the film be released during her lifetime, almost as if she were afraid of how vulnerable she looked—not the diva but a humble servant. Could it be that she saw in that younger spiritual persona a road less traveled, a path she had decided to leave behind? We will never know, but thank heavens it is now available for everyone to witness. As for my own journey toward an examined life, I was learning not to be ashamed of being vulnerable. It was time to learn again, knowing I didn't have all the answers.

19. Strangled by Harvey Weinstein

1996

That learning process in the early 1990s took the form of a passion for making long-form documentary series. Ken Burns's *The Civil War* had opened my eyes to the possibility that you could take nine hours to tell a great story. I decided to tell two big stories about the liquids that were driving civilization in 1990: oil and water. I didn't know a lot about these subjects, but luckily there were two important books that told the stories in detail. For the oil narrative, I optioned the book *The Prize* (1990) by Dan Yergin, which told the story of the oil industry from the 1860s to the present. It wasn't a pretty story and it was full of evil characters, like John D. Rockefeller, who manipulated the politicians to do their bidding. For water, I chose the book *Cadillac Desert* (1986) by Marc Reisner, which tells the story of how the desert regions of Las Vegas and Los Angeles both take water from other parts of the country. Here too there were villains a plenty, like William Mulholland. Both films were eight or nine hours long and made for PBS and the BBC.

After that I helped co-finance and executive produce Gus Van Sant's film *To Die For*, which came out of a wonderful script by

Buck Henry and was produced by my friend Laura Ziskin. The most astonishing thing about the film is the courageous performance by Nicole Kidman as the desperately ambitious central character. The film taught me the power of music to shape a film. When we first sneak-previewed the movie with no music, the film completely bombed with the audience. They didn't realize they were seeing something from the special genre known as black comedy. The composer Danny Elfman, who had worked with Gus before and was at that screening, came to us afterward, when we were stressing over the awful audience-response cards. He said he had a simple fix. He wrote a humorous little music cue that we put under Nicole's opening monologue, delivered straight to the camera. When we rescreened the film three days later, the audience's scores were wonderful. Danny's tune had given the audience permission to laugh at our twisted protagonist.

After that film was done and out in the world, my life took another abrupt turn.

Film festivals have always been slightly unnerving experiences for me. From the first showing of *Mean Streets* at the New York Film Festival in 1974, through the many screenings at Cannes, Venice, and Tokyo that helped my films find an audience, there was always the possibility that disaster could strike. A malevolent film critic, a broken projector, a bad job of subtitling . . . the perils were many and the pleasures were fleeting. To counter some of that, Robert Redford had, in the early eighties, set up Sundance with the specific purpose of reviving the independent (i.e., nonstudio) film business.

In January of 1996 (the first time I attended with a film), the Sundance Festival was not only still going strong at almost twenty years old but had succeeded beyond Bob's wildest imagination. The town of Park City, Utah, which had been a second-rung ski community, was now a permanent stop on the jet-set celeb calendar, and its happenings were chronicled by *Vanity Fair* and *People* magazine. More than most of the big Hollywood stars of the period, Bob was also committed to using his visibility to "give something back" to the world, not only by helping young filmmakers but by being a consistent voice for environmental sanity. Working on the six-hour documentary *The Native Americans* for Ted Turner in the summer of 1994, I spent a good deal of time with Redford, who was toying with the notion of being the series narrator. The subject matter was obviously close to his heart, and even though his lack of urgency was somewhat infuriating (he was known as "Easy Bob" to the crews that worked on his films), once he actually showed up he gave his attention; he was full-on, smart, and imaginative.

In the fall of 1995, I had been asked to run the American division of Pandora, a Paris-based distributor of independent films. The company was headed by Ernst Goldschmidt, who had distributed my films *The Last Waltz* and *Under Fire* when he was running foreign operations for both United Artists and Orion. Ernst reported to chairman Christian Bourguignon, who was a classic self-important French bureaucrat and seemed to know very little about the film business but a lot about the right Burgundy to drink at lunch. One of Pandora's main shareholders was Pargesa, a big French holding company run by my former Merrill Lynch partner Aimery Langlois-Meurinne, and in retrospect, I can see that Aimery's presence lulled me into a false sense of security about working once more with the French.

My experience with Anatole Dauman, a co-producer on Wim Wenders's *Until the End of the World*, had been so horrible that I had vowed I would never involve myself again with the French—forever paranoid of American cultural imperialism.

But Aimery was the most delightful international business-man I had ever met, like a combination of J. P. Morgan and Cary Grant in that he could move effortlessly from discussing matters of high finance to telling self-deprecating jokes and stories about his endless pursuit of the perfect wife. We sat up late one night at the Chez L'Ami Louis talking about how to revive the moribund film company, which was probably the smallest of Aimery's investments. The restaurant on the deserted rue de Vertbois was packed at midnight. The peeling brown paint on the walls belied the extraordinary quality of the foie gras. We had polished off an amazing Bordeaux with our côte de boeuf, and the warmth of the small room and the company was broken periodically when the door would open and a blast of the cool November air would follow in after some elegantly dressed couple come to this secret hideaway of refinement.

Pandora was one of a number of a relatively new type of entity, called a foreign sales company, that was at the heart of the current resurgence of the independent film market. When I had financed *Mean Streets* in 1974, there were only two ways to get an American film financed: one of the major studios would put up the investment or a producer like myself would assemble the money from family and friends, hoping to sell the finished film to a major studio when it was done. But in the late eighties, thanks to an entrepreneurial agent at William Morris named John Ptak, an English lawyer named Nigel Sinclair, and an enterprising Dutch banker named Alexander Gelderman, an alternative system of finance was created. The key to that system was the foreign sales company, which would either put up a guarantee letter or pre-sell certain territories. The banks would then loan against the pre-sales to the producer, and the producer could then finance most of the film out of the foreign sales budget and make a deal for U.S. rights while still retaining ownership. Some producers, including Dino De Laurentiis and Mario Kassar, occasionally abused the system. The classic example was Dino's 1976 remake of *King Kong*. The production manager confided to me that they had made two budgets: the actual budget was $65 million, but the one they showed to the foreign distributors was $90 million. Because foreign sales guarantees were usually based on a percentage of the budget, a producer who falsified that information was out and out trying to cheat the system. Dino didn't own the biggest estate in Beverly Hills and the largest villa in Rome because he always played fair.

In 1996, I came to Sundance with an independent film that Pandora had financed. The movie was a little Australian gem called *Shine*, a curious project that had been one of those true labors of love for a director with a passion. Scott Hicks, who was in his early forties, was no spring chicken in the film industry, having directed one forgettable film eight years earlier but also a good number of documentaries for Australian television. For ten years he had shopped the idea behind *Shine*, the story of David Helfgott, a child piano prodigy who had descended into schizophrenia in his late teens. With the help of the Australian Film Commission and the BBC, Hicks had gotten the film developed, but he had been unable to secure a U.S. distribution deal or the final financing. Pandora had come in at the last minute with $1.5 million in return for all worldwide rights except Australia and the UK. When I arrived at Sundance, I had no idea that this film would lead me to a situation in which I would find myself being screamed at by one of the founders of Miramax, Harvey Weinstein.

Like myself, the two Weinstein brothers (Harvey and younger brother Bob) had gotten their start in concert production in the 1970s and then migrated to New York City to start distributing foreign films. But whereas the films of Fellini, Truffaut, Bertolucci, Godard, and Antonioni had been the central cultural artifacts of the seventies, by 1986 French and Italian cinema did not seem as important. I can still recall the first time, in the late 1960s, I saw films like *Jules and Jim, Shoot the Piano Player, La Strada, 8½,* and even *Blow-Up*—they are imprinted in my brain because their energy and originality seemed so human compared to bloated American hits like *The Sound of Music*—but now, with the exception of a few Germans like Wim Wenders and Werner Herzog, and the occasional "touching memoir" from an old Italian master, there were very few "must-see" European films. It was in this milieu that Bob Redford's efforts to revive the American independent film entered into a symbiotic relationship with the little company that Harvey and Bob Weinstein had named after their parents, Miriam and Max.

It all came together in 1988, when Miramax acquired a low-budget American independent film (developed at Sundance) made by an unknown director: *Sex, Lies, and Videotape* by Steve Soderbergh. Miramax took it to the Cannes Film Festival, where it was awarded the Palme d'Or. That was the year Wim

Wenders was president of the Cannes jury, and as I had been hanging out with him, I know that the decision to award this unknown American the highest European film honor was extremely controversial. I believe Wim won over the rest of the jury by pure force of passion and will. It didn't hurt that he had an amazing amount of clout in Europe, due in part to his having won the same prize two years before, for *Paris, Texas*. Whatever the fights might have been in the jury room, it came out in Soderbergh's favor, and the win put Miramax in the big time.

Harvey, older than brother Bob by two years, was even then a man of Falstaffian proportions and appetites. His shirt was a road map of spilled food and cigarette ashes, and perhaps he was the spiritual heir to the moguls of 1930s Hollywood, as his publicity department insistently whispered to any journalist willing to listen. He had that strange ability to become different characters with different people. To a young star like Gwyneth Paltrow he may have seemed like the lovable papa bear, showering her with gifts and the first choice of his scripts. It was only years later that the dark secrets of Harvey's sexual assaults were revealed to the wider public.

But even before that, to many a director he was Harvey Scissorhands, unable to *not* meddle in the editing room, and always willing to browbeat into submission anyone who stood in his way. He was supremely competitive, and in the small world of distributors of foreign and independent films, he took no prisoners. His brother Bob was a more moderate influence, with a total bottom-line perspective, and in the years to come, he would secure Miramax's future by making a string of horror and genre films that the public loved.

But in the early nineties, almost running out of money after a spending spree, Harvey and Bob sold their company to Disney through a brilliant negotiation by William Morris agent John Ptak, who managed to play a winning poker hand with Michael Eisner, even though his clients had no credit at the bank. In the ensuing years with Disney's bankroll, Miramax managed to dominate the indie film world and buy up every film in sight.

A week before the Sundance Festival started in 1996, I screened *Shine* for Tony Stafford, the head of acquisitions for Miramax. I had done it as a courtesy to Pandora head Ernst Goldschmidt, who always wanted to keep Harvey Weinstein on his good side. Stafford viewed the film in a screening room with only myself in attendance, and at the end he thanked me and walked out without a word about what he thought of the film. For the rest of the week I didn't hear from him, and with Ernst I turned my attention to other studios, figuring we might be able to get $500,000 for U.S. rights from Fine Line or Fox Search-light, if we were lucky. Ernst said he would have one last conversation with Harvey before the festival started.

To not have Miramax in the bidding for *Shine* was a problem. No one else knew that a Miramax rep had seen it before the festival, and if Harvey Weinstein had wanted to be cruel, he could have leaked the information that they had already passed on the film. Because Miramax was clearly the gorilla of the business, that kind of blow would have killed any potential buzz we might have had.

Despite Miramax's lack of interest, however, I thought *Shine* had an amazing emotional impact. I had set the screening at Sundance for the first Sunday night of the festival in the

Egyptian, which was the biggest theater in Park City. The night of our screening, it was packed with buyers, agents, publicists, and "civilians," and I was nervous. About one hour into the screening, I saw Ruth Vitale, the head of Fine Line, get up from her seat and go out into the lobby. Four minutes later she was back in her seat. Then I saw an executive from Fox get up and do the same thing. I peered through the lobby curtain and could see him talking excitedly into the lone payphone. I realized that buyers were leaving their seats to get permission to bid on the film! By the last fifteen minutes of the film, all those hardhearted agents and cynical film executives were in tears, and I knew we had a winner on our hands. The themes of Jewish angst and great artistic triumph had struck a chord, and by the time that Scott Hicks and I were receiving congratulations in the lobby, I knew we would sell the film.

The next morning, the first buyer rang at 7 a.m. By 9 a.m. I had two bidders up above $1.2 million for the U.S. rights: Fine Line and Fox Searchlight. By the afternoon, Mark Ordesky and Jonathan Weisgal of Fine Line had moved into my condo with a computer and printer, determined not to lose another film to Harvey Weinstein. By 4:30, I called Ernst at home in Paris to report that we had passed the $2 million guarantee mark and that I was going to sell the film to Fine Line. At this point, Tony Stafford from Miramax called in a panic. He had gotten to see the film before anyone and could have easily taken it off the market *before* the festival for something less than $1 million, but now he realized he had screwed up. He said he would top any offer.

Scott Hicks, who had fought for eleven years to get the film made, told me that years before he had waited for six hours in the Miramax office in L.A. hoping to line up financing, and the arrogance of the Weinstein operation still rubbed his Aussie pride the wrong way. Beyond that, we all knew that Miramax had bought more than fifteen films in the last eighteen months that they had still not released, and for Scott especially the thought of *Shine* sitting on the shelf was too much to bear. Finally, at 6:30 p.m., we decided to sign a contract with Fine Line, complete with guarantees on marketing budgets and the timing of the release. We drank some Champagne and I called Stafford to tell him he had lost.

The terror in his voice was almost more than I could stand.

"You can't do this! Harvey's jet is landing in fifteen minutes. You have to wait until he gets here to make your final decision."

"The deal is done, Tony. We're going out to dinner."

"Harvey is flying in just to make this deal." (I knew that was bullshit.)

"You had your chance early, Tony. The filmmaker and I have made our decision and signed a contract."

"Harvey's not going to like this."

I didn't know what to say, so I hung up and went out to dinner with two old friends, Deb Newmyer and Linda Lichter. Deb ran all of the development at Steven Spielberg's Amblin Entertainment, and Steven leaned on her taste mightily. She was married to Bobby Newmyer, who had produced *Sex, Lies, and Videotape*. Linda was the fastest-rising attorney for actors and directors, and her husband, Nick Marck, had been an assistant director on several of my productions. Linda's law partner Carlos Goodman also came along. We went over to the Italian restaurant Mercato Mediterraneo and got ourselves a nice table upstairs. Halfway through the main course we heard a murmur from down below, and before we knew it Harvey Weinstein was standing in front of our table screaming at me.

"Motherfucker, you bid me up."

"So what?"

"That film is mine."

"You had your chance a week ago."

"You asshole, you're not going to make a fool of me."

"We're trying to have dinner here, Harvey. Why don't you come back later?"

"You're not going to give that film to Fine Line. We're going to get Ernst out of bed in Paris and make a deal with him."

At this point Deb Newmyer decided to enter the fray. "Why don't you take the high road for once in your life, Harvey?"

He turned his awesome stomach toward her. "Fuck you, bitch." He obviously didn't know whom he was talking to.

Linda stood up. "You apologize to her."

"Screw you."

I stood up then, signaling for the maître d', who had been hovering in the background, to get the unwanted guest away from our table. Harvey grabbed me by the coat lapel and hauled me over into the corner.

"I'm going to cut you a new asshole. You're going to need an army of lawyers when I'm finished with you."

"Harvey, I just signed a binding contract with Fine Line. You can call Ernst all you want, but he'll back me up."

The maître d' reappeared with two burly bus boys who looked like they worked on ski patrol during the day. Harvey knew he was outmatched and let himself be escorted out of the restaurant, followed at a distance by his associate Meryl Poster, who evidently had watched the whole show from the stairway. When they got in Harvey's car, she told him that he had just called Steven Spielberg's most trusted employee a bitch and that he ought to try to apologize quickly. Harvey wrote out a short note of apology, and Meryl sheepishly brought it to our table. There was not a word of apology to me but, as I was to learn the next morning, Harvey had already done me and the film the biggest favor imaginable.

I crawled out of bed at 7 a.m. to a call from Paris. Ernst had already fielded several calls from international distributors wanting to buy the film. Had I seen *Daily Variety*? I set down the phone and went to the door, where the trade magazines were distributed to everyone. There it was, as the lead story— the entire saga of the fight, the Fine Line victory, the Miramax defeat. Evidently, Ruth Vitale's publicity machine had worked long into the night to make sure that the world knew of their triumph. By noon Ernst and I had offers of more than $6 million for major foreign rights. Among the bidders were Jerry Hufstader and Anne Sterling of Walt Disney International, and when Harvey got word of that he begged Michael Eisner to make sure Disney got the deal. His face-saving maneuver would be to get a Miramax credit listed below Disney on all of the foreign prints. He didn't have anything to do with Disney's foreign distribution, but that didn't prevent him from trying to meddle in it. In the end, we sold the European rights to Disney for a record amount. We had gone to Sundance with the idea of getting $500,000 out of *Shine*, and we had come away with more than $9 million in guarantees, a 700 percent return on our investment.

Ultimately, the decision to go with Fine Line was a good one. Harvey already had so much money invested in *The English Patient* that year that when it came time to submit films for Academy Award nominations, it was clear where his campaigning efforts would be focused. *Shine* got five Academy Award nominations, and its star, Geoffrey Rush, won for Best Actor. In the end, it was one of those films that worked out well for everyone involved with its production and distribution.

20. Conclusion

As I am finishing this book, it's been more than twenty years since my cage match with Harvey Weinstein at Sundance. I've now been happily married for more than two decades to the photographer Maggie Smith, and the three wonderful children of my earlier marriages have grown into brilliant careers and relationships of their own. In that period, I have also had three more careers. I was the founder and CEO of Intertainer, the first streaming video-on-demand service. Then I was a professor at the University of Southern California and director of its Annenberg Innovation Lab. Finally, I became an author. All of these roles have related to wrestling with the intersection of technology and culture. When I think that my father had one career in his life and that I have had at least six, it tells me a lot about the changing world we inhabit. I don't know if my father loved his work, but, with sole exception of the end of my short career in investment banking, I have loved every job I've had. Sometimes my students would ask how I had managed to navigate these different worlds, and all I could think to say was, "When a great opportunity presents itself, don't be afraid to take it."

These days I spend a lot of my time giving talks about the role technology will play in both our democracy and our creative culture. I was recently invited to a seminar at Google, where they were debating whether they could create artificial intelligence to write and edit hit movies. (They were at least humble enough to believe the director should be a human.) I suggested that all we would get would be formulaic versions of what has already been successful. For the folks at Google, that seemed like a good outcome. A safe bet. But questions about the potential effects of widespread adoption of AI go far beyond whether screenwriters and editors can continue to make a living. The ability of AI to create the illusion that, for instance, a politician said something he or she never said—a "deepfake"—will be a bane to our democracy. The basic notion of shared facts—a concept that has underpinned democratic consent—is disappearing.

As I write this in the summer of 2020, we are living under the weight of a deadly pandemic, a stalled-out economy, and a national reckoning on racial injustice. The battles we fought in the 1960s over civil rights and the militarization of American foreign policy were never resolved, and so they haunt us to this day. From my perspective, we're living in uniquely worrisome times; my generation's dreams of how to make a better society have remained woefully unfulfilled, leaving many of us cynical and disillusioned, and yet my children's generation has been saddled with the wreckage of our attempts, and many are now facing what may seem to be insurmountable odds, only compounded by the crippling student debt many are on the hook for from the very beginning of their working lives. From the day I was old enough to vote until the present time, our country has been fighting somewhere in the world. And that same American Exceptionalism that my father's friends expressed in 1960 still seems (at least in the minds of the politicians) to flow from what Trump calls "our wonderful modern weapons." But as I saw in Berlin in 1989, it really flows from our culture, which for almost 250 years has reflected the young Thomas Jefferson's belief in equality and liberty. In an age when there is so much fear around the rise of autocratic regimes, as in China and Russia, we need to remember our source of power is in these ideas of freedom, not technology and weaponry. As long as we allow the military to take 60 percent of our discretionary budget, we will never be able to build the society we have dreamed of for half a century.

I know we are better than this, better than *them*—the dystopian wannabe autocrats ruling many of our failing democracies. Ultimately I have faith that our country can reform itself and that the techno-determinists can be brought to heel. And I believe that artists can be part of that effort.

Here is why I am optimistic: America is largely an immigrant culture, and has been since two hundred years before Jefferson wrote the Declaration of Independence. The people who came here, whether by their own volition or in the chains of slavery, brought their own cultures with them, and insisted on hanging on to their traditions, sometimes in the face of strong efforts to erase them. And so American art in all forms—sung, painted, captured on film, you name it—reflects these immigrant histories, desires, and dreams. You cannot separate the songs of Robert Johnson from the slave experience, just as the films of Martin Scorsese and Francis Coppola are deeply embedded in the Italian immigrant experience.

And yet, America is about the new. The Puritans who arrived here believed in the new—John Winthrop's New Millennium "city upon a hill"—that would usher in a new world order. So we hold on to our past as a way to anchor us, and yet we are forever banishing it in search of the latest trend. This tension seems to be the dynamic that defines our culture. The folk music movement, with its reverence for the past, was uprooted by the electric power of rock, and yet many of the musicians, Dylan included, found their way back to the "old-timey music" that had been their initial inspiration. But then we go through periods when forgetting is the main impetus for culture. We set our movies in fantasy worlds that never existed—and never will. So we have lost our faith in the future. A recent Pew poll showed that seven in ten Americans are unsatisfied with the future direction of the country. Without the call of the future, we get a society in stasis, unable to bring about the dreams of people like Martin Luther King, or art that can "make it new." Without the call of the past, we get a society with no deep purpose and no shared home. Perhaps it is when the tension between the old and the new is strongest, and when the artist engages most deeply with both at the same time, that the most profound and galvanizing art is made.

The problem we face today is that the firehose of the new that pours into our brains from our smartphones makes it hard to even consider our cultural history and the lessons it might teach us. In 2019, journalist and filmmaker Bilge Ebiri wrote an introduction to the newly released long version of *Until the End of the World* and specifically addressed that its characters are addicted to their devices.

The characters drown in self-absorption as these devices reflect their selves back at them. In this sense, Wenders saves his greatest, most alarming prophecy for last: What if all the promises of technology and of the road—indeed, of cinema itself—came true, and all the doors of perception were opened, and at the end of it all, in finding ourselves, we found nothing but paralysis and despair? What if the arrival turned out to be more perilous than the journey? What if the end of the road was the end of our dreams?

We have to acknowledge that "paralysis and despair" have become prominent characteristics of American life. The most startling evidence of this is what the economists Anne Case and Angus Deaton call the startling rise in "deaths of despair," which include accidental drug overdoses, suicide, and alcohol-related deaths. A Senate Joint Economic Committee report charts the scale of this increase—a doubling from 22.7 deaths of despair per 100,000 Americans in 2000 to 45.8 deaths per 100,000 in 2017, easily eclipsing all prior records from the twentieth and twenty-first centuries. Reading this report, my mind raced back to Bobby Kennedy's prophetic speech in the spring of 1968, when he noted that, "even if we act to erase material poverty, there is another greater task, it is to confront the poverty of satisfaction—purpose and dignity—that afflicts us all."

But the despair of our current era is not just in the death statistics; it is embedded in the popular culture. Read the nihilistic lyrics of young rappers like Juice WRLD or Lil Peep, both now dead from overdoses. In early 2020 critic Jon Pareles wrote in the *New York Times*, "Atomized, solitary music-making reflects broader cultural currents: a ruthlessly individualistic winner-take-all economy; the troll onslaught of social media; siloed and tribalized politics. It's no wonder so many singers and rappers sound mournful, defensive or belligerent, even when they're boasting." But it's not just music.

Who are the current protagonists in the most popular TV shows? Look at the vicious factions of *Game of Thrones* and *Succession*, or the scheming meth dealer of *Breaking Bad*. *True Detective, Stranger Things* . . . everywhere you look is cynicism and darkness. And some would point to Donald Trump as the ultimate TV reality show antihero. As the *New York Times*'s TV critic James Poniewozik recently wrote, "The key is to remember that Donald Trump is not a person. He's a TV character."

Some will say that our current pessimistic television universe is a reaction to the events of 9/11 (*The Wire* debuted in June of 2002) and to the lies that led to the Iraq War. Or perhaps it came out of the fact that none of the bankers that caused the Great Recession of 2008 went to jail. Critics have pointed to the parallels between the current media entertainment landscape and film noir in the early 1950s—a genre that similarly emerged as a reaction to war, the Hiroshima bomb, and the paranoia of the McCarthy era. The cultural critic Sam Wasson has seized upon a more recent noir film, 1983's *Chinatown*, as the perfect metaphor for our cynical age. "What makes *Chinatown* so uniquely disturbing as an American metaphor is that it is so unlike the whiteness of Ahab's whale or the greenness of Gatsby's light," he writes. "However illusory, these are totems of aspiration, of possibility." In contrast, in *Chinatown* the fix is in. The bad guys have already won and there is nothing you can do about it—"Forget it, Jake. It's Chinatown."

The writer Ben Lerner, in his 2011 novel *Leaving the Atocha Station*, seemed to speak for his Gen X and millennial peers when he has his autobiographical character, Adam, muse, "I had long worried that I was incapable of having a profound experience of art. . . . I was intensely suspicious of people who claimed a poem or painting or piece of music 'changed their life' . . . . The closest I'd come to having a profound experience of art was probably . . . a profound experience of the absence of profundity." I can imagine that if all your protagonists are deeply cynical, catharsis may be impossible, but the sadness inherent in Lerner's words is extraordinary to someone like myself, who has had many profound experiences, from my first Dylan concert in 1964 up to the last frame of Alfonso Cuarón's 2018 film *Roma*.

In late October of 2019 a brutal wildfire roared up the canyon below our home in Pacific Palisades, California. As we evacuated our home while firemen pulled hoses up our driveway, the flames were twenty yards from our porch. For three days we lived in fear as the firefighters who were camped out in our backyard fought to extinguish the blaze. I fed them coffee and toast every day at 6 a.m. On the fourth day, as the trucks were leaving, having saved our house, I surveyed the burnt remains of the land below and remembered that I had tickets that night to the Los Angeles Philharmonic's performance of Mahler's Second Symphony ("Resurrection"). I decided to go. At the beginning of the fifth movement the one-hundred-voice choir begins a passage that is so soft and so tender it is on the very edge of audibility. As the voices began to swell, I felt a tear on my cheek. I didn't really expect it, but this amazing feeling of both sadness and relief flooded over me. I looked up at the supertitles projected above the choir.

> *Rise again, yes, rise again,*
>
> *Will you, my dust,*
>
> *After a brief rest!*
>
> *Immortal life! Immortal life*
>
> *Will He who called you, give you.*
>
> *To bloom again were you sown!*

The whole week of near tragedy and extraordinary blessing made sense through Mahler's transcendent music. That is what art can do, if you let it. Mahler was wrestling lyrically (in German) with the great religious themes of death and resurrection, and yet I understood it through the music first, not the words.

Is Lerner (or at least his character) so cynical that he refuses to believe that art still has power? Or is it that his generation's access to art's power is limited because the smartphone is their main source of media? As sad as I am contemplating that reality, I know that Lerner is wrong. Great music, film, and literature can profoundly change people. Why would governments still be trying to ban books like *To Kill a Mockingbird* if they didn't hold such power? Ultimately, it is up to the artists to counter this nihilism. Culture precedes politics.

Francis Coppola announced in late 2019 that he is going to make a new movie about a modern utopia called *Megalopolis*.

He told the *Wall Street Journal*, "What I want to say has to do with this very misunderstood concept of utopia—the idea that the world of the future could be beautiful and fulfilling. This notion that man brings with him perforce war and slums and wealth disparity and violence, and that all these bad things that we know happen—that these are necessary. I don't believe in necessary." This brings us back to Marcuse's concept of the role of the artist in society—to be the one who refuses to "forget what can be." The great music producer Jimmy Iovine posed this question in a 2019 interview with the *New York Times*: "So why do visual artists like Mark Bradford, Kara Walker, Ed Ruscha, Jenny Holzer make such powerful statements on where we are today in our culture, like Marvin Gaye, Public Enemy, Bob Dylan or Rage Against the Machine did? What has changed?"

What has changed is that we are living in a cynical and dystopian era in America, and the utopian dreams of the 1960s are fading from memory, only ever recalled when we celebrate fiftieth anniversaries of events like Woodstock and the moon landing. But we should not despair; the history of American culture has been a constant battle between our nostalgic past and our desire to "make it new."

In thinking about our desire for a brighter future, I am reminded of a quote from Albert Camus's *The Rebel* (1951), his long meditation about the role of the artist in rebellion. He wrote, "We are at the extremities now. At the end of this tunnel of darkness, however, there is invariably a light, which we already divine, and for which we have only to fight to ensure it's coming. All of us, among the ruins, are preparing a renaissance beyond the limits of nihilism."

I am confident that our culture will renew itself. In 1999 the Coen Brothers made a movie called *O Brother, Where Art Thou?* It was set in the 1930s, and they called upon their friend T Bone Burnett to create a soundtrack for the movie. T Bone enlisted traditional folk, bluegrass, and country artists like Ralph Stanley, Gillian Welch, Alison Krauss, and Emmylou Harris to create authentic mountain music from the period. When T Bone went to get a record deal for the soundtrack, he was turned down by most companies, but then an independent label called Mercury Records picked it up. It went on to sell 7.9 million copies, win two Grammys, and be one of the most successful records of the decade. The music was called Americana.

I sit on the board of the Americana Music Association, and every year we have a festival and awards ceremony in Nashville that rekindles my confidence in music's ability to renew itself by returning to the past. Recently I was entranced by Rhiannon Giddens, an African American banjo player and singer who explores the history of enslaved persons' use of the banjo in the United States and its direct connection with use of the African akonting, a three-stringed instrument from Gambia. What I find interesting is that, in an ironic way, her access to the past was made possible by the tools of the future; technology—and specifically access to the "celestial jukebox" of music-streaming services—had allowed Giddens to do, in a matter of months, the kind of anthropological work that had taken folks like Alan Lomax ten years in the field to accomplish. (Spend some time on the Library of Congress's website titled "Lomax Recordings: Iconic Song List" (https://www.loc.gov/folklife/lomax/lomaxiconicsonglist.html) and you can hear these original (sometimes scratchy) recordings from the 1930s that carry all the splendor and despair of American folk culture.)

The word "authentic" is badly misused in our present moment. Consumer brands are heralded as being authentic. Even incredibly calculating politicians are called authentic. The two main definitions of the word tell us that something is authentic when it is (1) trustworthy and (2) not an imitation. That sounds like Rhiannon Giddens to me. What she is trying to create is a kind of solidarity between America's past and present. She, as an African American woman, has found beauty in the slave songs played on the banjo without ever forgetting the painful legacy they represent. Giddens's songs, like Alan Lomax's recordings, are a way to not forget. That is part of art's role, and the Americana renaissance is helping preserve it.

Acknowledging not just our past but our present is the key to moving forward, and there are always creators who are doing the hard work of making sure we don't forget that our country has a long way to go to get to the promised land. A film like *Harriet*, for example (directed by Kasi Lemmons and produced by my daughter Daniela), takes us deep into the world of the Underground Railroad, and in showing us our past helps us look toward the future. Or consider the work of actor Donald Glover, who sings under the moniker Childish Gambino; he rocked the music world with his video for the song "This Is America," which takes a stark look at the topics of gun violence and what it means to be Black in America today.

The problem in the current entertainment economy is that the forces more interested in making money than making art have no real desire to "make it new." What is valued above all else is "IP"—intellectual property—on which the owner can collect rents. The highest form of IP right now is superhero movies, which, as the screenwriter Alessandro Camon pointed out in a 2019 essay for the *Los Angeles Review of Books*, are more a product of a board of directors, rather than a single director with a creative vision.

> As to what kind of artistic worldview is governed by a Board of Directors, it's interesting how, despite their message of inclusivity, these movies created a modern Pantheon of interplanetary royalty, demigods, tycoons, tech masters, and genetic elites, in charge of the fate of mankind.

It is no wonder that Google, Facebook, Apple, and Amazon are entering the entertainment content business; collecting rents on IP is a business they completely understand. They also believe in the supremacy of "tycoons, tech masters, and genetic elites."

Martin Scorsese recently caused a furor among the fans of the Marvel Cinematic Universe (MCU) when an interviewer asked him whether he was an MCU fan. "I don't see them. I tried, you know? But that's not cinema," Scorsese told *Empire* magazine in 2019. "Honestly, the closest I can think of them, as well made as they are, with actors doing the best they can under the circumstances, is theme parks. It isn't the cinema of human beings trying to convey emotional, psychological experiences to another human being." I think Marty is right and that moviegoers will get tired of the comic book formulas, and, like the Americana music fans have, gravitate back to stories that deal with real emotions and real human dilemmas. The days of exploiting the universe of characters with superpowers might just run its course.

The future of the culture I would like to see involves not executives managing IP or even superhumans accomplishing wondrous feats but rather individual artists taking risks. This is why I cautioned my students not to heed the siren song of the techno-determinists, who say their future is the only one worth considering. The high schools and universities are putting all their money into STEM (science, technology, engineering, and math) and trying to convince students that if they know how to write code they will be set for life. But anyone who actually studies artificial intelligence knows that within ten years the machines will be writing their own code. And what we will desperately need then (as now) is humanists—people who have studied history and poetry, people who have empathy. Of course my poetic hero, W. H. Auden, foresaw this in 1946 when he came to Harvard to read his poem "Under Which Lyre: A Reactionary Tract for the Times." Auden imagines the new technology elite, empowered by the atomic age, decimating the humanities on campus and rewriting the curriculum.

> Unable to invent the lyre,
>> Creates with simulated fire
>> Official art.

> And when he occupies a college,
>> Truth is replaced by Useful Knowledge;
>> He pays particular Attention to Commercial
>> Thought,

Public Relations, Hygiene, Sport,
In his curricula.

Auden was right; in many contexts, the humanities have been relegated to a minor curiosity—our memory of the great works of the past, banished. For seventy years the idea of a resistance mounted by the humanists against the tech masters of the universe was just that, an idea. But now it is our reality, and the artists have to go deeper if they want to win. I realize we are at a crossroads. The world I have written about in these pages, where technology played much less of a role in our lives, is never going to return. As Emerson once wrote, "Things are in the saddle and ride mankind." We have crucial decisions to make about our future, and whether the outcome is good or bad, any decision is going to involve some leap into the unknown.

Though I am a humanist at heart, I totally believe that technology can help us escape the "coming anarchy." While I have criticized Facebook for being a disinformation tool, I am equally aware that real participatory democracy can be greatly enhanced by the organizing instruments embedded in Facebook Groups and similar structures on other platforms. Thus, the technology barons have a choice: be part of the problem or part of the solution. And yet we can't sit back and leave our future to the mercy of the techno elite, hoping they do the right thing. It matters what we *all* do to create the kind solidarity that Dr. King taught us fifty years ago:

Power without love is reckless and abusive, and love without power is sentimental and anemic. Power at its best is love implementing the demands of justice, and justice at its best is power correcting everything that stands against love.

Like Epicurus, Dr. King is saying that love and faith are the antidote to the cynicism of our contemporary culture. I know this is counterintuitive in an age of online mob shaming, but I believe it deeply. What used to be a country full of people eager to pave a path toward equality and freedom, and toward cultivating technology that would hold answers to some of our most urgent problems, has given way to a dark and discordant new America. Our one hope is finding a way to bring the generations together in a way that kindles (or rekindles) our dream of a better life for everyone. Now, perhaps more than ever, we will need our musicians and filmmakers to join with us to fight against the fatalism that currently envelops our culture.

Acknowledgments

First of all, to my wife, Maggie, for her loving support and good advice. To my children, Daniela, Nicholas, and Blythe, and my grandchildren, Rose, Beatrice, and Walter—may they continue our quest for liberty and equality.

To Steve Wasserman at Heyday for believing there is wisdom in the battles we fought. And to Emmerich Anklam at Heyday for his wonderful editorial guidance and Lisa K. Marietta for her wonderful copyediting. In my last book I said that I thought that independent, regional distributors would be the solution to the bane of centralized media that haunts us. Working with Heyday has proven to me that my hunch was right.

To Robbie Robertson, Lindsay Holland, Nick Hoff, Cam Ferenbach, Geoff Muldaur, Peter Kaminsky, John Ptak, Wim Wenders, Ron Shelton, and T Bone Burnett for helping me refresh old memories.

Some of these stories I told in an experimental video e-book I self-published in 2011. It was called *Outlaw Blues* and was an attempt to blend video and print. Even though I had the technical support of Apple Books, the file was almost 500 megabytes and so took almost an hour to download. Ultimately we stopped the experiment because the technology wasn't quite ready.

Finally, I want to express my thanks to Simon Lipskar for his steadfast advice and counsel, and to James Ward for his friendship and wise feedback.

Playlist

1. Bob Dylan, "Maggie's Farm," from *The Bootleg Series Vol. 7: No Direction Home: The Soundtrack*

2. Bob Dylan, "It's All Over Now, Baby Blue," from *Live 1962–1966: Rare Performances from the Copyright Collections*

3. Bob Dylan, "Baby, Let Me Follow You Down," from *The Bootleg Series Vol. 4: Bob Dylan Live 1966, The "Royal Albert Hall" Concert*

4. Joan Baez, "Silver Dagger," from *Joan Baez*

5. Jim Kweskin and the Jug Band, "Jug Band Music," from *Jug Band Music*

6. The Charles River Valley Boys, "Rocky Island," from *Bluegrass and Old Timey Music*

7. Tom Rush, "No Regrets," from *The Circle Game*

8. Bob Dylan, "The Times They Are a-Changin'," from *Live at Carnegie Hall 1963*

9. Son House, "John the Revelator," from *The Original Delta Blues*

10. The Paul Butterfield Blues Band, "Shake Your Moneymaker," from *The Paul Butterfield Blues Band*

11. The Doors, "Light My Fire," from *The Doors*

12. The Jim Kweskin Jug Band, "Gee Baby, Ain't I Good to You," from *Garden of Joy*

13. Louis Armstrong, "West End Blues," from *Hot Fives and Sevens*

14. Jimi Hendrix, "Purple Haze," from *Are You Experienced*

15. Big Brother and the Holding Company, "Ball and Chain" (live at Winterland), from *Sex, Dope & Cheap Thrills*

16. Otis Redding with Booker T. & the M.G.'s and the Mar-Keys, "Try a Little Tenderness," from *Captured Live at the Monterey International Pop Festival*

17. Bob Dylan, "Sad Eyed Lady of the Lowlands," from *Blonde on Blonde*

18. Bob Dylan, "Ballad of a Thin Man," from *The Bootleg Series Vol. 7: No Direction Home: The Soundtrack*

19. Bob Dylan and the Band, "Tears of Rage," from *The Basement Tapes*

20. Judy Collins, "Suzanne," from *In My Life*

21. Woody Guthrie, "This Land Is Your Land," from *This Land Is Your Land, The Asch Recordings, Vol. 1*

22. Pete Seeger, "We Shall Overcome," from *We Shall Overcome*

23. Bob Dylan, "I Ain't Got No Home," from *A Tribute to Woody Guthrie*

24. The Band, "The Weight," from *Music from Big Pink*

25. The Band, "The Night They Drove Old Dixie Down," from *The Band*

26. The Band, "Chest Fever," from *Music from Big Pink*

27. Muddy Waters, "Mannish Boy," from *His Best, 1947 to 1955*

28. Bobby "Blue" Bland, "Who Will the Next Fool Be?," from *Greatest Hits, Vol. 1: The Duke Recordings*

29. Junior Wells, "Little By Little (I'm Losing You)," from *Calling All Blues*

30. Crosby, Stills, Nash & Young, "Woodstock," from *Déjà Vu*

31. Derek and the Dominos, "Layla," from *Layla and Other Assorted Love Songs*

32. The Band, "Don't Do It," from *Rock of Ages*

33. George Harrison, "My Sweet Lord," from *All Things Must Pass*

34. Dizzy Gillespie "Groovin' High," from *Groovin' High*

35. Marvin Gaye, "What's Going On," from *What's Going On*

36. The Rolling Stones, "Tumbling Dice," from *Exile on Main St.*

37. The Rolling Stones, "Jumpin' Jack Flash," from *Through the Past Darkly (Big Hits Vol. 2)*

38. Bob Dylan and the Band, "All Along the Watchtower," from *Before the Flood*

39. Bruce Springsteen and the E Street Band, "Thunder Road," from *Live/1975–85*

40. Joni Mitchell, "Coyote," from *Hejira*

41. The Alpha Band, "Interviews," from *The Alpha Band*

42. Jackson Browne, "The Pretender," from *The Pretender*

43. The Eagles, "Hotel California," from *Hotel California*

44. U2, "Where the Streets Have No Name," from *The Joshua Tree*

45. Pat Metheny and Lyle Mays, "September Fifteenth," from *As Falls Wichita, So Falls Wichita Falls*

46. Jane Siberry and k.d. lang, "Calling All Angels," from *Until the End of the World: Music from the Motion Picture Soundtrack*

47. Childish Gambino, "This Is America"

About the Author

Jonathan Taplin is an author and director emeritus of the USC Annenberg Innovation Lab. Taplin's book *Move Fast and Break Things: How Facebook, Google, and Amazon Cornered Culture and Undermined Democracy*, published by Little, Brown and Company, was nominated by the *Financial Times* as one of the Best Business Books of 2017. Taplin has produced music and film for Bob Dylan and the Band, George Harrison, Martin Scorsese, Wim Wenders, Gus Van Sant, and many others. He was the founder of Intertainer, the first streaming video-on-demand platform in 1996.

Taplin graduated from Princeton University. He was a professor at the USC Annenberg School for Communication and Journalism from 2003 to 2016. He is a member of the Academy of Motion Picture Arts and Sciences. He currently sits on the boards of the Authors Guild, the Americana Music Association, and Los Angeles mayor Eric Garcetti's Technology and Innovation Council. Taplin's commentary has appeared in the *New York Times*, the *Washington Post*, *Time* magazine, the *Huffington Post*, the *Guardian*, *Medium*, the *Washington Monthly*, and the *Wall Street Journal*.